DISABILITY
PRIDE

DISABILITY PRIDE

DISPATCHES FROM
A POST-ADA WORLD

BEN MATTLIN

BEACON PRESS, BOSTON

BEACON PRESS
Boston, Massachusetts
www.beacon.org

Beacon Press books
are published under the auspices of
the Unitarian Universalist Association of Congregations.

25 24 23 22   8 7 6 5 4 3 2 1

This book is printed on acid-free paper that meets the uncoated paper
ANSI/NISO specifications for permanence as revised in 1992.

Text design and composition by Kim Arney

Portions of this book appeared, in very different form, in the *New York Times*,
the *Washington Post*, and *USA Today*, and on my blog posts for Facing
Disability and Aging with Dignity.

Library of Congress Cataloging-in-Publication Data

Names: Mattlin, Ben, 1962–author.
Title: Disability pride : dispatches from a post-ADA world / Ben Mattlin.
Description: Boston : Beacon Press, [2022] | Includes bibliographical references
    and index. | Summary: "An eye-opening portrait of the diverse disability
    community as it is today and how attitudes, activism, and representation
    have evolved since the passage of the Americans with Disabilities
    Act (ADA)"—Provided by publisher.
Identifiers: LCCN 2022024698 | ISBN 9780807036457 (hardcover) |
    ISBN 9780807036464 (ebook)
Subjects: LCSH: People with disabilities—United States—Social conditions.
    | People with disabilities—Civil rights—United States. | People with
    disabilities—Legal status, laws, etc.—United States | Discrimination
    against people with disabilities—Law and legislation.
Classification: LCC HV1553 .M3725 2022 | DDC 323.3/70973—dc23/eng/20220610
LC record available at https://lccn.loc.gov/2022024698

For M.L., Paula, and Miranda—
again, always, and forever.

we, young folk in the disability rights movement, are called the ada generation because we grew up with rights older disabled people fought for. we, for the most part or at least a higher proportion, were allowed in schools and in public. many of us who are labelled as ada generation have also been given opportunities. . . . what we do with these opportunities is going to define the future of our movement and community.

—STACEY PARK MILBERN (1987–2020),
"dear ada generation," *cripchick's weblog*

CONTENTS

TOO DEFIANT?

In the summer of 2018, in the heart of bustling, jam-packed, pre-pandemic Times Square, a giant billboard for the skin-care brand Olay might have gone unnoticed. But for anyone who looked up and saw, anyone who knew, who understood, it was revolutionary. Over the words "TOO DEFIANT," with *too* crossed out, was the luminous face of a rising young model named Jillian Mercado. A native New Yorker of Dominican descent, Mercado was born less than thirty years earlier with a variation of muscular dystrophy. (Later, on Instagram, she'd describe herself as "a latinx model, who is queer af [as fuck] and happens to have a disability.") Five years before, she'd unexpectedly won an open modeling call for Diesel, the clothing brand that sells jeans starting at roughly $200 a pair. Campaigns for Nordstrom and Target followed. In 2016, she appeared in merchandising for Beyoncé's world tour. Her career trajectory was meteoric, if unlikely. No one thought anyone who used a motorized wheelchair could go so far or so fast. No one had before. In the beauty business, some big-name companies had included plus-size and older models, but showcasing disability was unheard of.

Soon after her work with Diesel and Nordstrom, Mercado signed with IMG Models, the agency that represented supermodels Kate Moss, Gisele Bündchen, and Heidi Klum. Following the Times Square splash, she was featured on a *Teen Vogue* cover and, later, did runway work at New York Fashion Week. Then she landed a supporting role in the Showtime series *The L Word: Generation Q*, moved to Los Angeles, and signed with Creative Artists Agency in Beverly Hills. "I had to prove myself,"

Mercado shares, trying to explain her ambition and success. "I had to overcompensate to prove to them I was worthy. And thankfully the Diesel campaign went viral, so that helped tremendously."[1]

It also opened a few doors for others.

About a month before the Olay billboard, apparel retailer American Eagle boldly promoted its Aerie lingerie brand with an "empowerment" campaign featuring women we hadn't seen before. One was Abby Sams, then just twenty, a bespectacled dark-haired Alabama native with muscular arms and a girl-next-door smile, seated in her wheelchair in a black lace bra and black leggings. Another was Rajee Aerie (yes, her surname and the brand name are coincidentally the same), a glowing thirty-four-year-old Chicagoan in a camo-blue bralette and matching yoga pants, grinning rebelliously as she stood with crutches from childhood polio in India. A third was Gaylyn Henderson, a fit Atlanta resident, then thirty-three, looking calm and supremely self-assured in a navy blue bra and panties, brandishing a colostomy pouch. Yet another model wore an insulin pump. Some of the women had stretch marks; others had scars.

"Aerie Continues Its 'Real' Streak, Casting Models with Illnesses and Disabilities," declared Adweek, noting that "new images feature women with health conditions."[2] Aerie later reported that its empowerment campaign helped generate double-digit sales growth in the first quarter of 2018 and took market share from rivals such as Victoria's Secret.[3]

The door was now more than ajar. In the summer of 2019, Aaron Rose Philip, a then eighteen-year-old transgender woman who uses a motorized wheelchair because of cerebral palsy (CP), appeared in ads for Sephora, Dove, and designer Marc Jacobs and in a Miley Cyrus video and on TBS's Full Frontal with Samantha Bee. Philip had emigrated from the Caribbean nation of Antigua and Barbuda as an infant and gone through the New York public school system. Along the way, she'd snagged representation by Elite Model Management, the onetime home of Linda Evangelista, Monica Bellucci, and Tyra Banks. By the end of 2020, Philip became "the face of Moschino," the Italian luxury fashion brand. Her star was rising at such a spectacular pace that, before this book was finished, she'd advanced to runway work and changed agencies.

"To my knowledge, fashion has not been the most welcome space," she says, "even when it comes to things like race. So disability was definitely uncharted territory for the industry. Agencies didn't embrace it until Jillian Mercado, until she had her Diesel campaign, which was major. After she did that and got signed, there was me."[4]

In October 2019, Abercrombie and Fitch—the retailer known for displaying only the sexiest of models—featured photos of author and YouTube sensation Shane Burcaw, then twenty-seven, who has spinal muscular atrophy (SMA), with his disabled fiancée, Hannah Aylward, twenty-four. They were part of the retailer's rebranding for "diversity" and "inclusion"—words and concepts that have become such overused hallmarks of modern media, and, indeed, of the broader society, that at times you might wonder what they really mean.

This is what they mean: something new that can redefine your view of "normal."

The trend is certainly not unique to fashion and advertising. In April 2019, just as the hit ABC sitcom *Speechless*—about a goofy yet "typical" family with a teenage son with CP—was canceled after its third season, Netflix launched a comedy series called *Special*, about the coming of age of a twenty-something gay man with CP. Written by and starring Ryan O'Connell, himself a gay man with CP, it lampooned his vain attempts to hide or at least minimize his disability, and introduced mainstream audiences to notions such as "internalized ableism"—a kind of self-hatred that many disabled people experience, based on an acceptance of society's prejudices against those who have disabilities.

Not long after, Ali Stroker, a thirty-two-year-old paraplegic actor and singer, became the first wheelchair user to receive a Tony Award. Her winning role for Broadway's top prize wasn't a little old retiring granny or an outcast such as Laura Wingfield, the disabled loner who pines for a gentleman caller in the Tennessee Williams classic *The Glass Menagerie*. Rather, she won for playing Ado Annie, the happy-go-lucky town flirt in the musical *Oklahoma!*

For Stroker, a blonde powerhouse, it was the pinnacle of a career full of firsts. Paralyzed from the chest down due to a car accident at two years old, the mezzo-soprano was the first actor in a wheelchair to graduate from the theater training program at New York University. Stroker started gaining attention in 2012, at twenty-five, when she appeared on the reality TV competition *The Glee Project*. In 2015, she debuted on Broadway—the first actor in a wheelchair to do so—winning rave reviews for her role in a revival of *Spring Awakening*. After the Tony, she told the *New York Times* she felt excited and proud to be not just successful but a "symbol."[5]

Fast-forward to the spring of 2021. *Crip Camp: A Disability Revolution*, a documentary about the early days of the disability rights movement, codirected by disabled filmmaker Jim LeBrecht, was nominated for an Oscar. Though it didn't win, that year's ceremony was the first in the Oscars ninety-two-year history to show several wheelchair users on the red carpet at the same time. It was also the first time the Oscars stage was ramped.

The trend of high-profile disability inclusion even infiltrated politics. In January 2020, Ayanna Pressley—the first Black woman elected to Congress from Massachusetts—announced she has a form of alopecia that causes complete hair loss. "I want to be freed from the secret and the shame that that secret carries with it," she said, removing her wig.[6] Afterward, she shared that her diagnosis was "an opportunity to shed light on disability issues."[7] Then, in late 2020, US senator Tammy Duckworth, Democrat of Illinois—a woman of Color whose legs were blown off in combat in Iraq—was on the short list to become Joe Biden's vice presidential running mate. Though in the end she was not selected, it was an unprecedented degree of disability visibility in the highest spheres of power.

These events may have been a convergence of coincidences, but something new appeared to be happening. The worlds of fashion, Hollywood, Broadway, and government seemed to be moving away from squeamishness about disabled people and toward acceptance—maybe even a readiness to celebrate them. Major businesses and media outlets had already sought to signal a deeper sense of equity and democratization, including more people of different ages, colors, gender identities, and sexual orientations, but now people of all *shapes* and *body types* and *capabilities* were demanding—and receiving—greater representation and conspicuousness. What once might have been thought undesirable, even repulsive in some circles, was suddenly not just admirable but alluring.

This transformation was evident at the grassroots level, too, especially on social media. Instagram is now bursting with selfies of people with all kinds of disabilities, people who strut their stuff any way and anywhere they want. Check #DisabledAndCute, #WheelsNoHeels, #Disabled_Fashion,

#Wheelie_Good_Life, #DisabilityIsDiversity, #JustAWheelchairGirl, and others to take in a steady stream of the hottest, most daring, most blatant expressions of disability moxie and glamour. Young people with facial deformities, prosthetic limbs, tracheostomies attached to ventilators, or a combination of these, are posing at home, in busy marketplaces, at golden beachfront oases, in elegant urban settings, and on snowy mountaintops. They are laughing, kissing, dancing, shopping, eating and drinking, or just voguing in fabulous sundresses and cut-off jeans, in ball gowns and tuxedos, or in bikinis and sportswear. YouTube has multiple channels devoted to interabled couples, wheelchair "pimp my ride" techniques, Spinraza and Evrysdi diaries (referring to relatively new treatments for SMA), and critiques of stereotypical media portrayals. Some of the more inspiring or humorous YouTubers, such as Zach Anner, snag impressive endorsements. Anner, a comedic wheelchair-using entertainer with CP, starred in the *Rollin' with Zach* series, which was broadcast on the Oprah Winfrey Network.[8]

The only thing these folks have in common is a beguiling mixture of unapologetic self-confidence and, perhaps, unabashed exhibitionism. Whatever their physical, sensory, psychological/emotional, or cognitive/intellectual capabilities; body shape; or appearance, they are saying, "Look at me!"

These developments were particularly striking given the country's sociopolitical climate during most of that time. Donald J. Trump was in the White House, a man who during the 2016 campaign made fun of a disabled journalist, *New York Times* reporter Serge Kovaleski, who has arthrogryposis, a genetic lack of muscular development and joint contractures. Trump's mocking pantomime was shockingly offensive, though Kovaleski himself brushed it off, telling the press, "My strongest reaction to his behavior at that campaign event was pity—pity for Mr. Trump."[9] Trump also published a campaign manifesto called *Crippled America*, shamelessly wielding the C-word in a disparaging manner. In short order his administration slashed programs that benefit disabled Americans—including rescinding seventy-two policy documents related to the rights of disabled students, delaying a rule that required states to examine how well they serve minority students with disabilities,[10] cutting nearly $1.5 trillion from Medicaid and $600 million from mental health and substance abuse treatment programs, and putting programs and services disabled people rely on "on the chopping block," as Tom Ridge, then chairman of the National Organization on Disability, put it.[11]

Not all these proposals came to pass, but a very real fear was implanted in much of the disability community. Trump and his followers seemed intent on trying to turn our nation into an approximation of *Leave It to Beaver*, where everyone is white, middle class, cisgender, heterosexual, and most definitely not disabled.

Altogether, whether they meant to or not, the breakout, pioneering disabled people in mainstream and social media, politics, and elsewhere were bucking the trend and defying traditional perceptions. They practically made disability feel cool. There was much press praising the models and performers as "inspirational." But that's the easy interpretation. It's a cliché. All disabled people have at one time or another—probably many times—been called inspirational for just living our lives. Buying a quart of milk at the corner store is inspirational, apparently, if you happen to use a wheelchair or crutches or a service dog. This kind of attention can make going out for that quart of milk unpleasant. Sometimes folks just don't have the energy—the "spoons," to use the term coined by the writer Christine Miserandino, who has lupus—to be called "inspirational" one more time.

Problem is, the alternatives can be worse: To be called "crippled." To be talked down to as if a child. To be overlooked and ignored as if invisible.

~

I'm a lifelong wheelchair user, and my reaction to all this public disability is somewhat complicated. To me, these new celebs and cyber icons are just disabled people taking their rightful place at the adults' table. They're exhibiting body/mind positivity, an unabashed assertiveness in claiming their fair turn not just among the grown-ups, so to speak, but in the limelight, at center stage, on the front page, in the public eye. What's amazing is that they're not being blocked from doing it—or so discouraged by prejudice and other access barriers as to self-censor. By my lights, they exemplify disability pride.

I was born with spinal muscular atrophy in 1962, which at the time was practically a death sentence. According to the National Institutes of Health, SMA refers to a group of hereditary conditions that deplete motor neurons, the cells that power activities such as walking, swallowing, and breathing.[12] It's really a kind of umbrella term because it describes a variety of related situations. I have what's considered the intermediate variety, also known as type II, meaning I first manifested symptoms as an infant. I was a "floppy baby," unable to sit myself up and easily knocked over. I've never walked or stood, but my life expectancy nowadays is close to a nondisabled man's, as long as I'm careful and remain lucky. One bad cold, however, could easily develop into a terminal case of pneumonia because I can't cough with enough force to clear my lungs.

SMA is progressive. I'm forever losing strength, though the deterioration is so gradual as to be noticeable only every ten years or so. Today, at nearly sixty, I can no longer hold a pencil or feed myself. I'm writing this with voice-recognition software. I'm not complaining. I have a pretty terrific "normal" life. My wife and I have been married for more than thirty years (and counting), and we have two daughters in their twenties. I've had every advantage. When I was growing up, my parents were open-minded and possessed the resources to procure all the medical, psychological, and technological assistance I required, and some I probably didn't. They believed I could do or be anything I wanted when I grew up, and they made me believe it, too, at least till I got older and discovered it wasn't quite true.

How you define yourself in a world full of judgments and challenges can be vitally important. But your outcome depends, too, on your circumstances, your resources. Can you afford the supports you need to live a good life? And if you can afford them, do you have access to them?

One day, when I was perhaps five, my parents introduced me to the jaunty songs of the British comedy team Flanders and Swann. I was struggling to memorize the months of the year, and they thought Flanders and Swann might help. Mom pulled out an old LP of the duo's London revue called *At the Drop of a Hat*, which I believe she and Dad had seen performed live on an overseas trip before I was born. She put the needle down on the black vinyl disc. I was to pay particular attention to the opening number on side two, a track called "A Song of the Weather." It was a sardonic lilt about climatic discomforts throughout the year, month after month. This is how I learned the months. Later, she told me that Michael Flanders—whose mellifluous baritone did most of the talking and singing—was in a wheelchair. He'd had polio as a young man. Of course, you couldn't tell from the record. Even the album cover blurred his image. I still have it. It features a black-and-white photo of a burly, bearded man (Flanders) in the foreground and a high-foreheaded and bespectacled man (Donald Swann) seated behind him at a piano. Most of Flanders's body—from his shoulders down—is covered by a superimposed image of piano keys.

As a child, I made nothing of the news of his disability, other than registering mild surprise. Mom was always pointing out successful disabled people to me. She told me about Christy Brown, the Irish writer and painter who could only control his left foot. She said that Bill Cullen, a frequent host and contestant on the TV game shows I loved, actually walked with a limp because he, too, had had polio, though you wouldn't know it, thanks to strategic camera angles and editing. This information was supposed to give me hope and encouragement, but I never felt I needed either. I *was* kind of inspired by *Ironside*, though—the police procedural about a gruff chief detective in a wheelchair, played by the nondisabled Raymond Burr, which Mom recommended I watch.

What my young mind gleaned from all these examples wasn't so much the limitless possibilities for those of us with mobility impairments, as Mom no doubt intended; it was instead the need for or at least tradition of keeping disabilities at bay, covered up, unseen, private. I inadvertently picked up on a kind of disability code that was common then: minimize the impact, hide it, sweep it aside as a mere personal detail—and get on with your life.

This, I see now, was the opposite of disability pride.

These old impressions came flooding back to me as I witnessed what young disabled people are up to today. Perhaps things don't have to be as they were anymore. Perhaps young disabled people are growing up in a different reality, with less restrictive expectations, more and better support systems, and a greater sense of entitlement. But how had that happened? How did we get to this point? I could not connect the dots.

For many disabled folks, myself included, the kind of chutzpah these young people exhibit can be hard to muster. Most days are filled with slights and conundrums, unnecessary inconveniences, and unjust and possibly illegal encounters. At times, our lives feel hostage to the careful rationing of our wits, our wherewithal—the necessary "spoons" for calculating and recalculating how long till the van service shows up, say, or the next chance to pee in an accessible bathroom. Some problems involve our own minds and bodies, such as a rebellious limb that refuses to cooperate with the brain, or a brain that's not wired to react to certain social cues and customs. Other problems involve the needlessly complex and often unfair social welfare system or the garden-variety architectural and attitudinal obstacles. The daily trials become familiar, in a sense. No big deal, unless and until something makes us want to scream. Makes us want to change the world.

But there is a difference between wanting and doing. What had empowered today's disabled people to bust loose from the strictures of the past? In truth, the disability community has always changed the world, or tried to, but maybe especially over the past half century. That's partly because we're living longer, healthier, more active lives than in years past. Today, the average person diagnosed with multiple sclerosis (MS) may live to nearly seventy-five, just seven years shy of the average for the non-MS population, whereas in the 1980s the survivability odds were much lower.[13] Birth difficulties aren't necessarily the tragedies they used to be either. In December 2018, for example, a baby girl in San Diego was born prematurely at just twenty-three weeks, instead of full-term at forty weeks, and weighed only 8.6 ounces—setting a new record and making her the world's smallest living preemie ever.[14] She will likely grow up with chronic illnesses and disabilities, but her life was not lost.

Surviving premature births, accidents, illnesses, and congenital conditions to live longer and more active lives is a starting point. It's helped create a critical mass of disabled people in society. When their combined energy—or outrage—boils up, changes get set in motion. For my generation of disabled people, the crowning achievement was the Americans with Disabilities Act of 1990, familiarly known as the ADA. It's so monumental that the act is invariably preceded by the word "landmark." The ADA made discrimination against disabled people illegal. It granted unprecedented equality and access and accommodations for nearly a quarter of the US population. It changed our national landscape. People are now used to seeing wheelchairs, service animals, ramps, and sign language interpreters. This reappraisal of disabled people's right to take part fully in society became the global standard, one that extends beyond national borders. Disability, after all, cuts across all nationalities, races, orientations, genders, socioeconomic groups, and religions—perhaps the most democratic of all minority cohorts. In 2006, the United Nations adopted a treaty called the Convention on the Rights of Persons with Disabilities (CRPD) that was designed to "promote, protect and ensure all human rights and fundamental freedoms for all persons with disabilities."[15] It's a pledge, nothing more—a promise to extend rudimentary civil liberties to anyone with a disability. As of this writing, it's been endorsed by 180 nations plus the European Union, but not the United States; President Barack Obama signed it in 2009, but so far the Senate has failed to ratify it. That's ironic, considering the CRPD was based on and inspired by the ADA.

The ADA enabled disabled people to imagine a better, more open, more accepting tomorrow. The law made such a future seem almost within reach. "Never has the world of disabled people changed so fast," wrote journalist Joseph Shapiro in his seminal text about the early days of disability rights, *No Pity: People with Disabilities Forging a New Civil Rights Movement*, published in 1993. "More disabled people are seeking jobs and greater daily participation in American life."[16]

Yet, for all its strengths, the ADA did not—could not—guarantee fair play or full inclusion. It did not automatically change people's attitudes or, in some cases, make institutions comply. Countless barriers to parity and full social involvement remain. Disability activists have had to keep going, keep advancing their agenda and their priorities because many disabled folks are still oppressed, struggling, suffering. Unemployment, poverty, loneliness, lack of access to needed medications and devices and medical care, even senseless ableist violence, remain hallmarks of life for many disabled people. "It's one thing to have our rights," says Judy Heumann, the polio survivor, author, and activist who is often called the mother of the disability rights movement, "but that doesn't mean you have justice."[17]

I came of age on the tail end of the effort to make the ADA happen. I closely, anxiously followed the progress of the better-known disability rights pioneers like Heumann. I wrote letters to senators, congressional representatives, and newspaper editors urging its passage. I went on protest marches. I gave testimony at a local community "hearing" about how I'd been discriminated against and why the law was so important. But then I got married and had kids. I lost touch with much of the disability community and the movement. While I wasn't looking, everything changed, evolved.

In the more than three decades since the ADA became law, a new generation of disabled people has come of age. They've seized the prerogatives my generation (and the ones before that) had fought for and they built on them, made them their own. They took the "greater daily participation" Shapiro referred to and doubled it, tripled it, pushed it in all kinds of ways and directions their forebears never would've thought possible. The ADA wasn't the endpoint we supposed it to be; it was actually a beginning.

What started for me as a quest to understand how these glowing, daring disabled models and performers had managed so young to overcome or evade disability shyness and shame—and prejudice—became a broader, deeper mission. The disability community had grown into something I no longer knew much about but to which I felt intrinsically akin. The group had continued to spread and blossom, drawing new battle lines and forming new alliances.

This book is an account of my journey as a reporter and disabled person to reacquaint myself with that community—*my* community—and to learn from its wisdom, to better understand where disability culture is today, how we arrived here, and where we might be going next. It is an exploration, not a primer. Not *Disability A to Z*. I am not trying to represent the entirety of cripdom. As a white, heterosexual, cisgender man, I couldn't if I tried. I know my limits; my purview is incomplete and imperfect. My intent is to center these stories on the people who made them happen and are making them happen today; I am not speaking for them. I hope to use my privilege to amplify as much as possible this varied group of human beings and their multifarious efforts to shake up and improve the world, to render it more accepting and embracing of all humankind, with all of its wonderful differences. Maybe think of this as an update of Shapiro's *No Pity*—or simply as one disabled reporter's take on a diverse and growing culture. As such, it's subjective as all get-out.

As for my methods, I've attempted to ensure that a wide-ranging assortment of people and interests and views contributed to this narrative, each in their own ways. If I could not interview someone personally, I quoted from posted and published works, with full citations in case anyone wants to explore further, including Internet links whenever possible. I'm indebted to the research that's come before me, the labor involved in unearthing rich veins of disability history, culture, and consciousness, and I've endeavored to give credit where it's due. Forgive me if I fail to represent as fairly and honestly as I should.

One thing binds these stories together: Despite the progress that's been made, as good as things may seem at times, this group knows there are still too many obstacles, still too much subjugation and cruelty, still too great a need to make life better, safer, more accessible, more just. We're not resting on our laurels.

PART I

THE ADA GENERATION GROWS UP

CHAPTER I

CREATING RIGHTS

(Content note: This chapter contains descriptions of abuse.)

In a 2018 TED Talk, the disability activist and scholar Rebecca Cokley explained the term "ADA Generation," which she'd coined nine years earlier in a speech she wrote for then US secretary of education Arne Duncan. The phrase, originally proposed as a somewhat academic concept—she was an assistant for the Education Department's Office of Special Education and Rehabilitative Services at the time, appointed by President Obama—stuck. It resonated. People started using it everywhere—from student groups to the floor of the US Senate, from disability magazines to the *New York Times*—though often with only a partial understanding of its import. She'd intended it, she says, to refer specifically to those who, like her, were in school when the Americans with Disabilities Act of 1990 became law. She was only eleven when it passed. Born with achondroplasia, a congenital condition that causes dwarfism—both of her parents had the condition, too—she already knew firsthand about disability oppression. But Cokley, who is currently the Ford Foundation's program officer for US disability rights, says the ADA's impact on her peer group in particular was "both subtle and powerful."[1]

Thanks to the earlier Education for All Handicapped Children Act of 1975—reauthorized in 1990 as the Individuals with Disabilities Education Act—she and other kids like her had been educated alongside nondisabled kids, in integrated schools, unlike generations before them. This imbued them with a sense of belonging. It gave them the tools to move into society, prepared them to become part of the thrum of life—or, more likely, to be disappointed. That's because, before the ADA, they had little to no expectation of actually being able to fulfill those expectations, that promise. "Preparation falls short without access," observes Cokley.

The ADA gave this first wave of fully educated disabled young adults equal access to the adult world, at least theoretically. It opened the door to possibilities that had been little more than pipe dreams before. As a result, disabled kids could begin "transition planning," Cokley says. At school, they might now be asked, "What do you want to do or be when you grow up?" That was huge. Before the ADA, she notes, only 2 percent of disabled people went to college. Today that number is closer to 11 percent. Many disabled people were stuck in their homes because they simply couldn't get out. Many parents were pressured to give up their disabled children at birth "for their own good," only to have them warehoused in massive, cold institutions where countless numbers perished from neglect and abuse. Cokley says her own mother, a teacher, was denied tenure in 1989 because, ostensibly, she couldn't reach higher than the bottom few inches of a chalkboard. Eleven years later, post-ADA, she became the director of diversity outreach for President Obama— one of five disabled women professionals in the White House at that time. "We've seen disabled people achieve great things that would have seemed impossible before [the ADA]," Cokley says.

In addition to creating opportunities via access, the ADA sparked something much more ideological—a cultural shift in how we as a society regard the disability community. For many Americans, the image of a disabled person was (and often still is) a white cisgender man in a wheelchair. Consequently, most people's concept of "accessibility" remains stuck on ramps. The imagination might stretch to canes, guide dogs, and braille; closed captioning and sign language interpreters; emotional support animals for people with invisible, psychological disabilities such as depression, anxiety, or post-traumatic stress disorder (PTSD); or speech-to-text and text-to-speech functions. But probably not to the height of counters at cafeterias, banks, or doctors' offices, or the way doctors' exam tables rarely have grab bars, or how medical masks that proliferated in the COVID-19 pandemic prevented lip reading and social cues for those who depend on them.

All told, 61 million adults in the US live with a disability, according to the Centers for Disease Control and Prevention. That's 26 percent of the adult population. Disabled children number another 3 million. Altogether, that includes some 43 million people who live with a mental health condition, 37 million who deal with migraines on a regular basis, 30 million who have eating disorders, 25 million with inflammatory bowel syndrome, 15 million with endometriosis, 1 million with chronic fatigue syndrome, and so forth.[2] Cokley, who is a white cisgender woman, points out that it includes people of all colors, religions, ethnicities, gender identities, and sexual orientations—many of whom also deal with sexism, racism, homophobia, transphobia, anti-fatness, and other forms of bigotry, on top of ableism. She calls this diversity "the power of the community."

Nevertheless, she laments, many nondisabled people are hung up on the idea that the ADA is about special privileges—parking placards and so forth. Not true, she says. It's about rights. It's about ending disability oppression, which of course hasn't really ended. Not even close. "There are still so many people facing ableism, audism, and structural barriers," she stresses, quickly explaining that "ableism" refers to bigotry against disabled people, "audism" to the oppression and discrimination faced by the D/deaf community, and "structural barriers" to basic, physical inaccessibility.[3] The ADA has brought these issues out from the shadows and pushed them into the mainstream. But it hasn't erased them. "The work of the ADA is not done," says Cokley.

Still, the ADA generation and those who came after it have a different frame of reference from their elders. Younger people have never known a time when they didn't see people in wheelchairs or with service dogs everywhere. "They have a different way of looking at things," observes Joseph Shapiro, NPR correspondent and author of No Pity.[4] "They are much more ready to claim a disability, to claim that identity, even if they don't have to, such as if they have hidden disabilities. They talk about them and embrace them as parts of their identity. It's a very different mindset."

That mindset is predicated on the certain knowledge that they can't— or at least shouldn't—be discriminated against or otherwise treated prejudicially. They're protected by law. "Even if it's imperfect," says Shapiro, who doesn't have a disability but has been covering the disability beat for more than four decades, "the ADA gives people a way of challenging discrimination, which makes them freer to *identify* with disability."

efore that—from the beginnings of American society—the role of disabled people was always at issue. Kim E. Nielsen, a professor of disability studies and history at the University of Toledo and author of *A Disability History of the United States*, among other books, finds that the question of how disability is valued is something that permeates much of our heritage.[5] Before Europeans colonized the Americas, she says, many Indigenous tribes didn't separate out or judge people by their physical or cognitive differences; they valued people for their contributions to others, not by *how* they contributed or how they looked. For instance, sign language was a common attribute of several Indigenous cultures. European settlers, however, interpreted this method of communication as primitive and uncivilized. In other words, they brought over their prejudices (along with their diseases).

In fact, the Europeans tended to block their physically or mentally "unfit" members from coming to the New World in the first place. There were soon plenty of disabilities, though, because of diseases, injuries, and battle wounds—some more stigmatizing than others. We know that, in 1866, a kind of internment camp for people with leprosy, now called Hansen's disease, was set up on the Hawaiian island of Molokai,[6] followed by similar "colonies" in Massachusetts, Louisiana, and elsewhere, where residents were deprived of basic civil liberties. Many of them were people of Color. These segregated communities continued for decades after a cure was developed.[7] Intellectually disabled and/or neurodivergent folks—particularly those of Color—were frequently incarcerated in "sanatoriums" or prisons, as is still true today.

Still, Nielsen says that, in the early years of the emerging capitalist economy, many of those who could be put to work *were*, regardless of disability. "We have a lot of historical evidence that, for example, people with mobility disabilities did a lot of work in the shoemaking industry," she says.[8] Those who could not work were often cast aside as useless, sometimes quite literally. She tells a harrowing story of a slave ship called *Le Rodeur*, which, for some reason, was beset with an epidemic that caused blindness among the crew and human cargo. Shortly before landing in the Americas, the captain decided to throw many of his enslaved captives overboard and collect insurance on them as lost or damaged goods rather than selling them at a reduced rate, devalued as they were because of their blindness.

A number of well-known abolitionists had less well-known disabilities. Harriet Tubman, one of the leaders of the Underground Railroad that helped escaping enslaved people relocate to the North to obtain freedom, had a head injury that caused seizures and narcolepsy.[9] Sojourner Truth, the formerly enslaved woman who went to court to sue for her son's freedom, recruited Black soldiers to fight for the Union army during the Civil War, and became an outspoken champion of feminism and human rights—particularly well known for her iconic "Ain't I a Woman?" speech—lived with a disabled hand and other lasting effects of physical and emotional abuse.[10]

The connections between disability and slavery were complicated and often contradictory. Many slaveholders used disability as a partial justification for slavery, since they crassly deemed Africans to be mentally inferior or otherwise unfit to become part of society. In effect, Nielsen says, they "combined ableism and racism." The rigors of slave labor caused many physical disabilities and, as on that ill-fated slave ship, an enslaved person who became too disabled to work was considered worthless and often discarded as trash. Some abolitionists used this fact to argue that enslaved Africans should be liberated from slavery just to get them out of such disabling conditions. In her book, Nielsen finds that the 1830 census was the first to record the number of "slaves and Colored persons," who were D/deaf, blind, or nonverbal, a blatant attempt to corroborate a correlation between disability and slavery; ten years later, the census asked about "insanity" and intellectual capabilities. The numbers were inaccurate, she contends, but they were nevertheless used to categorize people—in some cases to further justify slavery, in others to justify building institutions. It's a complex, mind-twisting history.

In any case, disabled people weren't just victims; they were active participants in the culture and history, if sometimes unrecognized as such. At the end of 1876, for instance, in Bureau County, Illinois, a girl named Eliza Suggs was born to two formerly enslaved people. She was born with osteogenesis imperfecta, also known as brittle bone disease—she herself called it "an extreme case of the rickets." In addition to having frequent fractures, she couldn't walk and grew to weigh about fifty pounds and measure less than three feet tall. In 1906, at the age of thirty, she published a book of memoirs and poems called *Shadow and Sunshine*. In it, she describes rejecting repeated solicitations to display herself in carnivals as an oddity, which would have enabled her to earn a living. "It has never been a temptation to me to want to go with a show or to be in a museum for money," she wrote. "Such places are not for me." Instead, she lived a quiet life of religious faith. She died in 1908, at thirty-one.[11]

As the US economy charged ahead—from farming to mining to laying railroad track to factory work—disabling injuries remained frequent but not necessarily life-threatening. There was an increased reliance on doctors to determine who could work and who couldn't—and what to do with those who couldn't. Medicine became the solution to dealing with disability in a way it really hadn't before. Alas, this wasn't always a good thing. In 1927, in a case called *Buck v. Bell*, the US Supreme Court ruled on a situation involving an intellectually disabled teenager named Carrie Buck, who had been raped while in foster care at the Virginia State Colony for Epileptics and Feebleminded. The state sought to forcibly sterilize her, in case she ever had sex—or, presumably, was ever raped—again. The state won. The high court ruled that compulsory sterilization of those deemed "unfit," particularly people with intellectual disabilities, was not only constitutional but salutary. It did not violate due process protections because it was essential for the safety and, in particular, the *health* of the community. Justice Oliver Wendell Holmes Jr., writing for the majority, effectively rubber-stamped eugenics on the pretext of public well-being. The state of Virginia's sterilization statute was finally repealed in 1974, but the Supreme Court has never expressly overturned *Buck v. Bell*. Forced sterilization of disabled people could still be permissible in the court's eyes.

In 1932, in another example of blatant abuse of disabled people, particularly disabled people of Color, government-sanctioned scientists began the infamous Tuskegee Syphilis Study. The program singled out hundreds of Black men who were debilitated from the disease to monitor the effects if left untreated. The ghastly experiment went on for forty years, even though penicillin, a known cure, became widely available in 1943.[12]

As frightening as these examples sound, a concerted push for disability rights didn't get moving until money became the central issue.

In 1932, nearly twenty thousand World War I veterans—many of whom were disabled—marched on the White House grounds to demand the cash bonus for military service that Congress had promised in 1924. They arrived on foot, by freight train, on top of boxcars, and any other way they could, some in their tattered military uniforms, some with their families, all of them destitute, many of them homeless. The government responded by calling out no less than the US Army—soldiers in tanks, others wearing gas masks and lobbing tear gas, a battalion led by future war heroes Douglas MacArthur and Dwight D. Eisenhower (who would later become president). The next day, the headline in the *Washington Post* read "ONE SLAIN, 60 HURT AS TROOPS ROUT B.E.F. [Bonus Expeditionary Forces, sometimes called the Bonus Army] WITH GAS BOMBS AND FLAMES." A reporter for Hearst newspapers named Bess Furman described the scene as "a blaze so big that it lighted the whole sky . . . a nightmare come to life."[13]

Nationwide shock at the horrible spectacle may have contributed to the defeat of one-term president Herbert Hoover in November 1932. The poor, battered ex-soldiers were due what the government had promised, after all. Protests continued intermittently until 1936, when Congress finally gave them their payments—overriding then president Franklin D. Roosevelt's veto.[14]

Roosevelt, a polio survivor himself, sought to combat the Great Depression with a variety of public works programs. One of the biggest was the Works Progress Administration (WPA), which employed out-of-work Americans in artistic, educational, and infrastructure construction projects. Though it ostensibly reached out to include ethnic and racial minorities, the WPA explicitly excluded disabled job seekers. Their applications were marked "PH" for *physically handicapped*. When this was discovered, a New York–based group called the League of the Physically Handicapped launched a series of demonstrations. The first, in May 1935, was small but attention grabbing. Three men and three women, all on crutches, occupied the New York City office of the Emergency Relief Bureau, a satellite of the WPA. The agency's director refused to meet them, so they staged what today might be called a sit-in. "WE ACCUSE!!! The administration of unjust discrimination against the handicapped," reads a flyer from that protest.[15]

"The next day," writes the late disability historian (and polio survivor) Paul K. Longmore, "a large crowd backed the demonstrators and demanded jobs for themselves."[16] The sit-in petered out without resolution, but the League kept going until it grew to several hundred members nationwide. They spoke at various progressive political gatherings and joined labor union picket lines to garner public support. Finally, in 1939, the WPA awarded more than five thousand jobs to disabled people around the country, and the League dissolved.

In a sense, another paradigm-shifting event for organized disability activism occurred in 1932 with the invention of the folding steel wheelchair. An engineer named Harry Jennings built the first one for his friend Herbert Everest, who was paralyzed from a mining accident. Together they went on to form a successful wheelchair-making business, Everest and Jennings, which would become so dominant that it would eventually come under fire for price fixing.[17]

Some twenty years after, in 1953, a Canadian inventor named George Klein, at the National Research Council of Canada, developed a battery-powered wheelchair to aid injured World War II veterans.[18] The Everest and Jennings company adapted that prototype to its standard wheelchair, and by the mid-1960s it was mass-producing motorized wheelchairs. A new generation of physically disabled Americans began enjoying greater mobility. Soon they demanded access to more places.

But it wasn't just physically disabled Americans who were beginning to gain attention. Public outrage over inhumane conditions at psychiatric hospitals was rising. Some large state-run institutions housed tens of thousands of people, greatly outnumbering the often ill-trained staff, according to Wesley Sheffield, an attorney with the Young Minds Advocacy Project, a nonprofit organization dedicated to children and young adults with unmet mental health needs. "Most patients were warehoused in these institutions for long periods of time without treatment or care," Sheffield says.[19]

In 1963, President John F. Kennedy signed the Community Mental Health Act. Spurred partly by the example of his sister Rose Marie (sometimes called Rosemary), who had psychological and intellectual disabilities, he urged Congress to help move people out of institutions and "return [them] to the community" to "restore and revitalize their lives." Kennedy argued for better mental health programs, educational opportunities, and rehabilitation services.[20] But the Community Mental Health Act never got very far. Kennedy's assassination and the growing war in Vietnam derailed the plans.

Meanwhile, the Black civil rights movement was growing increasingly visible and powerful. One leader of that movement was Fannie Lou Hamer, daughter of a Mississippi sharecropper and polio survivor who spent her early life picking cotton—until she was fired for trying to register to vote. When she was in her early forties, she was sterilized without consent while hospitalized for minor surgery. This only fueled her political rage. In 1963, on her way home from a voter registration workshop, she paused at a bus station's whites-only lunch counter and was swiftly arrested and beaten. The brutality left her with a lifelong limp, kidney problems, and a blood clot behind one eye. Nevertheless, a year later she helped organize Freedom Summer, which brought hundreds of college students to the South to fight for African American voter registration. She became a powerful voice within the Democratic Party, agitating for passage of the Civil Rights Act of 1964. Afterward, she was one of the first Black women to give testimony before the US Congress. She went on to run unsuccessfully for public office and spent the rest of her life raising awareness about the disenfranchisement of Black women in the South. Though Hamer was not a disability rights activist per se, her work highlights the link between disability oppression and related civil rights movements—a link that will only grow clearer and strengthen disability activism as it progresses. As the attorney, educator, artist, organizer, and "social justice engineer" Talila A. Lewis—who goes by T.L.—observes, systemic oppression, by definition, "leads to people and society determining who is valuable and worthy based on a person's appearance and/or their ability to satisfactorily [re]produce, excel and 'behave.'"[21] T.L. has dedicated much work to addressing "the inextricable links between ableism, racism, classism, and all forms of systemic oppression and structural inequity."

Without the civil rights movement, it's doubtful there would have been a disability rights movement. In 1968, four years after the Civil Rights Act, the growing number of disabled Vietnam vets compelled Congress to pass the Architectural Barriers Act, which mandated that newly constructed federal buildings be wheelchair accessible. This primarily meant constructing ramps and adequate doorway widths. The next problem was how to get disabled people *to* these buildings. So in 1970, newly mobile and vocal disability advocates—inspired by the civil rights movement—pressured Congress to pass the Urban Mass Transportation Assistance Act, to make transit systems wheelchair-friendly, too. The act lacked adequate enforcement provisions, though, and soon a group of activists who called themselves ADAPT (American Disabled for Accessible Public Transit) began blocking city buses to demand the installation of wheelchair lifts.

An activist named Brad Lomax, who had multiple sclerosis, took up the challenge. He had been a member of the Black Panther Party, the Oakland, California–based revolutionary political organization dedicated to Black nationalism, since the late 1960s. He'd helped found the Washington, DC, chapter in 1969 and helped organize the first African Liberation Day demonstration on the National Mall in 1972, where tens of thousands of marchers proclaimed solidarity with African nations that were casting off the shackles of colonial rule. In 1973, Lomax moved to Oakland and soon became immersed in local issues such as gay rights, Indigenous rights, and disability rights. He became particularly frustrated with the inaccessible public transportation system. To get on a bus, he needed his brother to lift him out of his wheelchair and carry him up the steps into a bus seat, then go back and retrieve the wheelchair. It was just one of the unnecessary obstacles disabled people faced then, and it galvanized Lomax to take action.[22]

The contributions of disability activists of Color, like Lomax, are often excised from standard tellings of disability history. But there were many. Conventional histories focus on people such as Ed Roberts, the wheelchair- and ventilator-using polio survivor who popularized the idea that disabled people could live independent lives if they had adequate support systems. Roberts amassed a ragtag crew of like-minded folks in motorized wheelchairs who called themselves the Rolling Quads. In 1972, they lobbied for and won the first curb ramp, at the corner of Bancroft Way and Telegraph Avenue in Berkeley, California. Shortly thereafter, they launched the Berkeley Center for Independent Living, the first independent living facility in the world.

In 1975, Lomax approached Roberts about working together. The center's mission was—and remains—to give disabled people the means to control their own lives, have full and equal access to everything society has to offer, and live outside institutions, in their own homes, with the assistance of personal aides they hire and control themselves. Lomax suggested that the Berkeley center and the Black Panthers join forces to help the mostly Black and Brown disabled people in Oakland. The alliance would prove mutually beneficial.

A few years later, in 1979, an activist named Johnnie Lacy who had worked at the Berkeley Center for Independent Living became the executive director of its younger counterpart, the Community Resources for Independent Living, in nearby Hayward, California, a largely Black area in southern Alameda County. Lacy had contracted polio at nineteen (she'd actually first met Roberts at the polio rehab hospital) and remained paraplegic. Years later, looking back on her career, she told an interviewer that she'd started as a kind of "ethnographic guide," helping to bridge the white and Black disability communities. She frequently observed that she'd felt excluded from the Black community because of her disability but also from the disability community because of being a person of Color. Different racial and socioeconomic cultures, she added, tended to have different attitudes about the meaning of "independence" and the role of community and family—attitudes that were relevant to the growing independent living movement. The white and often professional-class activists at the Berkeley center, for instance, "came from backgrounds where . . . they just didn't have that much exposure to people of Color, and they truly did not know how to outreach with these folks," she said. "They just felt that if you're disabled, that's the only thing, you know, that's important."[23] Lacy is credited with improving community outreach and recruiting more activists of Color. She retired in 1994 but remained active in Hayward community affairs, serving terms on the Commission on Personnel and Affirmative Action and the Mayor's Disability Council for San Francisco.[24]

Separately but simultaneously in New York City, Judy Heumann, another polio survivor, was organizing a group called Disabled in Action. A decade earlier, she'd gone to court to win the right to teach from her wheelchair in the city's public schools. Later, she would join Roberts, Lomax, and the other disability activists in Berkeley.

Thanks in part to Heumann, the problem of educational segregation for disabled kids began receiving more and more attention. Professor

Robert L. Burgdorf Jr., yet another polio survivor, says that in 1971 a New York judge described people with disabilities as "the most discriminated [against] minority in our nation." Around that time, a million school-aged kids with disabilities were completely excluded from public education, while another three million who did attend public schools weren't provided the necessary services to meet their needs. "This meant that well over half of all kids with disabilities were not receiving minimally adequate education," Burgdorf writes.[25]

In 1972, a federal court ruled that Washington, DC, could not exclude disabled children from its public schools.[26] That was the first domino. Shortly after, a Pennsylvania court struck down state laws that had been used to exclude disabled children from public education.[27] These cases, however, only set precedents. They did not apply beyond their local districts. That would come later. In 1975, Congress passed the Education for All Handicapped Children Act, which leveled the playing field for millions of disabled children. It not only enabled them to be educated alongside their nondisabled peers; it actually required school systems to identify disabled children in their districts and figure out ways to integrate them in regular classrooms. It required periodic evaluations of those efforts and established legal protections for families who felt they were not well served. It also provided financial assistance for school districts to comply.[28] In time, it would lead to in-class aides and "shadow teachers" to provide one-on-one support for students who need it for their academic, social, and behavioral development.

Before addressing educational disparities, though, Congress had other priorities. In 1973, spurred by the wave of disabled Vietnam vets who were desperate for vocational training, Congress passed the Rehabilitation Act. More than anything that had come before, the Rehab Act of '73 addressed the problem of disability unemployment head-on. It banned access barriers in most federal buildings and programs. It mandated affirmative action for disabled workers in some, but not all, federal agencies. Its reach was limited to places and services under the federal purview, but it was the first federal law outlawing discrimination against disabled people. It became a model for the ADA.

In particular, Section 504 of the Rehab Act barred *all* organizations that receive any kind of federal funding from discriminating against any "otherwise qualified handicapped individual." That included many educational institutions, even private colleges and universities that offer federal tuition grants and student loans, but it did not cover public elementary, middle, or high schools, which are not under the federal purview. At that point, Congress was apparently still content to leave local school districts alone.

It took several more years to iron out the Rehab Act's details. Blame the political bureaucracy, or perhaps nobody really wanted to figure out how to become accessible. By 1977, four years after President Richard Nixon signed the Rehab Act, Section 504 had still not been fully implemented. Disability activists were losing patience. That spring, independent living centers and ADAPT groups in Atlanta, Boston, Chicago, Denver, Los Angeles, New York, Philadelphia, San Francisco, Seattle, and Washington, DC, staged sit-ins at their respective local offices of the US Department of Health, Education, and Welfare (HEW), which had been tasked with overseeing Section 504. Jimmy Carter was president by then, and his appointed point person at HEW, Secretary Joseph Califano, was refusing to sign the necessary regulations to put 504 into action. Why is not entirely clear, but he refused even to listen to the disability activists' concerns. Some three hundred demonstrators blocked his office in Washington, DC. In San Francisco, more than 120 activists camped out in the federal building in their wheelchairs, with their aides and necessary supplies, for twenty-five days straight.[29] Dennis Billups, a blind African American activist who was dubbed the "chief morale officer" of the San Francisco sit-in, says many of the participants didn't even know that their comrades were protesting in other cities. "It was like an awakening, you know," he recalls in an online interview for Soul Machine, an activist video channel.[30] "A group of disabled persons had never got together before in that large number to speak, to talk, or to even protest anything." The government tried to get the protesters out. It restricted movement in and out of the federal building, switched off the water and phone lines. But D/deaf people didn't need phone lines. Volunteer sign language interpreters— among them, Lynette Taylor,[31] who grew up with a D/deaf mother, and Joe Quinn,[32] whose boyfriend at the time was D/deaf—relayed messages between the fourth floor windows of the San Francisco federal building and comrades in the courtyard below.

Brad Lomax was a key figure in that action; in addition to leading many followers in the San Francisco occupation, Lomax helped arrange for the Black Panther Party to donate daily hot meals, which many attendees credit with enabling the demonstration to last as long as it did. Important alliances with other progressive causes paid dividends, too. The Salvation Army provided mattresses and blankets. Letters of encouragement came from Cesar Chavez, leader of the United Farm Workers, and other labor union organizers.

After three weeks, Lomax, Billups, Heumann, and about twenty other San Francisco protesters flew to Washington to confront Secretary Califano face-to-face. The Black Panthers paid their way. Finally, on April 28, 1977, Califano okayed the regulations to guarantee Section 504 implementation. Made famous to a new generation in an episode of Comedy Central's *Drunk History*, the San Francisco action remains the longest sit-in at a federal building to date.[33]

The impact of Section 504 cannot be overstated. Disability historians like to say that before it was passed, disabilities were seen as deficits and medical problems. Access was something you had to solve yourself. After it became law, the nation and indeed the world began to perceive access barriers as civil rights issues. One was "handicapped" only by the obstacles put in place by society.

The ADA took these ideas further.

In the immediate aftermath of the Section 504 sit-ins, in 1978, Congress amended the Rehab Act to include Title VII, which provided federal funding for a nationwide network of independent-living centers modeled after the one in Berkeley. The centers were tasked with helping implement much of the rest of the Rehab Act through a combination of peer support, skills training, advocacy, and information and referral services.[34] The same year, Congress also established the National Council on the Handicapped, a small advisory group within the Education Department. The council's workload kept growing until it became an independent federal agency in 1984. Two years later, the new agency—now made up of fifteen members appointed by the president—published a study called "Toward Independence: An Assessment of Federal Laws and Programs Affecting Persons with Disabilities." The document weighed in at nearly five hundred pages and included a draft of what would become the ADA.

This draft introduced a new terminology: "persons with disabilities." Objections to the word "handicapped" were many and varied. It sounded like a beggar's "cap in hand." It referred to a player's disadvantage in a competitive sport. It just seemed out of date. "Disabled," on the other hand, could be construed as a legal term describing those who have been left behind or excluded. Putting "persons" or "people" first felt appropriately respectful of this population's humanity. Most activists today insist on the shorter, more direct "disabled people," which, they say, is a matter of unabashed pride in being disabled. They often object to the "person first" formulation, which buries the disability designation at the end of the phrase. (Both variations are used interchangeably in this book, in deference to different generations of activists.) Euphemisms such as "handicapable," "differently abled," and having "special needs" are generally frowned upon for further diminishing the idea of disability pride. In any case, in 1988 the ten-year-old council changed its name to the National Council on Disability (NCD). (Ironically, the name change was ratified via a bill that clung to the old label: the Handicapped Programs Technical Amendment Act of 1988.)[35]

Almost immediately upon receiving its new name, the NCD submitted its ADA draft to Congress. Senator Lowell Weicker, Republican from Connecticut, and Representative Anthony Coelho, a Democrat from California, who has epilepsy, officially introduced the bill in 1988. Despite this bipartisan support, the ADA proposal was hotly debated. Disability groups around the country began a vigorous campaign to keep it from being forgotten. A series of "discrimination diaries" was collected and sent to members of Congress. These testimonials not only raised consciousness about the barriers disabled people endure in their daily lives but served as proof of a systemic and multilayered pattern of disenfranchisement.

Also in 1988, students at Gallaudet University, the Washington, DC–based private university for D/deaf and hard-of-hearing students, walked out of class to protest the installation of a new university president, Elisabeth Zinser, who, like all her predecessors, was not D/deaf or hard of hearing. Soon alumni, faculty, and staff joined the demand to replace Zinser with a D/deaf person. In about a week, Zinser resigned; the Board of Trustees appointed I. King Jordan as the school's first D/deaf president since its inception in 1864.[36] He served the next eighteen years, retiring at the end of 2006. The turmoil, the mini-revolution, was over pretty quickly, but it registered as a major historic moment for disability empowerment.

Not long after, Congress created a Task Force on the Rights and Empowerment of People with Disabilities, a body expressly tasked with collecting and investigating the evidence vis-à-vis the proposed ADA. It was chaired by Justin Dart Jr., a member of NCD and the son of a pal of and to President Ronald Reagan advisor. Dart was also a scion of the wealthy family that founded the Walgreens pharmacy chain,[37] among other accomplishments, and a polio survivor. A Republican who, like Reagan, had started his career as a Democrat, Dart had bipartisan appeal. In his wheelchair, with his signature cowboy hat and boots, he traversed the country meeting disabled people and their families to hear their stories of discrimination.[38]

In September 1988, a joint hearing of the recently formed Senate Subcommittee on Disability Policy and the House Subcommittee on Select Education convened in the Capitol. A broad spectrum of disabled people—some blind, some D/deaf, some with Down syndrome, some with HIV, some with mobility impairments—and their close relatives were invited to testify. They testified about architectural and communication barriers and the pervasiveness of stereotyping and prejudice. There was testimony from a disabled Vietnam vet who couldn't get out of his housing project without help, or on the bus, or off the curb at his street corner, or get a job, because of disability prejudice. D/deaf people testified about communication obstacles that kept them from procuring necessary services. Parents of a child who had died of AIDS-related complications explained how they couldn't find an undertaker to bury their child because of the stigma around the disease. A breast cancer survivor testified that she was fired from her job and couldn't find new work because of prejudice about her history of illness.

Combined, the impression these stories left was that violations of disability civil rights are harmful to everyone—our whole society—not just to a few individuals.

Some business leaders protested that accommodating disabled people would bankrupt their industries. Many of their Republican allies in Congress agreed. A new Consortium for Citizens with Disabilities, a grassroots hodgepodge of progressive advocates and organizers, insisted on presenting a unified voice. "Even at the eleventh hour . . . the disability community held fast with the AIDS community to eliminate an amendment which would have excluded food-handlers with AIDS, running the risk of indefinitely postponing the passage or even losing the bill," reports the Disability Rights Education and Defense Fund.[39]

Among the politicians who soon pledged to push for the bill were Senator Edward (Ted) Kennedy, Democrat of Massachusetts, who spoke about his son who was an amputee; Senator Tom Harkin of Iowa, a Democrat with a D/deaf brother; Senator Robert Dole, Republican of Kansas and a disabled World War II vet; then vice president George H. W. Bush; and his Democratic rival for the presidency, Massachusetts governor Michael Dukakis. It seemed a shoo-in, but the pace of legislative debate was mind-numbingly glacial. In March 1990, some one thousand disability activists gathered at the Capitol for a final push. They came from thirty states, and some threatened to stay the night if they didn't win immediate action on the bill without any weakening amendments. In the afternoon, to dramatize the urgency of the cause and their determination, dozens of demonstrators dropped their crutches or left their wheelchairs to crawl up the Capitol steps. "Spectators' attention focused on 8-year-old Jennifer Keelan of Denver, who propelled herself to the top of the steep stone steps using only her knees and elbows," the *Los Angeles Times* reported. "Nearby, sprawled on her back and inching ahead slowly, was Paulette Patterson, 33, of Chicago. 'I want my civil rights,' Patterson said. 'I want to be treated like a human being.'"[40]

In disability lore, the Capitol Crawl remains "a very important moment," says Aimi Hamraie, associate professor of medicine, health, society, and American studies at Vanderbilt University and author of *Building Access: Universal Design and the Politics of Disability*. Hamraie, who uses they/them pronouns and identifies as multiply disabled and Iranian, adds that using disabled bodies to demonstrate the lack of access to the built environment is a tactic with a long lineage.[41] Still, they add, there is some debate as to whether the Capitol Crawl was actually necessary. It may have served another function—an important social and performative one. The news coverage it generated, and the mythology around it that continues to this day, helped create a sense of community and identity that, over the years, has proved key to understanding the post-ADA generation.

As Lennard J. Davis, professor of English, disability studies, and medical education at the University of Illinois at Chicago, points out in his book *Enabling Acts: The Hidden Story of How the Americans with*

Disabilities Act Gave the Largest US Minority Its Rights, the Senate had already passed the ADA, and the House was likely to as well, despite rumors to the contrary. "Grassroots [activists] were often left uninformed of inside-the-Beltway happenings," writes Davis, who isn't disabled but whose parents were D/deaf.[42] In any case, Bush, now president, had repeatedly pledged to sign it. He believed in it, and he had to be thinking about his legacy.

Not long after the Capitol Crawl, Congress approved a final draft of the ADA. On July 26, 1990, in a public ceremony on the White House South Lawn, President George H. W. Bush signed it into law.

CHAPTER 2

SUCCESSES, DISAPPOINTMENTS, AND SHORTCOMINGS

The day after the ADA became law, the *New York Times* ran an unsigned editorial titled "A Law for Every American" that dubbed it "the most sweeping anti-discrimination measure since the Civil Rights Act of 1964," a comparison that still echoes today.[1] We were told to expect ramps everywhere, restaurant menus in braille, fire alarms that would not just sound but flash—in short, a complete change in the American landscape.

That wasn't far wrong. Today, the changes brought by the ADA *can* be seen everywhere—not just in ramps and braille signs but in public transit lifts, emotional-support animals, sign language interpreters at many large gatherings such as political rallies and sporting events, electronic listening devices in movie theaters, "reasonable accommodations" by employers such as flextime and telecommuting, and myriad other adaptations. You see disabled people out and about, interacting with society in ordinary ways.

Yet the changes were as much qualitative as quantitative. There was a new national interest in the lives of people with disabilities—a large, heretofore unappreciated minority that had seen oppression and been subject to systemic discrimination. The ADA validated the community of disability and gave it a kind of cultural identity. It wasn't long before society in general began studying and hearing about the history of disabled people's marginalization and victimization, of institutional prejudices that had once relegated "unsightly" people to attics, basements, and institutions. It was an altogether new awareness.

Perhaps chief among the ADA's successes is the simple fact that so many people now accept the idea of equal rights for disabled folks. In itself, this very notion "approaches disability in a new, unfamiliar way," write Doris Zames Fleischer and the late Frieda Zames in the *Disability Studies Quarterly*. The old approach, they explain, was the "impairment model," which essentially presumed you couldn't expect equality if you couldn't do certain things to function effectively in the world. After the ADA, however, disability was redefined in terms of a struggle for social equality.[2]

But the ADA didn't solve all our problems either.

The legislative document itself is complicated—comprehensive yet full of compromises. It defines disability as any "physical or mental impairment that substantially limits one or more major life activities," a broad definition that leaves no one out (or so it seemed). It also applies to family members of the disabled, and anyone who appears to be or is thought of as disabled.[3] Specific diagnoses are irrelevant. It's the extent to which an impairment impacts your life, or is perceived to impact your life, that matters. It's about your inability to accomplish tasks in traditional ways, as well as any stigmas related to being physically or mentally different.

That comprehensiveness is the good news. But in order to appease certain anti-ADA (read: business) interests, the law's protections don't apply to every place all the time. Moreover, many of its requirements are open to interpretation in the courts.

Broadly speaking, the law is made up of five main parts, or "titles." Title I concerns employment discrimination. Title II covers fair and equal access to state and local government facilities and services. Title III bars discrimination in public accommodations and commercial facilities. Title IV governs telecommunications, and Title V clarifies that this law does not invalidate other disability protections.

In all cases, enforcement is solely through the courts. No one is going to give you a ticket for an ADA violation. Someone must first feel their rights have been violated and pursue a lawsuit. No one wants to be sued, of course, but many have taken their chances. After all, every aspect of the ADA has loopholes—or so the violators hope.

Employment discrimination, as defined in Title I, refers to any entity—public or private, for-profit or nonprofit—that maintains *fifteen or more* employees and *could* achieve equal access through a "reasonable accommodation" (read: a modification that doesn't cost too much). No one is required to make an alteration that would incur an "undue hardship," the definition of which—an "action requiring significant difficulty or expense"—is vague at best.[4] It makes it illegal to discriminate against *qualified* disabled applicants in hiring, firing, training, compensation, advancement, and all other terms and privileges relating to employment. (It also covers employment agencies and labor unions.)

It does not include any mention of so-called sheltered workshops, where disabled people are paid a subminimum wage.[5]

Legally speaking, employment discrimination cases are overseen by the US Equal Employment Opportunity Commission (EEOC), which enforces most civil rights protections in the workplace, not just ADA-related complaints. But the ADA caseload alone is huge and growing. In 2019, the year with the most recent data available, more than 24,000 disability-related employment suits were filed with the EEOC, or 33 percent of its total annual caseload. Ten years earlier there were fewer than 21,500 such cases, just 23 percent of the total roster.[6]

One example: In 2019, a woman named Amanda Peal was fired from her job as a pet-waste technician in Rockville, Maryland, after she requested an accommodation for a "pregnancy-related lifting restriction" that was ordered by her doctor. She asked to take periodic breaks, as long as she still completed her rounds. Her employer—DoodyCalls, a Charlottesville, Virginia–based animal poop disposal company—chose instead to fire her.[7] Peal complained to the EEOC, which agreed she had a valid grievance. It attempted a conciliation, but when that failed the agency filed suit in US District Court. On December 14, 2020, the case of *EEOC v. DoodyCalls* was settled in the plaintiff's favor: DoodyCalls had violated Title I of the ADA by refusing to grant a reasonable accommodation for a medical condition. (It also violated Title VII of the Civil Rights Act of 1964, as amended by the Pregnancy Discrimination Act of 1978.) As a result, the company agreed to rehire Peal, pay her $40,000 for lost wages and damages, train its staff on the relevant nondiscrimination requirements, and take appropriate disciplinary measures—including termination—against any managers who discriminate in the future.[8]

Title II applies not just to local government offices but to the very streets themselves. All cities must have curb ramps for wheelchair users and audible traffic signals (the kind that make different sounds for red and green lights) wherever and whenever practical. Public transportation systems must be made accessible, too. The only exception is the federal government's own buildings and services, which for the most part were already covered by the Rehab Act of 1973.

One of the biggest alleged Title II offenders is New York City. In 2017, under threat of a class-action lawsuit, New York officials acknowledged they had failed to maintain adequate curb ramps. Too few were properly sloped, were free of potholes, and included little tactile bumps so low-vision and blind people could tell when they were about to leave the sidewalk and enter the street. Fully 2,246 intersections weren't ramped at all. Michelle Caiola, an attorney for Disability Rights Advocates, told *City Limits*, a local newsletter, that New York's curbs were in such bad shape that they're not only difficult but dangerous. "We have stories of people actually tipping over in their wheelchair and falling into the street," she said.[9]

In 2019, after seemingly endless haggling and appeals, New York officials agreed to overhaul all 162,000 street corners throughout the five boroughs and bring them up to full accessibility requirements by 2034.[10]

New York is also under fire for its subways. Of some 472 stations, only 124 are ADA compliant, according to an *AM New York* report.[11] In January 2020, a federal judge ruled that the Metropolitan Transportation Authority (MTA) must add elevators to every subway station that undergoes renovation. So far, there is no clear timeline for such changes, and progress has been slow,[12] though an MTA spokesperson says the department had allocated some $5.5 billion to make an additional seventy stations fully ADA accessible by 2024.[13]

Title III cases have generated a great deal of press and acrimony. Perhaps more than any other type of ADA suit, these allegations pit business interests against the public interest. If a store has a few steps out front, it should ramp them whenever possible—and ramps cannot be steeper than a one-to-twelve grade. Appropriate signage must be put up to direct disabled customers to an accessible entrance, if it's not obvious. Doorways must be thirty-six inches wide, and aisles can't be blocked with boxes.[14] Menus must be available in braille or recited aloud by waiters. Elevators should have tactile buttons. Hotels ought to maintain a certain minimum number of rooms with a degree of accessibility, though how much and what type depends on the total number of rooms. Historical buildings might get an exemption, but new constructions and most major renovations must meet these accessibility codes to be greenlighted.[15] You could be forgiven if your brain went wobbly trying to keep these regulations straight. It's little wonder that some businesses can and often do try to skirt the law.

Even where Title III does apply, nothing is required that would cause "undue" hardship on the business, which is why some ancient facilities simply can't be brought up to code. But the excuse that "I don't get any disabled customers anyway" doesn't hold water.

Nevertheless, there are a few categorical exceptions to Title III. Insurance companies aren't included, for instance. Their lobbyists argued that ignoring customers' physical or mental impairments would essentially imperil their business model. (Thanks to the Affordable Care Act of 2010, however, health insurers can no longer discriminate against preexisting conditions.) As a result, if you feel you've been discriminated against by an insurance company because of your disability, chances are you can't sue them—at least not successfully—under the ADA. "Most insurers will include some type of 'discrimination exclusion,'" explains a 2017 white paper from New York–based insurance broker Marsh, a subsidiary of Marsh and McLennan Companies. It goes on to say that this includes an exemption from "any claim that cites the ADA as the basis for relief."[16]

Airlines got out, too, on the pretext that they already can't discriminate against disabled passengers because of the Air Carrier Access Act of 1986. That older legislation, though, is far less stringent.[17] Unlike buses, trains, and taxicabs, airplanes only have to accommodate to the extent they deem appropriate or "safe." So wheelchair users still must be lifted into a plane seat while their wheelchairs are stowed with the baggage and invariably returned damaged or in pieces, if they're returned at all.[18] Sometimes the consequences are fatal—such as in November 2021, when a Los Angeles–based disability advocate named Engracia Figueroa died from complications of injuries caused by an airline-damaged wheelchair.[19] And never mind using the restroom while in flight if you need assistance or extra space. What's more, airlines continue to push back against allowing service animals in the passenger cabin. In December 2020, the Transportation Department acceded to industry demands and narrowed the regulations: Only specially trained dogs (such as guide dogs for blind people) and other certified service animals that are small enough to fit on a person's lap or under the seat can travel in airplane cabins. Emotional support animals for people with chronic anxiety, panic attacks, depression, or other psychological disabilities may be rejected or forced to travel in the baggage compartment—and their handlers may be charged extra fees—at the airline's discretion. Prairie Conlon, a psychologist and clinical director of Therapetic, an organization that advocates for acceptance of emotional support animals, calls this ruling "textbook discrimination."[20]

Notwithstanding these exceptions, the caseload of Title III lawsuits is large and growing. In 2018, there were 10,163 Title III suits filed. That's more than triple the number of similar suits just five years earlier.[21] With such large numbers, it's not surprising that several websites keep track of this data. UsableNet, a corporate technology consultant firm, found there were more than two thousand federal lawsuits related to website accessibility alone in 2018, nearly triple the count a year earlier. Online commerce, of course, is an area the ADA framers never imagined.

Some of these suits have gone all the way to the US Supreme Court. In October 2019, the high court let stand a lower court ruling in favor of a blind man named Guillermo Robles, who sued Domino's Pizza because he was unable to order from its website and mobile app, even with his screen-reading software.[22] The idea is that a company's website and mobile app have to be as accessible as its physical stores—that is, they must be compatible with screen-reading technology, which essentially speaks the electronic links out loud, along with tags or text descriptions of images.[23]

Another target of rising Title III complaints is gift cards that don't have braille-embossed writing. In October 2019, a Brooklyn woman named Kathy Wu, who is legally blind, tried to buy a Disney stores gift card that had braille. A Disney employee told her (correctly) that no such item exists. Wu called an attorney. A "proposed" class-action lawsuit was subsequently filed in New York, charging that the Walt Disney Company was essentially denying visually impaired customers full and equal access to its products and services. No decision has been reached as of this writing, but the lawyers hope to win an injunction to compel the Burbank-based entertainment conglomerate to produce braille gift cards and pay unspecified compensatory damages to all claimants in the class action.[24]

To disability activists, the sheer number of ADA lawsuits is due to the fact that there are so many violations. Businesses and municipalities have had plenty of time to get with the program. At this point there is little excuse for failing to meet accessibility requirements. These litigants are pursuing nothing less than justice.

Not everyone agrees with that assessment. Many reactionaries—frequently, businesses that don't want to spend the money to make accommodations or are afraid of being sued (though not so afraid as to do the right thing)—have tried to knock the ADA down bit by bit, if not wholesale. In 2017, for example, a Texas Republican congressman named Ted Poe proposed the ADA Education and Reform Act, which effectively would allow businesses to ignore accessibility regulations unless very specific complaints were made in writing and, even then, action could not be pursued for at least sixty days. It passed the House and went to the Senate, where it expired unresolved.[25] But it could always come up again. Some states have taken potshots at the ADA, too. In 2017, Florida passed a law allowing property owners to apply for ADA compliance certifications that would make lawsuits against them unwinnable.[26] Also in 2017, Nevada state attorney general Adam Paul Laxalt attempted to curb what he called "abusive litigation" against local businesses for ADA violations; he sought to consolidate and then dismiss nearly two hundred separate cases brought by a single plaintiff, a wheelchair user named Kevin Zimmerman, who he claimed was out for money and unduly harming the public interest. Zimmerman's complaints involved a variety of violations including narrow store aisles and a lack of proper signage to indicate van-accessible parking. Zimmerman admitted he'd rushed to sue without first notifying the businesses or giving them a chance to fix the alleged problems.[27] But does that mean the charges were unfounded, malicious, or motivated by financial gain, as Laxalt contended? Does it mean the businesses weren't unnecessarily blocking disabled customers? In the end, Laxalt's motion to consolidate and dismiss the cases was denied. Zimmerman reportedly settled most of the cases individually for between $50 and $100 apiece.[28]

There's no question the ADA hasn't been a complete triumph. One problem came to light rather quickly via a series of high-profile court cases. In 1992, two nearsighted twin sisters, Karen Sutton and Kimberly Hinton, who were pilots for a regional commuter airline, applied to United Air Lines (now United Airlines) to become regular, long-haul commercial pilots. With glasses, their eyesight was fine. But because they couldn't pass the test for adequate vision without glasses, United Air Lines turned them down. They filed an ADA discrimination suit that eventually ended up at the US Supreme Court. In 1999—in a case known as *Sutton v. United Air Lines*—the high court ruled against the sisters. Justice Sandra Day O'Connor delivered the verdict. In short, because their nearsightedness was mitigated by wearing glasses, the sisters didn't qualify as *disabled* under the ADA and therefore weren't entitled to its protections.[29]

In 2002, another case before the high court—*Toyota Motor Manufacturing, Kentucky v. Williams*—was decided on similar grounds. An auto assembly-line worker named Ella Williams sued her employer, Toyota Motor Manufacturing of Kentucky, for failing to adequately accommodate her carpal tunnel syndrome and tendinitis. She won her case in the lower courts, but Toyota appealed to the Supreme Court, where she lost. Again it was Justice O'Connor who delivered the ruling: Williams was not protected by the ADA because her impairments didn't "substantially limit" a "major life activity," standards that were vague and ill-defined in the ADA.[30]

In both cases, and others like them that were adjudicated in lower courts, the focus was on whether the plaintiff actually counted as disabled, rather than whether discrimination had occurred. A broad group of disability activists protested. The National Council on Disability—the federal agency that advises the government on disability policy—issued a report suggesting ways to fix the ADA so it would be interpreted more fairly, as originally intended. In September 2008, Congress passed and President George W. Bush signed the ADA Amendments Act to correct this shortcoming. It expanded the legal definition of disability, explicitly stating that "major life activities" can include caring for oneself, performing manual tasks, seeing, hearing, eating, sleeping, walking, standing, lifting, bending, speaking, breathing, learning, reading, concentrating, thinking, communicating, and working, among many other things. In determining whether an impairment "substantially limits" any of these (and other) activities, the courts must not consider mitigating measures such as eyeglasses, assistive technology, or medications. In so doing, it overturned both the Sutton and Toyota cases.[31]

The ADA amendments of 2008 primarily affected Title I, employment issues. But two years later, just in time for the law's twentieth anniversary, the Justice Department updated certain terms related to Titles II and III—that is, related to government services and public accommodations, respectively. There were new design standards for restaurants, schools, parks, stadiums, hotels, theaters, and hospitals. Besides setting a schedule for architectural renovations, the new rules would ensure that ticketing procedures for sporting events and theatrical performances accommodated those who can't see or hear. They also addressed access to broadband Internet and websites, which didn't exist when the ADA was passed, as well as communication access for 911 emergency services. Calling the package "one of the most important updates to the ADA since its inception," President Barack Obama said that allowing the injustice of inaccessibility to stand deprives "our nation and our economy of the full talents and contributions of tens of millions of Americans with disabilities."[32]

A year later, on the twenty-first anniversary of the ADA, Obama addressed the "many technological barriers," as he put it, that impinged disabled people's ability to interact with the federal government, an area that was exempt from ADA protections. In fact, it's an area that was supposed to be addressed in Section 508 of the Rehab Act of 1973 (as amended by Congress in 1998), but the regulations adopted then had become outdated or were poorly enforced. So Obama proposed beefing up the standards. "Making electronic and information technology, such as websites, 508 compliant will ensure that applicants have equal access to apply for job opportunities," he said in a press release. Moreover, it would provide greater access to "all the information the federal government has placed online." The US Access Board, an independent federal agency that oversees much of the Rehab Act, finally updated its standards and guidelines for information and communications technology in January 2017.

These moves were long overdue adjustments that helped make disability antidiscrimination laws all they promised to be. Yet obstacles to full access would continue. For instance, the ADA doesn't address the ongoing problem of institutionalization. Whether an accidental oversight, a compromise to expedite the law's passage, the result of pressure from the nursing home industry to maintain the status quo, or some other reason, the omission quickly gained activists' attention—again because of a court ruling.

In 1995, two women with disabilities sued the state of Georgia to receive their necessary treatments at home rather than in a state-run institution. Lois Curtis, an autistic Black woman, was the primary plaintiff; her co-plaintiff was Elaine Wilson, a white woman who had intellectual disabilities from a brain injury in early childhood. The women had been in and out of mental hospitals for years; each time they were allowed to go home, they would end up institutionalized again because they couldn't get the help they needed at home. Their doctors agreed they were capable of living in the community *if* appropriate supports were provided; in fact, they'd be better off that way. Inexplicably, the state said no. Curtis and Wilson appealed and won, but Georgia officials appealed the decision. The case ended up before the Supreme Court.[33]

On June 22, 1999, Justice Ruth Bader Ginsburg delivered the final verdict. The women won the right to receive treatment outside of institutions. The court held that mental illnesses, including cognitive and emotional impairments, are ADA-protected forms of disability, and unjustified separation in institutions is a form of discrimination. Segregating disabled people this way, without valid justification, is a violation of Title II, which applies to state agencies and public entities such as state-run institutions. These public entities must offer services that are integrated within the community whenever possible.[34]

Disability advocates hailed the ruling, which became known as the *Olmstead* decision after Tommy Olmstead, who was then Georgia's commissioner of human resources, the defendant in the case. Some point out that it should have been named after Lois Curtis, the primary plaintiff and the true hero of the story. Not doing so erases an important autistic Black woman from her due place in disability history—and from the consciousness of the community that owes her a great debt of gratitude. Hereafter, this book will refer to it as the *Olmstead-Curtis* decision.

But there was another problem. *Olmstead-Curtis* left out people with physical disabilities. So in 2001, President George W. Bush issued an executive order that extended the ruling to all people with disabilities. Ostensibly aimed at helping states comply with the Supreme Court decision, the order required federal agencies to support states in their efforts to free disabled and chronically ill folks from institutions. The goal, said Bush, was "to place qualified individuals with disabilities in community settings whenever appropriate."[35]

That would prove harder to enact than it seemed. This is why many of today's activists are fighting for passage of the Disability Integration Act (DIA), which would prohibit government entities and insurance providers from denying services that would enable disabled people to live in the community.[36] Sponsored by Senator Chuck Schumer of New York in 2019, DIA remains in abeyance.[37]

～

Despite the ADA's safeguards for disabled employees and job seekers, the unemployment rate for disabled people remains terribly high. The Bureau of Labor Statistics, which primarily measures those who are actively seeking work, estimates that unemployment among working-age disabled people totals about 8 percent, more than twice that of those with no disability. Weighed against the overall working-age population, the percentage of disabled folks who are employed is just 19.1 percent, whereas 65.9 percent of those without a disability are employed.[38] There's no clear measure of what the disability unemployment rate was *before* the ADA, but these figures are certainly disappointing and somewhat puzzling.

No one can say for sure why employment remains such a problem. It may be that employers are afraid of the costs of accommodating disabled workers or refuse to even consider disabled candidates for fear of being sued if they don't hire them. Many claim liability concerns, assuming disabled people represent a greater risk than their nondisabled peers. It's an excuse disabled people have heard all their lives. Before the ADA, it was common to hear safety and liability raised as reasons for keeping wheelchairs and walkers and service dogs out of theaters and shops and public transit. Another similar excuse, at least early on, was that hiring disabled employees would raise the company's health insurance premiums. But the Affordable Care Act made it illegal for insurance carriers to charge more for preexisting conditions, so that excuse is no longer valid. Maybe it just comes down to prejudice, whether conscious or unconscious. Employers prefer applicants who look and talk a certain way. "People with disabilities are being screened out because they don't present in ways that are considered normative," suggests Azza Altiraifi, a research associate and advocacy manager for the Disability Justice Initiative at the Center for American Progress, in an interview with CNBC.[39]

At the same time, ride-sharing services such as Uber and Lyft continue to resist making more of their vehicles accessible. They are open to hiring disabled drivers, their apps are accessible to people with vision impairments, and their drivers are required to take disabled passengers (and their service animals). But very few of their vehicles can accommodate a wheelchair. In New York City, Uber's biggest market, only 554 of nearly 118,000 active ride-share vehicles were wheelchair accessible as of 2018, according to Molly Taft of *Bloomberg City Lab*.[40] Joseph Rappaport, executive director of the Brooklyn Center for Independence of the Disabled, says, "Uber has fiercely opposed accessibility in its services, particularly for people who use wheelchairs. They've lobbied against proposals, they've sued, and they've spent millions of dollars to prevent a requirement that they provide accessible service." Legally speaking, Uber and the rest employ independent contractors, not full-time staffers, which becomes a convenient excuse for evading federal employment laws such as the ADA. Uber and Lyft have reportedly entered negotiations with specialty transportation companies to provide more wheelchair-friendly vehicles, at least in New York. Rappaport isn't impressed. He says the only reason they're now considering this is the threat of further legal action.[41]

The ADA also doesn't extend to Indigenous reservations; no federal laws do. Besides impacting Indigenous disabled people, this exemption has ramifications for businesses operated on Native-run properties such as casinos. In 2019, a woman named Nadia Drake went to the Talking Stick Resort in Arizona, which is owned by the Salt River Pima-Maricopa Indian Community. She brought her service dog, which she needs for coping with extreme anxiety and occasional panic attacks, but the casino managers told her the dog had to go. She had a panic attack, and subsequently filed an ADA suit. The resort defended itself on sovereign immunity grounds—and won.[42]

It's hard to keep score, to tally the wins and losses for the disability community. There have been many definite victories. But activists can never rest on their laurels. They stay ever alert to new violations and shortfalls, always churning out (or reacting to) unexpected advocacy priorities as they arise. It's not unlike a game of Whac-A-Mole, only with more dire consequences. Randomly scattered and jagged-sharp particles of injustice remain untouched by the ADA.

For instance, in thirty-two states disabled parents can have their children taken away simply because of their disabilities, as if disabled people have no right to raise kids, cautions Rebecca Cokley at the Ford Foundation. Nationally, she says, disabled youths are three times more likely to end up in foster care than their nondisabled counterparts and six times more likely to end up in jail. Penalties for work and marriage continue to undermine federal benefits programs. As of 2022, recipients of Supplemental Security Income may lose partial benefits if they earn more than $65 per month;[43] they are completely disqualified if they earn more than $1,767 per month ($2,607 per month for married couples)[44] or have more than $2,000 in savings ($3,000 for married couples).[45] Recipients of Social Security Disability Insurance (SSDI) must earn less than $1,350 a month (or $2,260 if they're blind), after accounting for qualified disability-related work expenses.[46] If they're on the SSDI "survivors benefits" program—which is designed for those who had their disabilities before age twenty-two and have a deceased parent—they must also remain unmarried.[47]

Underreported, too, is the prevalence of police violence against those with sensory, intellectual, or neurological disabilities that may make them appear drunk or uncooperative. A study by the Ruderman Family Foundation, a nonprofit disability advocacy group, found that as many as half of the people killed by law enforcement officers had a disability.[48] Furthermore, activists attest to discrimination in the way disability policies are applied; disabled people of Color, say, are far less likely to be granted the full measure of the ADA. Anyone with intersectional identities—disabled folks who are queer, trans, Black, Indigenous, people of Color, or members of other stigmatized groups—face a combination of ableism and racism, sexism, homophobia, transphobia, anti-fatness, and other forms of oppression that the ADA doesn't address. It's clear, activists say, that we can and must do better.

CHAPTER 3

WHAT IS PRIDE—AND WHY DOES IT MATTER?

When you've grown up in a world not quite made for you or are forced into one from an accident or illness, and when you feel you should be able to do what everybody else seems to do, when you feel as if you've been inexplicably singled out for punishment, it can be utterly, achingly soul sinking. Worse still, it's hard to shake. "Internalized ableism" is believing the prejudicial assumptions and expectations thrust on you by society, believing you're inferior, undesirable, burdensome, don't fit in, and/or in need of repairing or healing or fixing or curing. "Internalized oppression is not the cause of our mistreatment; it is the result of our mistreatment," says the British disability scholar Deborah Marks. "It would not exist without the real external oppression that forms the social climate in which we exist. Once oppression has been internalized, little force is needed to keep us submissive."[1]

Another way to look at it is disability shame. "A great deal of my disabled friends hold onto the idea that we are fundamentally different from non-disabled [people]," says an unsigned 2013 post at the blog *Disability Rights Bastard*, which is subtitled "musings of yet another bitter cripple." "By refusing to see ourselves simply as people, we are implying that we do not deserve to be treated as equals."[2] Many disability blogs focus on this. On *Crutches and Spice*, the activist Imani Barbarin—who "writes from the perspective of a Black woman with cerebral palsy"—observes, "Discrimination from the outside world we can recognize, but the discrimination we are taught to apply to ourselves is harder to identify." She goes on to list some self-hating messages we tell ourselves, tagging them as symptoms of internalized ableism, such as *This person is only with me because they want to be seen as a hero,* or *I need to make other people feel at ease about my disability.*[3]

In 2021, the vlogger and author Shane Burcaw posted a video to YouTube titled "I was ashamed of my body." Because of his spinal muscular atrophy, he has severe scoliosis and reed-thin limbs. "Ten years ago," he explains, shirtless, to his hundreds of thousands of subscribers, "I would go to the beach and not take my shirt or my pants off because I was programmed by society to be ashamed of the way I look." Now, he continues, he enjoys posting photos and clips of himself in the pool or shower wearing nothing but a bathing suit. Still, even today, he braces himself for negative reactions and feels surprised when they don't come. It isn't easy, he says, to "overcome the belief that my body was shameful."[4]

As Burcaw's story makes clear, this kind of self-doubt can happen even when you know better. You may say it doesn't matter what other people think. You may try to bolster your self-esteem by recalling your accomplishments, the people who love and respect you. You may count the advantages your disability gives you. (No, not just the parking spaces!) You're a creative problem solver. You know how to cope, how to be sedentary, to be patient. If you've had to rely on regular personal—care help—what disability columnist Mike Irvin calls his "pit crew"—you know a bit about employee management, too. Recognizing the value in such experiences—the expertise they afford—is one way of boosting self-confidence.

But it only goes so far.

In her 2019 memoir, *Such a Pretty Girl: A Story of Struggle, Empowerment, and Disability Pride,* New York–based activist Nadina LaSpina, a polio survivor, describes her emotional battle with society's low expectations, how she learned from other disabled people to recognize prejudice and fight it. She participated in one of the first "disability independence" marches in New York in 1992, on the second anniversary of the ADA. (Bragging rights to the first march are a matter of some dispute. It may have been in Boston in 1990, with guest speaker Karen Thompson, the brain-injured coauthor of the 1989 memoir *Why Can't Sharon Kowalski Come Home?,* which was about one couple's fight against ableism, sexism, and homophobia.) LaSpina was one of the organizers of the 1992 New York march. Groups such as Disabled in Action, the grassroots advocacy team cofounded by Judy Heumann, had been mounting protests for years—first for the Section 504 regulations mandating accessibility in federally funded institutions and programs, then for the ADA. But once their goals had largely been met, they still had energy. They weren't done organizing. So they began focusing that momentum into a kind of victory celebration. "The first march, though small, kindled feelings of disability pride," LaSpina writes.[5]

The next year's parade grew to an estimated three thousand participants. They filled the streets of lower Manhattan in giddy celebration, and a version of the march has been repeated almost every summer since, on or near the anniversary of the ADA. There's a clip, a montage, of the 1993 event available online. People proceed on foot, with crutches, in wheelchairs, singing and shouting and laughing. A float rolls by with a huge banner reading PRIDE. Toward the end, a succession of speakers riles up the crowd. A demonstrator named Eric von Schmetterling declares, "It's so important for our people to show the world we are proud of who and what we are."[6]

Passage of the ADA may not have been the starting point for what would come to be known as disability pride, but it certainly gave it a big push. By 2015, the Disability Independence March had morphed into the Disability Pride Parade. New York mayor Bill de Blasio kicked off events by announcing he was proud that his city was "a national leader in supporting rights for disabled people," notwithstanding the ongoing lawsuits against the city for access violations.[7] A more recent celebration boasted some seven thousand revelers who gathered at Madison Square Park in lower Manhattan shortly after 10 a.m. and proceeded slowly to Union Square Park through early evening. Major corporate sponsors such as New York Life and T-Mobile joined in.[8] Even in 2020, when the parade was scrubbed because of the COVID pandemic—like many other public gatherings—the significance of "ADA day" wasn't forsaken. Some people took to calling the entire month of July Disability Awareness Month or Disability Pride Month.[9]

As the concept of disability pride gained traction, it wasn't always readily embraced, even by some activists. In the March/April 1998 edition of the movement's unofficial newsletter at the time, *Electric Edge*, LaSpina looked back on those first marches and explained the idea to editor/reporter Mary Johnson: "Nondisabled people always think about our lives as being tragic. . . . We are saying that being disabled can be a positive experience." Particularly surprising to her were the objections from other disabled folks. "People said, 'You may like disability, but I don't. You don't speak for me. I hate physical limitation. I hate losing function. I hate pain!'" she recounted. LaSpina acknowledged that it's not easy to live with a disability. There are aspects of it that she'd rather not have. But that doesn't mean she'd prefer to be nondisabled. She compared it to menopause. She may not like it, but that doesn't mean she'd rather be a man.[10]

For many people, disability pride remains a slippery, subjective concept; it connotes different things to different folks at different times. Pride in our accomplishments? Pride in our identity? Is it like gay/queer pride? Black pride? This lack of specificity may be surprising considering it's not really a new concept to the movement. In the early 1990s, Ed Roberts reflected that before he could go about trying to change the world, he had to alter his attitude about himself as a ventilator- and wheelchair-using polio survivor. He had to become proud of who and what he was.[11] Around the same time, the disabled writer Laura Hershey published a poem called "You Get Proud by Practicing" that became a kind of anthem, helping people understand how to achieve a healthy self-acceptance. It spoke directly to the shame and embarrassment many disabled people feel about their "broken bodies" or lack of a spouse or money or a job.[12]

But what are the limits and the benefits of this post-ADA identification with disability pride? Eli Clare, a Vermont-based author, essayist, and poet who describes himself as "white, disabled, and genderqueer," writes in an essay called "Shame and Pride" that pride is sometimes used by marginalized communities as an act of resistance. "We've rejected the idea that our body-minds are broken. We've learned lessons from the Black Power movement of the 1960s and the slogan 'Black Is Beautiful.' We've rallied around the value of pride," writes Clare.[13]

Emily Ladau, author of *Demystifying Disability: What to Know, What to Say, and How to Be an Ally*, says that disability pride is "not an isolated thing. It's more like a shared cultural identity."[14] Born after the ADA became law, she is a past winner of the Paul G. Hearne Emerging Leader Award for up-and-comers in the disability movement. She uses a wheelchair because she has Larsen syndrome, a genetic condition that can cause dislocations of the joints and other hand and foot abnormalities.

Ladau cohosts *The Accessible Stall* podcast—a (mostly) monthly production where she and her cohost debate and explore a variety of current issues—and, for a number of years, Ladau edited *Rooted in Rights*, a blog that highlights authentic, progressive disability perspectives "through an intersectional lens," or, as Ladau says, it "showcases perspectives that don't always get the mainstream attention they deserve."

Ladau's mother and uncle also have Larsen syndrome, which she says was important for giving her role models when she was growing up. That's rare. As the scholar Jennifer Natalya Fink observes, disabled children are often relegated to an *other* status, their disabilities regarded as personal traumas they and their families must cope with, rather than ordinary experiences. "Despite the fact that one-fifth of all the planet's people are formally recognized as disabled, meaning that more or less everyone else is related to a person with a disability, we continue to construct our sense of family and its lineage in such a way that we are stunned, shocked, and traumatized by the incredibly common, collective, and familial experience of disability," writes Fink.[15]

Authentic disabled role models can be crucial for helping disabled kids—and newly disabled adults—build pride. In mainstream media, there aren't many, and the few who do exist are far outnumbered by nondisabled icons, which can be counterproductive for disability pride, reinforcing unrealistic expectations of attractiveness and acceptability.

Surprisingly, Ladau says her personal convictions about disability pride solidified when she got to know more people with different types of disabilities. "It was really when I started to find myself surrounded by a lot of other disabled people, when I chose to surround myself with the disability community," she says. "By doing so, I understood I wasn't alone. That's when I was able to foster this stronger sense of identity and pride."

Feeling not alone can be difficult because there are so many different types and degrees of disabilities, including chronic health conditions. Beth Haller, a professor of media and disability studies at Towson University, outside Baltimore, has explored the many sides of the disability community. Her disability background is nuanced. "I have some ongoing chronic illnesses, but I have only more recently identified as someone with invisible disabilities/chronic illnesses," she says by email.[16]

She suggests that people with hidden disabilities or chronic illnesses may not have the same "relationship to disability" as others, especially if they weren't born with their conditions. It takes time to come to terms with one's own disability (or disabilities). Whatever your degree of disability or illness—and she adds that these conditions aren't always static; many people have intermittent and/or multiple disabilities—the concept of disability pride is important for combating ableist prejudices. Pride "counters the stigma that had been associated with disability," says Haller. Without pride, it's difficult or impossible to fight for your rights, for justice. But pride is not necessarily apt or fitting for everyone, she says. Many folks with hidden disabilities may not talk about them much if at all, or may not identify them *as* disabilities. Age-related chronic illnesses such as arthritis or hearing loss, for example, are often written off as "just part of aging" and don't tend to generate feelings of pride.

The younger generation of disabled people is more likely to understand many more forms of disability and disability discrimination. "They are fighting against [this discrimination] through social media, blogs, videos, even books and documentary films," says Haller. "They understand that getting better and more authentic disability representation in popular culture and media can help change society's attitudes. They're using modern tools to do their advocacy work."

In July 2020, the *New York Times* reported, "There are more young people with disabilities now than in the past, or, at least, more who are willing to accept the label." That may be partly because the definition of disability has expanded, particularly in this case to include a full spectrum of less visible impairments, including autism and anxiety disorders. "Today," the *Times* went on, "almost one in four college students report having had a diagnosis of depression, according to the American College Health Association. That's up from one in 10 college students in 2000."[17]

That figure doesn't include learning or other behavioral disabilities that are increasingly diagnosed in children. According to the US Centers for Disease Control and Prevention, the number of American children diagnosed with attention-deficit/hyperactivity disorder (ADHD) grew from 4.4 million in 2003 to more than 6 million by 2016, the most recent figure available. Of those, 64 percent also had another unspecified "mental, emotional, or behavioral disorder." Roughly half had "behavior or conduct" issues, and a third were diagnosed with anxiety.[18] In 2018, nearly 14 percent of American children between the ages of three and seventeen had been diagnosed with either ADHD or a learning disability.[19] Some of them may outgrow the disabilities, but others won't. It's estimated that more than 4 percent of US adults have ADHD.[20]

That young people are identifying with disability in so many different ways, not shying away from it as their elders might have, hints at a scope and speed of transmission of information that the pre-ADA generation never had. With these new forms of media, many folks know about offensive stereotypes and access violations the moment they occur or are spotted. "Many nondisabled people see these comments on social media, too, and they are siding with disabled people," says Haller. "The movement has done an excellent job of using the technology to educate everyone, disabled or not, about these issues."

An important part of that education, of that consciousness-raising, concerns language. In the decades since the ADA, the terminology around disabilities continued evolving. All sociopolitical movements are bound to get hung up on vocabulary at some point; it's almost unthinkable to talk about any marginalized group today without carefully weighing your choice of words. This isn't just a matter of political correctness or trendiness. It has to do with group identity. Being able to ascribe to yourself your own nomenclature, instead of accepting what the majority culture (or even a past generation) clapped onto you, is key to feeling agency over your fate and asserting your autonomy. But which words or phrases are best for expressing pride?

For many years kids with disabilities have been referred to as having "special needs." But they didn't choose that moniker for themselves. An offshoot of "special education," "special needs" is a term that was picked up by parents and educators who evidently didn't want to associate their kids with the larger disability community, or at least with the stigma of being part of that community. "The word *disability*, for some parents, is a label that makes them feel limitations have been placed on their child prematurely," writes Ericka Polanco-Webb, a reporter for *Chicago Parent*.[21] That's their right, of course. Nevertheless, it's fair to say that most disabled adults find "special needs" cringeworthy. Disability rights are not intended to be about special rights or privileges. They're about fairness and equality. "When I was thrust into parenting a child with a disability, I took the advice from doctors and other parents," says Jamie Davis Smith, mother of a multiply disabled daughter, writing in the *Washington Post*. These so-called experts told her to use the term "special needs" and a host of other euphemisms such as "handicapable." But she soon realized that her daughter's needs were the opposite of special. "She needs to eat, get around, be educated, use the bathroom and be entertained. These things take extra effort for her," Smith says, explaining that her daughter may always have to use a wheelchair, wear diapers, and be fed. "But the needs themselves are basic and ordinary."

For her, the final nail in the "special needs" coffin was realizing that "disabilities" are protected under the law—"special needs" and "developmental differences" and the like are not, at least technically speaking. They have to be translated to "disabilities" to fall within legal safeguards. "When parents use words other than 'disabled' to describe their child, they may be making it more difficult for their child to assert their rights," she says.[22]

Whether or not that's true at a practical level—most bureaucrats and courts recognize that "special needs" means "disabled"—there has certainly been a strong push for "disability" and "disabled" over all other descriptors. In the early 2000s, Lawrence Carter-Long, a disability activist with cerebral palsy, who is currently at the Disability Rights Education and Defense Fund, started the hashtag #SayTheWord to promote these terms. "The language we use mirrors the ways we think," he says. "Embracing the word 'disabled,' fighting the urge and the conditioning that demands we distance ourselves from it, is a powerful illustration of self-determination in action." Boldly proclaiming the word, he says, epitomizes how far the disability community has come. "By deciding what we want to call ourselves, owning it, we claim our power and celebrate the history and the community advocacy that made it possible."[23]

The post-ADA world also gave birth to another neologism: "ableism." Though the *Oxford English Dictionary* pegs the word's first usage to 1981, it doesn't appear even once in the legal language or in Joe Shapiro's *No Pity*. It didn't come into widespread practice until relatively recently, but the fact that it has entered the common vernacular is a testament to the broad recognition of the existence of disability discrimination.

Ableism means different things to different people, however. "The word does a lot of work for disability culture," Andrew Pulrang, a disabled blogger and past executive director of a Pittsburgh-based independent living center, writes in *Forbes*. "It carries the weight of the worst of what plagues disabled people the most, but can be so hard to express." He says that it "often adds as much confusion and dissension to disability discourse as it does clarity and purpose."[24]

Talila A. Lewis, the disabled attorney and "social justice engineer," has thought a great deal about its multifaceted connotations. Ableism is "a system that places value on people's bodies and minds based on societally constructed ideas of normality, intelligence, excellence, desirability, and productivity," T.L. writes. "These constructed ideas are deeply rooted in anti-Blackness, eugenics, misogyny, colonialism, imperialism, and capitalism." As such, T.L. goes on to say, "You do not have to be disabled to experience ableism."[25]

In any case, it's largely because of the ADA and disability pride that people today can easily speak of disabled people as they might other oppressed minorities, incorporating words such as "violations" and "prejudices." Half of the battle to put the ADA over in the first place was convincing legislators that there was actually a problem to address, that disabled people *are* discriminated against and *do* in fact represent a maligned, disparaged, and otherwise unfairly treated minority group. In other words, that ableism—systemic ableism—exists. Nowadays it's a little hard to imagine this was ever in doubt.

If the ADA enables us to cast disability problems in the same way we view racism, transphobia, sexism, homophobia, and other forms of discrimination, it's also turned the word "disability" from a negative descriptor to a politicized signifier. In disability-related social media forums, people engage in feisty debates about the pros and cons of words such as "impairment" and "disease," which many contend are not interchangeable with "disability." "Disability" is inclusive, the *most* inclusive choice. A disability can result from illness, injury, accident, genetics, and more. That broad base gives it power. Furthermore, identifying with disability connects you with a diverse array of other people and a common cause. There's nothing intrinsically shameful about "impairment" or "disease," but they pathologize; they hark back to an outmoded and repressive standard when those with atypical bodies or minds were either shunned and feared as monsters or studied as freaks and oddities, as puzzles to solve. Disability pride reflects a different kind of disconnect between disabled people and the nondisabled world, one that rejects these medical paradigms.

Rejecting medical paradigms means rejecting the "cure mentality." Eli Clare, who has written a great deal about the cure mentality, popularized the term "body-mind," which Clare defines as a rejection of "the dualism built into white Western culture." Body-mind, he says, recognizes "both the inexplicable relationships between our bodies and our minds and the ways in which the ideology of cure operates as if the two are distinct—the mind superior to the body, the mind defining personhood, the mind separating humans from nonhumans."[26] Disability scholar Jennifer Natalya Fink agrees with the concept, noting "how any nonphobic understanding of disability is predicated on an acknowledgment of that indissoluble relation."[27]

This is far from the end of the word wars. Just as the understanding of "disabled" has widened, the distinction between "nondisabled" and "able-bodied" has tightened; activists point out that "able-bodied" should not be used for "nondisabled" (sometimes shortened to "abled," with the people it refers to called "ableds" or "ables") because some able-bodied people *are* disabled—and some disabled people are able-bodied. People with learning, psychiatric, cognitive, autistic, and other invisible disabilities may be able to walk and lift weights and do jumping jacks. They might process or react to information according to a nonconforming blueprint, but their bodies function quite ably. To get the difference between "able-bodied" and "nondisabled" is to twig the full range of what the word "disability" encompasses; to use the words interchangeably—as many people inadvertently do—is tantamount to committing an affront against autistic people and many others with invisible disabilities.

Oddly enough, the oldest word for a disabled person—"cripple"—which was considered a slur for decades, has been reclaimed by many activists, at least among themselves. That was true even before the ADA, but it's become more acceptable now. It's not unusual for disabled people to bandy about the sobriquet "crip" with good-humored ease, unapologetic confidence, and more than a measure of acerbic, ironic pride.

～

An early test of the community's synergy and pride came in the spring of 1995. Word had gotten out that an official memorial to President Franklin D. Roosevelt in Washington, DC, was imminent. It would elevate FDR to the pantheon of Presidents Washington, Jefferson, and

Lincoln, the only others with a grand monument erected in their memory in the nation's capital.

As a concept, it had been discussed for decades; Congress had established an FDR Memorial Commission as early as 1955. "The first design, which called for eight towering slabs of marble, was approved in 1960 and then laughed out of construction by an article in *The Washington Post*, which characterized it as 'Instant Stonehenge,'" according to the *New York Times*. "In the years that followed, other designs were approved and then rejected."[28] But this time, it was finally about to happen, to coincide more or less with the fiftieth anniversary of FDR's death. A San Francisco architect named Lawrence Halprin had produced a plan that won the approval of the congressional memorial commission. That was in 1978. It took another twelve years for Congress to approve the funding. Then a sculptor was chosen.

The design called for four semi-separate outdoor spaces, each with its own statue or monument, to represent his four terms in office. Between these spaces would be a garden pathway. The walls of the spaces would be inscribed with Roosevelt quotations and related historical texts, including, carved in granite, the inscription, "1921, stricken with poliomyelitis—he never again walked unaided."

Construction began in October 1994 on more than seven acres in West Potomac Park along the Tidal Basin near the National Mall. Then the controversy began.

Roosevelt is considered a personal hero to many disabled people—a role model of sorts, even for those who were born decades after his death. He's the only president (so far) who used a wheelchair throughout his tenure (Woodrow Wilson used a wheelchair in part of his second term, following a stroke). And that was precisely the problem. That Roosevelt was a polio survivor was known during his presidency, but the full extent of his post-polio limitations was not. He couldn't keep it a secret, not entirely, so he and his spin doctors cast him as courageous and indomitable—a good, inspiring leader for a country trammeled by the Great Depression and then by World War II. In public appearances, he did his best to hide his disability. He used crutches and leg braces painted black, to be camouflaged by his dark suits and black shoes. He had Secret Service men stand close beside him to prop him on his feet. Outside, he often favored an oversized dark cloak that could easily drape over his seated form and cover his braces. At home, he had wheels attached to a wooden kitchen chair to turn it into an innocuous, nonmedical-looking wheelchair. The White House press corps was not like today's; it didn't challenge the president. It didn't expose secrets. It was in on the deception, though there are reports that any time a press photographer snapped a picture showing the president's infirmity, the Secret Service immediately snatched the camera and destroyed the film.[29]

If you go to YouTube, you can find a few silent clips of FDR walking. Or, rather, seeming to walk. His legs do not move. They are stiff and lifeless in leg braces. In his right hand he holds a plain black cane that he uses as a crutch, or it may actually be a cleverly disguised crutch. The way he clings to it looks jaunty and distinguished, but he plainly leans on it to swing his legs forward, both legs at once. On his left side is a broad-shouldered man holding his elbow, standing very close to support his frame. In one clip, FDR moves in this way to a White House terrace railing; once there, he leans on the railing and the aide on his left abruptly walks away. FDR rests the cane/crutch against the railing and then raises his right hand, now free of the cane, to wave at the crowd. After less than a minute, the bodyguard rematerializes at Roosevelt's left arm, and Roosevelt grabs the ebony cane with his right hand. He is swiftly whisked away. If you blink you might miss it. All you would register is that FDR walked to the railing, waved, and walked away. You couldn't be blamed for swearing you saw him walk. It's a brilliant bit of theater.

When the planners of the FDR Memorial decided to show him as he'd wished to appear in life—that is to say, standing grandly, sans wheelchair—many disabled people were in an uproar. They called it the disability equivalent of whitewashing. Revisionist history. Disability "was so much a part of who he was," Speed Davis, then acting executive director of the National Council on Disability, told the press, "and for them to continue to hide it kind of undermines everything we're trying to do. . . . It reinforces the idea of shame."[30]

Not all disabled people agreed with that. The late conservative columnist Charles Krauthammer—himself a wheelchair user, who often appeared on CNN in tight head-and-shoulders shots that avoided showing his wheelchair—thought the activist viewpoint was wrong. In his weekly column for the *Washington Post*, he wrote, "The weakness of the critics' case lies in its central premise: that FDR would have wanted himself portrayed in a wheelchair. . . . It is a nice argument. It is also nonsense." Krauthammer concluded, "You do not memorialize a man by imposing on him an identity that he himself rejected. Better no memorial at all."[31]

Eight of FDR's grandchildren wrote in support of showing his disability.[32] Later, eight other FDR grandchildren would concur. In time, President Bill Clinton and former presidents Gerald Ford, Jimmy Carter, and George H. W. Bush all came out on the pro-disability side. Bush, champion of the ADA, said, "It would be a shame if at least one of the figures in the memorial did not show him as a man who had a disability."[33]

There are other FDR monuments outside DC. There's a statue of him in Grosvenor Square, London, standing alone (though his cane is visible poking out from his cloak). There's one at his birthplace in Hyde Park, New York, that shows his wheelchair; the site is somewhat off the beaten path, though, receiving fewer than two hundred thousand visitors a year, according to the National Park Service. By comparison, some twenty million tourists come to the nation's capital every year.[34] This was sure to be a big draw.

In April 1997, two years after the first objections were raised and just days before the memorial was due to open, President Clinton announced he would send legislation to Congress for an additional sculpture of FDR *in his wheelchair*. The opening wouldn't be delayed; the modification would have to be made later. In May of that year, Clinton dedicated the memorial while he himself happened to be on crutches. He had recently injured a knee.

It took nearly four more years for the unveiling of the wheelchair statue that Clinton had ordered. In January 2001, in his final days in office, Clinton dedicated the additional dark brown bronze sculpture—a life-size version of FDR seated in his wheelchair, erected near the memorial entrance (called "the prologue room," distinct from the original four open-air "rooms"). It's accessibly level with the stone floor, without pedestal or barrier, and wheelchair-using visitors invariably take a selfie beside the seated president. "The chair in the statue depicts the one the president designed himself from a kitchen chair and tricycle wheels," states the memorial's official literature, which adds that private funds were raised to pay for the addition, not taxpayer dollars.

At the other end of the memorial, up a couple of steps, is a larger-than-life rendering of FDR seated under his cloak with his dog Fala at his feet.

It is less accessible than the one at the entrance, at least for those who can't climb steps. But the figure is most definitely not standing.

In May 2021, a report from the National Council on Independent Living charged that the memorial is not fully accessible for blind visitors. For instance, the braille signs are mostly unreadable.[35] What, if anything, will be done to correct the problems isn't clear. Neither is FDR's legacy as a disability role model. Because of him, any parent of a disabled kid can honestly say, "You can grow up to be anything you want—even president!" But it's complicated. FDR was the epitome of triumph over tragedy. He embodied the overachiever model, the "good patient" who fights the invading disability with pluck and valor. Many disabled people today are intimately familiar with that paradigm; sometimes it seems the only option for getting ahead in the world. It's not exactly disability pride, though. Minimizing or denying your limitations is merely a way of leveraging an awkward situation, of coping with how disabilities are often regarded.

"In many Western cultures, disability is predominantly understood [as] a tragedy, something that comes from the defects and lack of our bodies, whether through accidents of birth or life," say Australian scholars Gerard Goggin and Christopher Newell. "Those 'suffering' with disability, according to this cultural myth, need to come to terms with this bitter tragedy, and show courage in heroically overcoming their lot while they bide their time for the cure that will come. The protagonist for this script is typically the 'brave' person with disability; or, as this figure is colloquially known in critical disability studies and the disability movement—the super-crip."[36]

Disability pride is the opposite end of the spectrum. It's the idea of showing it all, not trying to cover it up, without shame or excuse or trepidation. That's why the FDR Memorial felt so important. Hide his disability and you're telling disabled Americans to hide theirs. But show it and you're proclaiming there's no embarrassment or dishonor about it.

CHAPTER 4

DISABILITY STUDIES AND THE AFTERLIFE OF CULTURAL ICONS

I n 2009, a scholarly journal called the *Disability Studies Quarterly* noted a surprising phenomenon: The number of post-secondary courses devoted to disability studies—a field that was then less than twenty years old—had nearly doubled in the preceding five years. Specifically, in the English-speaking world—the US, Canada, the UK, Australia, and New Zealand—such classes that were not part of a degree-granting program (the publication called them "standalone courses") had grown 93 percent in the prior five years. At the same time, those within degree programs (bachelor's, master's, and PhD) had surged even more: a mind-blowing 98 percent. In all, there were 528 disability studies courses offered in English-speaking countries, up from 268 just five years earlier. "The field is expanding at an exponential rate," concluded the authors, Pamela Cushing and Tyler Smith of King's College at the University of Western Ontario in Canada. They cited three "dimensions of growth"—independent disability studies departments, hybrid classes that combine disability studies with other disciplines, and disability studies curricula that are integrated within liberal arts programs, possibly alongside women's studies or ethnic/race studies.[1]

By 2020, interest in the field had grown so high that there was even a *U.S. News & World Report* ranking.[2] Not bad, considering there were exactly zero classes in disability studies in the US before 1994.

Americans raised after the ADA were subject to disability inclusion. They probably even had a partial awareness of disability politics. Perhaps it's only natural that in college and graduate school they would be interested in learning more about the subject, possibly even entering into disability-related careers. Such careers were no longer limited to health-care disciplines; they could include education, human rights, social justice, the law, and many other fields.

Yet disability studies actually has roots that extend pre-ADA. In 1982, Irving Kenneth Zola, a professor of sociology at Brandeis University and a survivor of both polio and a disabling car accident, joined with a group of other researchers to launch the awkward-sounding Section for the Study of Chronic Illness, Impairment, and Disability. It was mercifully renamed the Society for Disability Studies (SDS) in 1986. The fledgling society soon attracted academics not just in the social sciences but also in the arts and humanities—an interdisciplinary approach to a reality that cuts across all borders and demographics. To intellectuals, this may have seemed a logical step, coming as it did on the heels of the civil rights and women's movements. To the still young disability rights movement, it was groundbreaking and consciousness-raising.

"We began thinking more about America comprising specific histories, unique to groups of people," recalls Tammy Berberi, who is an associate professor of French at the University of Minnesota, Morris, and who has CP.[3] She's a past president of the society, which is still going strong. Currently based in Eureka, California, SDS is devoted to "the study of disability in social, cultural, and political contexts," according to its website.[4] Little has changed from its early days. Its core belief is that disability is a key aspect of the human experience and, therefore, studying it is essential to understanding humankind. Consequently, its goals are "to augment understanding of disability in all cultures and historical periods, to promote greater awareness of the experiences of disabled people, and to advocate for social change."[5] It also aims to promote leaders in the community.

SDS began making inroads into general academia after the 1990 publication of *The Politics of Disablement: A Sociological Approach* by Michael Oliver, a wheelchair-using sociologist in England who survived a spinal cord injury from a swimming accident at seventeen.[6] The book, first published in the UK, then in the US, discusses how disability often gets cast as a medical phenomenon rather than a sociopolitical one. Oliver is credited with coining the notion of the social model of disability.[7] He became the first professor of disability studies in the world, originally at Britain's University of Kent, where he "pioneered the teaching of what we now think of as disability studies to social work students," read his obituary in *The Guardian*. At his death in 2019, Oliver was emeritus professor of disability studies at the University of Greenwich.[8]

In the US, the first official disability studies curriculum was launched in 1994, four years after the ADA, at Syracuse University. It was taught by Steven J. Taylor, a professor at the university's School of Education and director of its Center on Human Policy. He'd taught courses in "special education," with a particular interest in intellectual disabilities, and was editor of the "Intellectual and Developmental Disabilities" newsletter published by the American Association on Intellectual and Developmental Disabilities. His idea, drawn on Oliver's work, was to study disability not as part of a medical or health-care curriculum—as had been done in the past—but as its own minority-based, civil rights–oriented discipline. He aimed to teach students to think critically about what it means to live with a disability and to research how to improve the situation, how to advocate for rights and resolve social inequities. He later won the SDS Senior Scholar Award for outstanding scholarship. "Disability studies starts with accepting the disability. Then it asks the question: 'How do we equalize the playing field?'" he said in 2013, a year before his death.[9]

The social model of disability is a primary element in today's understanding of disability identity. But completely scrapping the medical model isn't always a good idea. Many proud disabled people still battle with medical conditions and needs. The difference is in how one views those medical realities. Berberi at the University of Minnesota stresses that disability studies curricula challenge "deficit models" of disability, which define certain people as "less than" based on physical or cognitive differences, rather than on standard medical models. The social model of disability, in contrast, recognizes that disability isn't a problem to be remedied; instead, it's the ill-suited and unnecessarily closed-off environment that's the problem. Disability studies not only highlights barriers to full and fair inclusion but challenges students to question shopworn notions of who belongs and who doesn't. Academically, the field encompasses history, literature, anthropology, sociology, rhetoric, environmental studies, philosophy, art, and other disciplines. It also intersects with religious studies, women's studies, race studies, migrant studies, queer studies, and other similar areas. "These perspectives neither sync nor completely agree with each other," Berberi says, calling the field a "lively area" of academia that is "growing quickly by every measure."[10]

The popularity of disability studies may relate to the notion that more young people are identifying as disabled. They want to learn more about disabilities from a cultural and intellectual, or nonclinical, viewpoint. At the same time, disability studies courses help reduce the stigma. The possibilities for synergistic energy are powerful. With the knowledge gained on campus, fueled by other students with a similar interest, the spark of disability awareness can explode into action. A 2014 report by disabled scholar Allegra Stout and her nondisabled colleague, Ariel Schwartz, found that informal and student-run disability groups often have a symbiotic connection with official disability studies courses; that is, they feed each other. A campus survey showed "countless ways" in which student disability advocacy groups and disability studies classes—faculty and students, disabled and nondisabled alike—enrich one another. Students not only access disability studies on a theoretical basis but seem to build on it to keep developing their understanding and interpretation of disability experiences. "Additionally," the report says, "student groups educate their campus communities by advocating for the inclusion of disability studies in curricula, sharing their perspectives in the classroom, and hosting events related to disability studies. Through these activities, often in collaboration with faculty and staff, students forge reciprocal relationships between their activism and the field of disability studies."[11]

The piece goes on to tell how a group of undergrads at Wesleyan University petitioned for a quiet, accessible eating space in the campus center so students with sensory sensitivities, anxiety, and other disabilities could eat in peace. "We can't just grant special benefits to one student group. It wouldn't be fair," an administrator reportedly responded. But Wesleyan Students for Disability Rights, a mixed group of disabled and nondisabled students, replied, "This isn't a special benefit. This is about making sure that all students have equal access to the cafeteria."

Using ideas they'd learned in disability studies classes, spread and amplified over social media, the group articulated all the ways that disabled students were unfairly marginalized on campus, and the impact of that marginalization. Disability studies, they found, had "transformed the lens through which we perceive both disability and the rhetoric about disability" and given them the tools to counter this particular form of bureaucratic obstinacy.

In the end, they won their accessible eating space. Moreover, they reported feeling able to "change our realities."

~

O ver time, disability studies delved ever deeper into disability culture. Bit by bit, more truths about where we'd come from began to see daylight, some aspects of which were more pleasant than others. For instance, it's come out that there's been an unfair hierarchy in cripdom; as in other disenfranchised minorities, certain subgroups have enjoyed advantages or jockeyed for dominance—and not just along racial or gender lines. Impairments below the chest or waist are often considered "preferable" (by disabled and nondisabled people alike) to those that affect the head and face. Studies indicate that intellectual disabilities may bear the most stigma,[12] and that inborn impairments are more feared by the general population than acquired disabilities even if, on a functional level, they're equivalent.[13] Disabled people themselves debate who has it better, those with congenital disabilities or survivors of accidents and illness. This is not unlike a tendency among communities of Color, where lighter skin tones have often been taken to signify greater attractiveness, intelligence, or acceptability, as absurd and hateful as that may seem. "The stigmatized stratify their own because no one wants to be in last place," observes Duke anthropologist J. Lorand "Randy" Matory.[14]

The first group of disabled folks to become mainstream role models—outside of the occasional breakout stars—tended to be rugged, muscular, and white. Many were wheelchair basketball or wheelchair tennis players, their beefy arms propelling their stripped-down, aerodynamic sports chairs to great speeds and an almost brutal rigorousness. Very macho, they did the best job of emulating their nondisabled athletic peers. They were considered strong, independent, autonomous, tough, sexy—and they helped put at ease anyone who might be a little uncomfortable around atypical bodies. (They were also almost uniformly cisgender men.) That is, their pursuits were more recognizable and legible to the nondisabled world. Remember Oscar Pistorius, the Olympic and

Paralympic sprinter from South Africa whose prosthetic "racing blades" helped make him famous (and who was later convicted of murdering his girlfriend)? Remember the popular 2005 documentary *Murderball*, about quadriplegic jocks who play full-contact rugby?

Society's general acceptance of disabled people who are able to, in a sense, impersonate nondisabled people, or otherwise fit nondisabled expectations, runs through the history. Yet arriving at a unifying theme for disability icons is like trying to describe the most glamorous movie star or the most tragic event ever; it's slippery. It depends on your frame of reference. Similarly, there is no single resource, no pressing agenda or collection of concepts, that will inevitably jibe with every disabled person's biography or interests. Given that, you may wonder if it's even right to speak of "disabled people" as a distinct group. What, if anything, does it mean to be a member of that group? What exactly are the qualities that define "disability" as an identity? It's certainly not just about functional limitations or medical history. It's about exclusion and marginalization. It's about context and, often, a lack of respect and agency over one's own life. But beyond that, the traits are as widespread and diverse as humanity itself.

The international access symbol of a stick figure in a wheelchair is itself reductionist, some disability advocates say, since many disabled folks don't use wheelchairs, and those who do are rarely so stationary. It was adopted by the independent International Organization for Standardization in the late 1960s.[15] In 1994, an Irishman named Brendan Murphy proposed changing the image to show the seated figure leaning forward and with an arm cocked in back, as if to push the chair[16]; in 2013, Sara Hendren and Brian Glenney, Boston-area educators, further modified the icon to show the seated figure in an even more active position, to emphasize forward movement.[17] The latter became the official symbol in certain states and municipalities the following year. Still, not everyone is behind having a wheelchair represent all disabilities.[18] "It is a major cause of grief," says an unsigned post on the Nth Degree blog.[19]

The desire to reclaim the pillars of disability in America is one way of helping to define what the disability identity signifies. Disability studies has, among other pursuits, been devoted to unearthing the "secret history" of disability—the common threads in the lives of disabled people from the past, the through line that ties them together as a distinct cultural phenomenon or demographic body. This amplifies the sense of communal character while occasionally uncovering archetypes in the struggle against ableism.

It's through efforts to center erased people throughout history that we've learned about forebears such as Joice Heth, an enslaved disabled woman who went on to fame—if that's the word—in P. T. Barnum's circus. Barnum "leased" her for an alleged $1,000 (since slavery was technically illegal in the North, where Barnum operated) from a Kentucky slaveholder identified as R. W. Lindsay, in 1835, when Heth was probably seventy-nine years old. Lindsay had purchased her earlier that year from another Kentuckian named John S. Bowling, who had marketed her as an elderly woman with a connection to George Washington. Heth might have made that last part up. But under Barnum's control, she was hawked far and wide as Washington's 161-year-old childhood nursemaid.

Heth was reportedly paralyzed in both legs and one arm and mostly blind; Barnum added that she weighed forty-six pounds and had no teeth.[20] "Barnum went as far as to remove teeth from Heth and neglect her care to make her appear physically deformed, and by extension much older than she actually was," says the disabled historian who writes under the name Mwatuangi.[21]

Barnum's circus was more than your average minstrel show, but minstrelsy was about the only way out for many African Americans in those days, and that was especially true for those with disabilities. Consider Thomas Wiggins, known as "Blind Tom." Born into slavery in 1849 on a Georgia plantation, he soon made his masters (and, later, his "guardians") a fortune. Before reaching puberty, the young man who was born both blind and possibly autistic—his obituary calls him "weak-minded"—became a touring musical sensation, playing his own compositions on the piano and a variety of classical and popular tunes of the day. He could also recite famous political speeches with pitch-perfect mimicry.

At ten, Wiggins was invited to entertain at the White House for President James Buchanan, making him the first Black American to perform there.[22] At the height of his fame, Wiggins earned as much as $100,000 a year, the equivalent of more than $1 million today, though he got to keep very little of it. Still, he was among the highest-compensated performers of his time.

Exploited as he was, Wiggins was lucky. In 2008, the *Disability Studies Quarterly* revealed that most enslaved disabled people were *not* "liberated" by the Union forces as their nondisabled counterparts were. The Southern slaveholders spread the falsehood that Black people didn't have the mental or physical capabilities to handle freedom, and the Union bought it. After the Civil War, the North perpetuated the idea by circulating images of proud, robust, and distinctly nondisabled Black men (it was almost always men) joining the Union army, tending their own farms, and, eventually, voting. These images, writes history professor Jim Downs of Connecticut College, "obscured the experiences of hundreds of disabled, blind, and deaf freed slaves that were caught in the transition from slavery to freedom."[18]

Fifteen years after slavery was abolished, in 1880, Roger Demosthenes O'Kelly was born in Raleigh, North Carolina. He was nondisabled, but at nine he caught scarlet fever. He survived, but afterward remained D/deaf and partially blind. In 1898, O'Kelly applied to Gallaudet University. He was denied entrance because he was Black. So instead, he entered Shaw University in his hometown, a private liberal arts school that claims to be the first historically Black university in the South (founded in 1865). Some accounts say O'Kelly then suffered a football injury that exacerbated his blindness in one eye. In any case, he managed so well—communicating primarily with a pad and pencil—that, in 1909, he graduated with a law degree and subsequently applied to and got into Yale University, from where he received a second law degree in 1912. He worked odd jobs for several years, digging ditches and such, to earn a living. Between 1918 and 1919, he taught school for D/deaf Black children before opening his own private law practice in Raleigh in 1920, primarily for Black clients. His practice continued for the better part of three decades.

O'Kelly died in 1962 at age eighty-two. His obituary in the *Shaw University Bulletin* read, "He claimed the distinction of being the only Negro deaf lawyer in the United States and the second deaf person to graduate from Yale University in her history of over 250 years."[24]

Such distinctions alone should make him a hero, but his story is mostly forgotten.

In comparison, everyone has heard of Helen Keller, who was born the same year as O'Kelly, 1880, in Tuscumbia, Alabama. But Keller, who was white and perhaps most known because of the 1962 movie *The Miracle Worker*, grew up in completely different circumstances. Her family was well-to-do and had been slaveholders; her maternal grandfather was a Confederate general in the Civil War. At nineteen months old, Keller came down with a severe illness—like O'Kelly—that left her permanently D/deafblind. She went on to attend the Perkins Institution for the Blind (later renamed the Perkins School for the Blind), outside Boston, where she met Anne Sullivan, an instructor who was also visually impaired. Sullivan became her constant companion. For most of the next five decades, they helped each other navigate the world. But there's no question that Keller was well connected. She enrolled at Radcliffe College, and her tuition was paid entirely by a benefactor, Standard Oil head Henry Huttleston Rogers.

Keller became famous through her writing and speeches as a champion of braille, disability rights, women's rights, labor rights, and world peace. More than half a century after her death in 1968, she remains a role model for many. But some disability scholars have suggested reexamining her legacy.

Keller is known for the ways she learned to communicate with the nondisabled world. Besides writing and reading braille, she was able to understand spoken words by feeling people's lips and throats. She also used "fingerspelling," a way of representing letters and numbers with finger movements, primarily through having someone touch her hand. She took in music by placing her hands on vibrating tables or cabinets. She learned to speak orally, which enabled her to give lectures to the general public. As inspiring as her example may be, it's also polarizing. Some draw attention to her endorsement of oralism—that is, encouraging D/deaf people to communicate out loud so non-D/deaf people can hear them, instead of using sign language. They question her allegiance to the uniquely D/deaf culture and language. Others are alarmed by her longtime association with Alexander Graham Bell, the inventor of the telephone, whose mother and wife were D/deaf and who urged them to act like hearing people. Bell also argued that D/deaf people should not marry each other, lest their children turn out D/deaf. Keller herself "warned of the dangers of marriage" for D/deaf people, says the nondisabled disability scholar Deborah Marks, indicating a possible affinity for the eugenics movement.[25]

On the other hand, many modern-day D/deaf people don't want her erased from the collective memory or "canceled" for her ideologies. If anything, they say, we should understand more about her than her childhood efforts to cope in a hearing world. As an adult, Keller was a founder of the American Civil Liberties Union, a birth-control supporter, an early champion of the National Association for the Advancement of Colored People, and a strong opponent of lynching. Her politics was clearly progressive, which may be why, in 2018, the conservative Texas Board of Education voted to remove her name (and those of other liberal icons, such as Hillary Clinton) from the state's education curriculum. D/deafblind attorney and activist Haben Girma, among others, was outraged. Keller, she wrote in the *Washington Post*, "serves as a gateway to conversations about disability." Her life story can introduce young students to braille and sign language, she argued, while simultaneously demonstrating disabled people's capabilities and ingenuity. Girma acknowledged that Keller doesn't represent the only disability perspective; the disability community is naturally full of diverse views and accomplishments. But, she said, "students need to learn more about disability, not less."[26]

Two months later, the Texas education board rescinded the proposal.[27]

Touchstones of disability history like these help create a kind of latticework. But it's still under construction and ever shifting. To misconstrue, misjudge, or look past someone or something significant, a data point or unsung contributor to the disability ethos, is almost inevitable. No doubt more truths will be uncovered or reexamined in the future. Still, without an understanding of disability heritage, of disability culture, how can anyone understand their own disability experiences? As Emily Ladau, the disability activist and author, says about disability pride, it's something you feel inside that's derived from the culture and history of people who came before, perhaps many generations before.[28] It's knowing who you are as a person *within that context*, and in the ways you navigate the often inaccessible and unwelcoming world, just as other disabled people have done before you. It's important to educate disabled and nondisabled people alike about that context; it isn't dead history. Rather, it's background relevant to things going on today. People need to know their history, their roots, to understand what's going on in the disability community. They need to know about resources and supports. They need to know they're not alone and don't have to feel isolated or afraid.

This is one of the key impacts of disability studies programs—they help us better understand our roots through a disability rights lens and focus attention on other disabled lives and events that may have been erased from the mainstream narrative. By opening up and deepening our awareness of these histories, these cultural landmarks, the field of disability studies plays a major role in developing and expanding our understanding of what disability pride means.

PART II

PRESENTATION AND REPRESENTATION

CHAPTER 5

NEURODIVERSITY AND
AUTISTIC SELF-ADVOCACY

T hroughout much of the twentieth century, autistic advocacy was al- most exclusively about finding a "cure." Parents of autistic kids advo- cated on their behalf, or tried to, often unwittingly doing profound harm; autistic people themselves were scarcely recognized or acknowledged as full people. That was a recipe for disaster.

In the 1990s, in the wake of the ADA, a growing number of autis- tic people started connecting their experiences to the disability rights movement. They began self-advocating. One of the early advocates was Anita Cameron—who describes herself as a "fierce Black #BlackAutistic lesbian," among other things. In the 1980s, she joined ADAPT, the grass- roots disability rights organization that was then mostly about accessible transportation. "There wasn't even anyone there who was autistic that I knew of," she says.[1]

It took a few more years for the autistic community to get organized. In 2006, a group called the Autistic Self Advocacy Network was formed. In 2011, the Autistic Women's Network (AWN) was launched, partly in response to the male-dominated discourse on autism. Later renamed the Autistic Women and Nonbinary Network, it is today an organization dedicated to providing a supportive community and resources for autistic women, girls, transfeminine and transmasculine nonbinary people, trans people of all genders, Two Spirit people, and all others of marginalized genders. "People are not identical," says Lydia X. Z. Brown, who is AWN's director of policy, advocacy, and external affairs. "Their brains are not identical. How people function is not identical. People learn differently. They sense differently. They form relationships differently. They think differently. They perceive differently. That's a basic fact of human biology."[2]

Brown is a teacher, organizer, writer, and activist focusing on violence against multiply marginalized disabled people, especially those impacted by institutionalization, incarceration, and policing. An autistic Asian American who uses they/them pronouns, Brown has written for numerous scholarly and community publications and coedited (along with E. Ashkenazy and Morénike Giwa Onaiwu) *All the Weight of Our Dreams*, the first anthology by autistic people of Color.[3]

To encompass this understanding of the different ways people function, a new term entered the lexicon: neurodiversity. "A lot of people use the word 'neurodiversity' without knowing what it means," says Brown. Neurodiversity posits that there's nothing inherently wrong or defective about a person whose brain operates differently from another person's. "People are not *less than* because of how their brains function," says Brown. Such variation is in fact a key component of the rich patchwork of society. As such, advocates such as Brown disparage organizations that use person-first language; if an organization talks about "people with autism," as opposed to "autistic people," that's a pretty good clue it's not run by autistic people themselves. "There is nothing wrong with being autistic," says Brown, "so why would we say something that implies autism can somehow be separated from us and therefore *ought* to be?"[4]

Brown further rejects the term "autism spectrum disorder" as insultingly pathologizing. Autistic advocates, like other disabled activists, have fought against terminology that medicalizes. Equally maddening is the prominence of nonautistic "experts"—researchers, teachers, parents, and medical professionals who take it upon themselves to speak for autistic and other neurodivergent people. "These so-called authorities claim to be 'the voice for the voiceless,'" Brown says. "It's always better when people from marginalized communities take control of our own narratives. No one else understands what we experience better than *we* do, the people who experience it."[5]

Brown, who blogs at www.autistichoya.com, acknowledges that nonautistic folks *can* make valuable contributions to autistic lives; still, they warn, if you don't belong to a particular marginalized community, it is your responsibility to take the lead from the people who do. "Do your best to amplify their work and their leadership, rather than positioning yourself as the person who seizes all the attention," they advise.

Lately, no autistic person has seized more mainstream attention than Greta Thunberg, the teenage Swedish environmental activist. Brown has nothing against Thunberg, but separating out autistic "heroes" like Thunberg can be a distraction from normalizing neurodiversity. It "buys into the myth that if autistic people achieve something, something big, it makes them more worthy of respect," they say. "We all deserve respect and dignity for no reason other than because we're humans."

Brown says that rather than focus on those who need less day-to-day support, who tend to achieve a higher degree of social currency, we should pay attention to more urgent matters. For instance, they contend that to this day less than 1 percent of all federal research dollars spent on autism goes toward quality-of-life issues. The overwhelming majority is aimed at finding a cure, which Brown dubs "eugenicist research." In 2018, Brown launched the nonprofit Fund for Community Reparations for Autistic People of Color's Interdependence, Survival, and Empowerment—to provide the sort of direct support to autistic people of Color that the federal government doesn't.[6]

~

The word "neurodiversity" has its own history. It seems to have been coined in 1998 by an autistic Australian graduate student named Judy Singer. The idea was based on the ecological term "biodiversity," to make the point that invisible cognitive and intellectual disabilities are natural expressions of humanity's variations. "Judy started to think, what if, instead of thinking about how can we cure these conditions by discovering their cause, we focused on what these people actually need to participate more fully?" says Steve Silberman, author of *Neurotribes: The Legacy of Autism and the Future of Neurodiversity*.[7]

As a concept, neurodiversity was picked up and spread by a nondisabled American journalist named Harvey Blume. In the September 1998 issue of *The Atlantic*, Blume echoed earlier thinking by arguing that some people we might call geniuses—people such as Microsoft cofounder Bill Gates—could be regarded as part of the "neurodiversity spectrum." He underscored the proposition that a lack of fit between, say, traditional teaching modes and the ways autistic kids process information was what truly hampered them. Autism may be at least partly (if not wholly) genetic in origin, but that didn't mean it was a deficit.[8]

It wasn't long before "neurodiversity" became an umbrella term for an even broader variety of situations, including dyslexia, Tourette's syndrome, stuttering, bipolarism, schizophrenia, and obsessive-compulsive disorders. Some people objected to lumping together too many different types of folks. But Kassiane Asasumasu—a Hapa and Asian American autistic rights activist and blogger from Oregon, formerly known as Kassiane Alexandra Sibley—insists that "neurodivergent," a term she coined in 1999 specifically for individuals who are "neurologically divergent from typical," was always intended as "a tool of inclusion."[9]

Nevertheless, certain groups simply don't want to be associated with others. There have been efforts to differentiate between people whose cognitive functioning affects communication and those with medically treatable conditions such as epilepsy or hyperactivity. Some autistic people need constant support; others don't, and they achieve relative autonomy. But that, as Brown would say, is a distraction from the big picture affecting all neurodiverse people.

Even before these new words were coined, autism was already gaining mainstream attention. In 1986, Temple Grandin's memoir *Emergence: Labeled Autistic* became a big hit. Many readers considered it groundbreaking for its frank description of an autistic life. Grandin, an expert on animal behavior and a proponent of the humane treatment of livestock for slaughter, came out as autistic, which was a rarity at the time. For some, that act broke down years of stigma and shame. But her understanding of her own autism had problems she herself sought to correct in later years. For one, she referred to herself as a "recovered autistic," explaining that she had been effectively cured by the doting attentions of her mother and nanny; she did not speak until she was three and a half years old and credited their loving, devoted kindnesses with helping draw her out. In later years, she revised this account; in 1995's *Thinking in Pictures and Other Reports from My Life with Autism*, she writes that she had actually learned to adapt, rather than having "recovered." Later still, in 2013's *The Autistic Brain: Thinking Across the Spectrum*, she asserts that autism comes in many different forms and is often misdiagnosed.

Grandin won numerous awards and honors, and many autistic people credit her with helping them understand themselves. But her connection with autistic advocacy is often disputed. She may be a role model for some—particularly for older autistic folks; Grandin was born in 1947—but she doesn't speak for all.

Not long after Grandin burst on the scene, the movie *Rain Man* became a commercial hit. The comedy/drama/road picture about a self-centered young man (played by Tom Cruise) and his "savant" brother (Dustin Hoffman) was the top-grossing film of 1988 and went on to sweep the Oscars. Some disability activists protested that yet another nondisabled actor was performing in "crip face," but most viewers loved Hoffman's performance. His character was likable, intelligent, loyal, relatable, and altogether adorable. For many nonautistic people, that was their introduction to autism.

Interest in this disability was rising in academia as well. At that time, the prevailing theory on autism was an old one. In the early 1900s, a Swiss psychiatrist named Eugen Bleuler coined "autistic" for a kind of "social withdrawal and detachment."[10] In the 1920s, a Russian doctor named Grunya Efimovna Sukhareva used the word to describe "highly intelligent" boys who "showed a preference for their own inner world."[11] Then, in 1943, an Austrian American child psychiatrist at Johns Hopkins named Leo Kanner published an influential article titled "Autistic Disturbances of Affective Contact" in the journal *Nervous Child*, which concluded that autism was (a) extremely rare and (b) primarily attributable to stern, unaffectionate parenting.[12] This view continued to hold sway, despite passionate efforts to dispute it. As early as 1967, a woman named Clara Claiborne Park published *The Siege: The First Eight Years of an Autistic Child*, a first-person account of parenting her autistic daughter, which became one of the first books to challenge the idea that autism was caused by cold, detached parenting.[13] In particular, she challenged the teachings of Bruno Bettelheim, a Kanner adherent who championed using electric shocks to treat children with behavioral disabilities. (After Bettelheim's death in 1990, much of his work was discredited due to fraudulent academic credentials and allegations of patient abuse.)[14]

In the late 1980s and early 1990s, a British cognitive psychologist named Lorna Wing and her colleague Judith Gould picked up the thread. Wing had an autistic daughter, and, like Park, she knew that she and her husband weren't cold and austere. Moreover, she and Gould argued that autism was much more prevalent than most people surmised, in part because it encompassed a much broader array of behaviors than was generally acknowledged. They soon uncovered (and translated) a forgotten 1944 report by a German educator and researcher named Hans Asperger called "'Autistic Psychopathy' in Childhood";[15] Asperger ran a combination school and clinic in Vienna before the Nazi regime seized power, and he dedicated much of his career to studying and educating children with "mental deficiencies"—autism and learning disabilities. His specialty was adapting teaching methods to fit each child's particular abilities and strengths. Asperger believed there was a wide variety of autistic people, and he went so far as to posit that some highly intelligent, successful adults could be autistic—absent-minded-professor types who possess a single-minded devotion to solving knotty problems while utterly missing social cues. (There is also evidence suggesting he participated in the Third Reich's child-euthanasia program, which effectively aimed to eliminate young people deemed "impure" and "burdensome to society.")[16]

Wing and Gould took this overlooked research and ran with it. They developed new clinical tests for diagnosing autistic behavior and promoted the concept of an autism spectrum. They created the category of Asperger syndrome for those who did not have a significant language impairment—though nowadays, many who are proudly autistic reject that nomenclature. With this greater understanding came an explosion in the population of people identified as autistic. The broader definition simply included more people; it was not, as some critics alleged, evidence of an out-of-control "epidemic." Today, according to the Centers for Disease Control and Prevention, one in fifty-nine Americans is autistic.[17]

Soon after Wing and Gould's work, groups of like-minded autistic adults started joining together to empower one another. One leader of this effort was Jim Sinclair, a graduate student at Syracuse University, the school where disability studies originated in the US. Sinclair, assigned female at birth, did not speak until age twelve, at which point the young activist vociferously objected to the gender label they'd been given. Sinclair now identifies as intersex and uses they/them pronouns—"openly and proudly neuter," they wrote in "Self-Introduction to the Intersex Society of North America" in the early 1990s.[18] In 1992, Sinclair joined with fellow autistics (their word) Kathy Lissner Grant and Polly Samuel (known to much of the outside world by her nom de plume, Donna Williams) to form Autism Network International (ANI). It really started as a group of pen pals, or online pen pals, until they met in person and felt a profound connection to one another. The group grew with the speed of the Internet. It launched a newsletter called "Our Voice" and a series of autistic-only retreats called Autreats. Autreats were in sharp contrast to the autism conferences of the past, which had been primarily by and for medical professionals and parents of autistic kids.[19] Taking a cue from D/deaf culture—which essentially posits that D/deafness is not a deficit (or even, in some cases, a disability) but a communication difference, sign language being just another language—Sinclair and ANI developed the terms "neurologically typical" or "neurotypical" to describe those who are not neurodivergent. They were effectively satirizing the medical model. Autreats even had panel discussions where participants could "Ask a neurotypical." (Nonautistic people, who may still be neurodivergent because of dyslexia or ADHD or some other disability, are called "allistic.")[20]

Years later, this principle would be mirrored in the concept known as "disability gain." The idea, roughly speaking, is that if a disability is not a deficit, it is also not really a neutral characteristic either, at least not always. It can give people particular insights and advantages. Many disabled people boast of being unusually adaptable to whatever's thrown at them, to being creative problem solvers, for instance. Some autistic people are said to be especially adept at concentrating on details without distraction.

In 1993, in an essay titled "Don't Mourn for Us," Sinclair wrote:

> You didn't lose a child to autism. You lost a child because the child you waited for never came into existence. That isn't the fault of the autistic child who does exist, and it shouldn't be our burden. We need and deserve families who can see us and value us for ourselves, not families whose vision of us is obscured by the ghosts of children who never lived. Grieve if you must, for your own lost dreams. But don't mourn for us. We are alive. We are real.[21]

～

O ften, autistic people who are nonverbal feel the most devalued. Amy Sequenzia, for instance, is a nonspeaking, multiply disabled autistic activist and author who writes essays and poetry about disability rights, civil rights, and human rights. In one blog post, she discusses how "intelligence" is often used as an ableist weapon, as when nonspeaking people like her are pressured to vindicate themselves by proving their intelligence.[22]

Another "minimally-speaking autistic," as he describes himself, is Hari Srinivasan. A PhD candidate at the University of California, Berkeley, Srinivasan says that "access to higher education for individuals like me is hard-won." Which is at least partly why he's become an activist. To assert that he belongs.[23]

Sequenzia and Srinivasan have served as board members of the Autistic Self Advocacy Network (ASAN), the nonprofit cofounded in 2006 by autistic activist and scholar Ari Ne'eman. It started, Ne'eman says, in response to a lack of representation of authentic autistic voices. "A number of us in the autistic adult community were frustrated by the national conversation on autism that was taking place, which was almost entirely focused on researcher, provider, and family member perspectives, with little to no opportunity for the perspectives of—or even acknowledgment of the existence of—autistic adults. We really did not want an emphasis in autism policy that was exclusively on causation and cure. We wanted to ensure that autistic people ourselves were represented in the halls of power."[24]

ASAN borrowed a slogan from other grassroots disability rights groups: "Nothing about us without us." Although this motto originated in sixteenth-century Poland, with a political movement to shift power from a monarchy to an elected legislature,[25] its earliest known usage in disability circles was at an early 1990s disability gathering in South Africa, as described by author James I. Charlton.[26] It soon spread throughout the disability world.

By the time ASAN was forming, the fervor to "explain" autism had grown so nonsensical that, in 1998, the staid medical journal *The Lancet* published a now-debunked study by Dr. Andrew J. Wakefield and his team claiming autism could be caused by a vaccination.[27] It was retracted as a complete fraud in 2010.[28] Nevertheless, Wakefield, a proud anti-vaxxer, was supported by some parents of autistic people, primarily through groups such as Autism Speaks. ASAN and other autistic self-advocates protested strongly—and they continue to distance themselves from medical charities with little to no interest in autistic empowerment.

ASAN and Ne'eman, who is currently a senior research associate at the Harvard Law School Project on Disability and a visiting scholar at the Lurie Institute for Disability Policy at Brandeis University, went on to oppose the 2006 Combating Autism Act signed by President George W. Bush, which allocated $1 billion over a five-year period to identify the causes of autism and effectively wipe it out. To Ne'eman, it was tantamount to a declaration of war on autistic people. Many agreed, but others did not feel that way, particularly parents of autistic kids. Ne'eman and others lost that battle. The act was reauthorized in 2011 and again in 2014, when it was renamed the Autism Collaboration, Accountability, Research, Education and Support Act, commonly known as Autism CARES. In 2019, it was given another five-year extension.

However, Ne'eman credits ASAN with successfully "integrating the autistic community into the larger disability rights movement. Fifteen years or so ago, autism wasn't discussed in the context of disability rights. We've really changed that." He acknowledges that there's still a lot to be done, particularly in outreach to young autistic people. "Many autistic young adults have been struggling for years to understand who they are," he says. "They haven't had access to a paradigm that explains and values how their brains work, other than in a pathological sense." He wants to help more people form a healthy and positive autistic identity early in life.

To that end, ASAN produced a video, available on YouTube, called "Welcome to the Autistic Community," which is intended to help guide young autistic people to a better sense of self-worth. AWN and two other organizations—Little Lobbyists and Thinking Person's Guide to Autism—created a booklet called *Start Here: A Guide for Parents of Autistic Kids.*[29] Meanwhile, a group called Autastic—founded by Diane J. Wright, who identifies as a member of the autistic Black Indigenous people of Color community—posted an online guide called "The Basics."[30] And in November 2021, Haley Moss—one of the first openly autistic attorneys in the nation[31]—published *The Young Autistic Adult's Independence Handbook.*[32]

Another priority for autistic activists is ending the horrendous neglect and abuse that autistic people endure in institutions. Cal Montgomery—a trans, queer, autistic, physically disabled activist and writer—is a survivor of long-term institutionalization. Years ago, he joined ADAPT to fight disability oppression; now he's an ASAN board member. On March 4, 2020, Montgomery and other members of the neurodivergent community celebrated a rare victory: The US Food and Drug Administration (FDA) banned electric-shock devices used to alter (read: punish) the behavior of certain autistic and neurodivergent people. For years, activists had condemned the practice as torture; they had lobbied to ban using the devices to inflict pain, as opposed to using electricity for nerve stimulation or deep-brain stimulation (as in certain electroconvulsive or electroshock treatments). "We are relieved beyond measure that soon our community members will no longer be punished with dangerous electric shocks for doing things like standing up without permission, making noises, or crying in pain," said an ASAN press release.[33]

The practice is so widely derided as cruel and out of date that there is really only one institution left in the country that still practices electric-shock punishment for behavior modification: the Judge Rotenberg Educational Center (JRC), a residential institution for disabled people in Canton, Massachusetts.

A month after its electric-shock ban, though, the FDA issued a stay, ostensibly due to the coronavirus pandemic, and in July 2021 a federal appeals court overturned the ban completely, ruling it beyond the FDA's proper jurisdiction.[34] Activists were swift to condemn the ruling. "This decision is devastating and enraging for our community members," said an AWN press release. "Dozens of largely Black and Brown disabled people institutionalized in the JRC will continue to be subjected to torture in the name of treatment. In real numbers, that means 55 human beings will continue to be tortured because of their disabilities, and it will be legal."[35]

While the issue remains unresolved, progress seems to be marching on in other areas. In Vancouver, Canada, Fiji-born Dr. T. C. Waisman—who identifies as an autistic, Indigenous Pasifika, Southeast Asian and Nepalese woman—is conducting international autism outreach and education to promote a better understanding of autism on the global stage.[36] In South Africa, the Autistic Strategies Network is collaborating with autistic people throughout the continent and internationally to educate young people about autistic advocacy, raise awareness of disability rights, and generally improve opportunities for neurodivergent folks.[37] Closer to home, the Autism Intervention Research Network on Physical Health—a groundbreaking group in Los Angeles—is bringing a "neurodiverse orientation" to health care.[38] In Tampa Bay, Florida, Lourdes Quiñones, a physical therapist and consultant at the Center for Autism and Related Disabilities at the University of South Florida, launched *La Hora del Cafecito* (The Coffee Hour), an online program that brings discussions of autism-related issues to Spanish-speaking audiences.[39] And in January 2021, Jessica Benham became one of the first openly autistic politicians to hold office when she was sworn in to the Pennsylvania House of Representatives; Benham, a founder of the Pittsburgh Center for Autistic Advocacy, an activist group run by autistic people, promised to draw attention to the problems facing autistic and queer people (she's bisexual).[40]

In addition, recent appointments to the federal Interagency Autism Coordinating Committee, an advisory board under the Department of Health and Human Services, included eight professionals who are autistic—a record number, though still not enough, advocates say, considering there are thirty-one members in all.[41]

A better understanding of autistic people's needs and potential has begun to be recognized in corporate culture, too. Some companies are actively changing their intake processes to accommodate autistic jobseekers. They're realizing some autistic people may not interact socially along traditional behavior standards. They may not maintain eye contact. They may be uncomfortable giving a firm handshake. They may interpret sarcastic humor more literally than it was intended. In May 2013, German software giant SAP launched a program called "Autism at Work," which trains managers to better understand autistic traits and scout out talented autistic candidates. Interested applicants are encouraged to pursue any position available; they are not steered to specific areas, in recognition of the fact that autistic people have a broad variety of skills and interests.[42] Other corporations that have restructured their hiring processes for autistic talent include Microsoft, HP, Ford Motor Company, and UK-based insurance broker Willis Towers Watson.

Corporate initiatives to become more accessible for autistic people have gained so much traction that the *Harvard Business Review*—a bastion of un-fringe-y standards—addressed them directly: "Neurodiverse people frequently need workplace accommodations, such as headphones to prevent auditory overstimulation, to activate or maximally leverage their abilities," write Robert D. Austin and Gary P. Pisano. "Sometimes they exhibit challenging eccentricities. In many cases the accommodations and challenges are manageable and the potential returns are great." To realize these benefits, the article says, companies need to adjust their recruitment, selection, and career development policies to reflect a broader definition of talent. It further notes that many neurodivergent people have "higher-than-average abilities"; some of them, it observes, may have "special skills in pattern recognition, memory, or mathematics."[43]

Meanwhile, architects and designers are working to make buildings and cities more accessible to autistic people. This isn't exactly the same as the ADA architectural codes, but it's trying to achieve something similar. One example is an Egyptian architect named Magda Mostafa, who is an assistant professor at the Department of Architectural Engineering at the American University in Cairo. In 2002, as a student at Cairo University, she set out to plan her country's first educational center for autistic students. To her surprise, she found there were no guidelines. Six years later, after interviewing and surveying groups of autistic people and listening to what they wanted and needed, she completed an autistic-design study and devised seven design criteria for measuring the autistic appropriateness of any built environment. They included acoustical considerations to minimize background noise, echoes, and reverberations; avoiding other types of sensory overload by compartmentalizing different interior environments; spatial "sequencing" so that rooms are organized in a logical order that enables activities to flow seamlessly; the inclusion of "transition zones" such as plain hallways or anterooms to allow inhabitants to move from space to space gradually; and "escape spaces" to provide respite from overstimulation. In all, she called it the Autism ASPECTSS Design Index.[44]

Though Mostafa is not autistic, she says she felt the need to create some quantifiable standards for what she knew to be an underserved population. Her work was informed by the broader disability movement's impetus to smash expectations of "normative" body types and behaviors, she says.

Such supports and accommodations can encompass "a whole new world of 'universal design for learning' tools, many of them technology-based," explains Thomas Armstrong, executive director of the American Institute for Learning and Human Development in Cloverdale, California. Armstrong, who is not disabled, is the author of *The Power of Neurodiversity*, among other books. Accommodations, he says, might include "text-to-speech and speech-to-text apps, Augmentative Alternative Communication apps, et cetera."[45]

Augmentative Alternative Communication devices give nonverbal users the freedom to express themselves by pointing a laser or manually tapping at letters, words, or pictures. The simplest form is a board with the alphabet or basic graphics, but nowadays computers, tablets, and smartphones can perform the same function. Some people are hoping the next generation of the technology will make it easier to choose or customize the type or timbre of the speech output to better mirror diverse voices. These tools are not just for autistic people; they're also for anyone with a speech disability. For Armstrong, finding the right "tools that make autistic people better able to function in society" is crucial, even while simultaneously acknowledging "they're okay in their own right and don't need to be cured."

Perhaps the best expression of that concept comes from Mel Baggs, the autistic and nonbinary activist, filmmaker, and blogger who died in April 2020 at thirty-nine. Baggs was nonverbal and "genderless," using sie/hir pronouns. According to a remembrance posted on the blog *Chavisory's Notebook*, Baggs "wrote about times when people looked at hir and assumed that sie could not think, or had the mind of an infant. And sie wrote in a way that made me see myself in the world more vividly."

Baggs first came to public attention in 2007, when sie posted a short film online called *In My Language*. The film showed hir gesturing in the air like a symphony conductor while intoning "Eeeeeee," batting at a small chain, and repeatedly touching objects in a room—a door handle, a drawer pull, pages of an open book—without speaking words. Then a synthesized voice explains sie is communicating in hir "native language."[46]

In what may be the most perfect description of neurodivergence for the neurotypical world, the voice says: "My language is not about designing words or even visual symbols for people to interpret. It is about being in a constant conversation with every aspect of my environment, reacting physically to all parts of my surroundings. . . . [Yet] it is only when I type something in your language that you refer to me as having communication." It goes on to ask why hir failure to learn a traditional language is considered a deficit while our failure to learn hir language is considered "natural."

The film's intent, we're told, is to make clear "the existence and value of many different kinds of thinking and interaction." Only when the many shapes of personhood are recognized, says the voice, will justice and human rights be possible.

CHAPTER 6

DISABILITY JUSTICE

I n 2005, in response to the exclusion of queer, Black and Brown, and other intersectional perspectives from mainstream disability rights actions and disability studies conversations, a group of people in and around the San Francisco Bay area started discussing a "second wave" of disability rights. The group included Patty Berne, a Japanese Haitian queer disabled woman; Mia Mingus, a queer disabled Korean transracial and transnational adoptee raised in the Caribbean; and, later, Stacey Park Milbern, a queer disabled woman of Korean American heritage who'd moved to California from North Carolina.

Berne, who uses they/them pronouns, is the executive director and artistic director of Sins Invalid, a San Francisco–based performance project that's mainly by and for disabled artists of Color and queer and gender nonconforming artists with disabilities. Their training in clinical psychology focused on trauma and healing, and they've offered mental health support to violence survivors. They are also an advocate for immigrants who seek asylum and for alternatives to incarceration in the legal system. They've been a community organizer within the Haitian diaspora and supported the Guatemalan democratic movement. Berne advocates for LGBTQIA+ and disability perspectives within reproductive justice, including fair access to women's health services and family planning. They've worked to create "liberated zones" for marginalized voices.

Mingus, a writer, an educator, and a community organizer, is dedicated to ending sexual violence and creating a world where disabled children can live safely, with dignity and love. In 2011, Mingus coined the term "access intimacy" to describe intimate relationships that are free of bias and violence and other oppressions—"that elusive, hard to describe feeling when someone else 'gets' your access needs," she writes.[1] "I don't just want technical and logistical access," she tells the Disability Intersectionality Summit in a keynote address in 2018.[2] "I don't just want inclusion; I want liberatory access and access intimacy. I want us to not only be able to be part of spaces, but for us to be able to fully engage in spaces. I don't just want us to get a seat at someone else's table; I want us to be able to build something more magnificent than a table, together with our accomplices."[3] Mingus urges the centralization of marginalized people within disability studies and activism—that is, the dismantling of privilege. "We don't want to simply join the ranks of the privileged; we want to dismantle those ranks and the systems that maintain them," she says.[4]

Milbern, who died in 2020 at age thirty-three, was a community organizer and blogger who "called out the mainstream disability movement for marginalizing people of Color and nontraditional gender identities," as the *New York Times* puts it in an obituary."[5] Among the injustices Milbern zeroed in on were medical biases—doctors' tendencies to try to perpetuate "a 'good' body"—and the impact of everyday events on indigent disabled people. During widespread power outages in California, for instance, Milbern "helped organize a mutual-assistance effort called Power to Live to distribute generators and otherwise ensure that those who needed electricity for a ventilator or other medical devices were not cut off," the *Times* reports. In a podcast for KQED public radio, Milbern explained her vision for the future: "I would want people with disabilities twenty years from now to not think that they're broken. You know, not think that there's anything spiritually or physically or emotionally wrong with them." She added, "And not just people with disabilities, but queer people and gender nonconforming folks and people of color and all of the people I think that society really pushes down and out."[6]

The triumvirate of Berne, Mingus, and Milbern was later joined by Leroy Moore, an African American journalist, poet, rapper, radio programmer, and former New Yorker with CP who'd moved to Northern California to launch Krip-Hop Nation, a movement that opposes discrimination against disabled artists, especially Black musicians who have been marginalized by racism and ableism; Sebastian Margaret, an anti-ableism community educator originally from Yorkshire, England, who became part of the Oakland-based Transgender Law Center; and Eli Clare, the genderqueer disabled activist and author of *Brilliant Imperfection: Grappling with Cure*.

"Disability Justice activists, organizers, and cultural workers understand that able-bodied supremacy has been formed in relation to other systems of domination and exploitation," writes Berne.[7] Disability Justice, they explain, aims to right the wrongs of the disability rights movement. "The disability rights movement simultaneously invisibilized the lives of peoples who lived at intersecting junctures of oppression—disabled people of color, immigrants with disabilities, queers with disabilities, trans and gender non-conforming people with disabilities, people with disabilities who are houseless, people with disabilities who are incarcerated, people with disabilities who have had their ancestral lands stolen, amongst others."

Later, Berne and Sins Invalid would post the ten principles of Disability Justice. They include intersectionality, or the recognition that everyone comes from a mix of different backgrounds and experiences; leadership of those most directly impacted by prejudice and other forms of oppression; a rejection of competitive systems such as capitalism, which make one group get ahead at the expense of another; solidarity with other social justice initiatives; and the importance of mutual aid, in recognition of our interdependence on one another.[8]

In her 2018 collection of essays, *Care Work: Dreaming Disability Justice*, author and activist Leah Lakshmi Piepzna-Samarasinha unpacks these themes further. She's a Toronto- and Oakland-based queer disabled femme poet, organizer, performance artist, and educator of Burgher-Tamil Sri Lankan and Irish-Roma descent. "To me, disability justice means a political movement and many interlocking communities where disability is not defined in white terms, or male terms, or straight terms," she writes. "Disability justice asserts that ableism helps make racism, christian supremacy, sexism, and queer- and trans-phobia possible, and that all those systems of oppression are locked up tight."[9]

In this context, the basic civil rights guarantees of the ADA will never be enough because they're not up to the task of ensuring justice. "Our focus is less on civil rights legislation as the only solution to ableism and more on a vision of liberation that understands that the state was built on racist, colonialist ableism and will not save us," Piepzna-Samarasinha emphasizes.[10]

The interconnectedness of ableism and other forms of oppression is amplified by Lydia X. Z. Brown, the autistic activist and professor mentioned in chapter 5. As a movement, says Brown, disability rights has always been about using the law and policy to effect changes. But Disability Justice, by contrast, "understands that law and policy are necessary but not sufficient. We actually need to radically transform our society and culture, because you can't legislate morality. . . . The law will never disappear ableism," Brown says in an interview with *Marie Claire* magazine.[11] That's partly because the law and indeed the disability rights movement have been "primarily led by cisgender straight white men," they observe. Disability Justice, on the other hand, comes from disabled people who are "at the margins of the margins."

Conceptually, Disability Justice has many moving parts. One aspect—referenced in the ten principles—involves mutual aid. Brown believes that people within marginalized communities ought to care for one another in whatever ways they can, recognizing that "each of our own capacities and abilities to offer anything are constantly in flux," they tell *Marie Claire*. You can contribute from bed, if you have to. You don't have to travel, to walk and shout and raise a fist, in order to become involved. There are ways to get into the fray, to participate and serve and be heard, without physically joining the crowd if you're not able to.

Disability Justice also involves what Brown terms "redistributive justice"—the tenet that people of privilege ought to share their wealth and power with those who've been deprived. The haves gained their advantages "on legacies of stolen land and genocide and enslavement," says Brown. Disability Justice insists they return funds and power to "communities that have been exploited."

As for specific policy initiatives, Brown would like to see the Keeping All Students Safe in Schools Act passed.[12] It's a pair of legislative proposals introduced in Congress back in 2011 to protect school children from abusive restraints and seclusion; it failed to win enough votes to move forward. They would like to change how home- and community-based long-term support services are funded, and to shut all institutions, including prisons. Brown points to figures showing that a disproportionate number of disabled people are arrested and killed by law enforcement, such as the Ruderman Family Foundation survey which found that between one-third and one-half of all those killed by law enforcement officers are disabled.[13] Many of these disabled people may have been unable to earn a living wage and sustain a lifestyle that's compliant with societal norms, says Brown; they may have been unable to hear, respond to, or process an order to freeze and raise their hands. Many are neurodivergent.

Once incarcerated, their treatment is no better. A study by the advocacy group Helping Educate to Advance the Rights of Deaf Communities (HEARD) found that disabled inmates rarely receive the accommodations they need to survive. "Solitary confinement is often used as a substitute for [reasonable] accommodations," the organization concludes, calling it "a form of torture that leads to high incidences of mental illness and suicide."[14]

The onslaught of violence disabled people face from the law enforcement system dovetails with the Black Lives Matter movement. Eric Garner, the forty-three-year-old African American New Yorker who died in 2014 after a white NYPD officer put him in a chokehold for allegedly selling cigarettes illegally, had asthma, diabetes, and a heart condition—invisible health issues that made him especially vulnerable to such violence. In 2014, Tanisha Anderson was killed as a result of being physically restrained by white officers outside her Cleveland home; the thirty-seven-year-old Black woman had bipolar disorder, and her family had called the police for help because she was having a manic episode. The same year, in Los Angeles, a twenty-five-year-old Black man with bipolar disorder named Ezell Ford was shot dead by white police officers because he allegedly failed to obey their commands to keep still, which he physically could not do at that moment. In 2015, Freddie Gray, then twenty-five, of Baltimore, was arrested for carrying a knife and died after police gave him a rough ride in the back of a van; the young Black man had a cognitive disability from exposure to lead as a child, a disability that led him to misunderstand police, and they him. In 2016, Deborah Danner was having a schizophrenic episode while carrying a pair of scissors when police shot the sixty-six-year-old Black woman dead in her Bronx, New York, home. And George Floyd, whose killing by a Minneapolis police officer in the spring of 2020 sparked nationwide protests, had a heart condition, hypertension, and sickle cell disease, which made him especially vulnerable (though, of course, those conditions were not responsible for his murder).

The list goes on and on. Talila A. Lewis, the social justice attorney, who is a volunteer director at HEARD, says the US government uses "constructed ideas about disability, delinquency and dependency, intertwined with constructed ideas about race, to classify and criminalize people."

The problem is further exacerbated by the fact that Black Americans are more likely than white Americans to have untreated, even undiagnosed, mental and physical health-care needs. Haben Girma, author of *Haben: The Deafblind Woman Who Conquered Harvard Law*, adds that another part of the problem stems from the legal system's "compliance culture," which holds that anyone who doesn't immediately obey police orders is willfully not complying and must be stopped—which isn't the case for many neurodivergent people and others with disabilities. "Someone might be yelling for me to do something and I don't hear [it]," she says. "And then they assume that I'm a threat." Another disabled activist of Color, the writer and performing artist Teighlor McGee, started the Black Disability Collective expressly to raise awareness of the underreported disability component of police violence against Black people. McGee is a twenty-two-year-old Black autistic woman from Minneapolis.[15]

Lydia Brown argues that we cannot talk honestly about disability or ableism without talking about race or racism, respectively. In an essay in the collection *Resistance and Hope: Essays by Disabled People*, they write, "This nation was founded on stolen land, genocide, and myths of white (abled, male) supremacy that led to laws and 'traditions' based on the supposed inferiority and undesirability of anyone who didn't fit that mold, whether because they were Black, Indigenous, women, or disabled (among other things)."[16] The underlying tenet of racism, of course, is that whiteness is "the epitome of health, strength, sanity, intelligence, and beauty," says Brown. Ableism essentially says the same thing about those who are not disabled—in other words, that disability disqualifies you from all those advantages. If you're disabled, ableism avows, you categorically cannot participate in the idealized vision of personhood. "Disability Justice helps us understand the ways in which

disability and race have always been deeply intertwined in their defini-
tions, as well as their treatment within the law and within society and
culture," Brown writes.

Nearly all disabled people are marginalized, but white disabled people experience privilege over—and often at the expense of—disabled
people of Color, says Brown. The problem stems in large part from prejudice *within* the disability community—a community that's shot through
with the same biases and privileged attitudes as the rest of society, if not
more so, says Brown. People who don't have much, who have been left
out, often must scramble for vital resources. They must compete to get
what they need, and when they succeed they don't want to share. "Disabled people of Color and queer and trans people of Color have been
organizing and doing disability advocacy for many, many decades. We
just don't see the same amount of support or recognition," says Brown.[17]

Occurrences of multiply marginalized disabled people—particularly
those who are queer, trans, or nonwhite—being ignored, overshadowed,
or erased in mainstream disability narratives are many and varied. For
instance, in 2016 Jennifer Mizrahi, president of RespectAbility—a nonprofit that purports to fight disability stigma and advance opportunities
for disabled people by working with employers, elected officials, policymakers, media, and others—told CNN that Hillary Clinton was wise to
address disability issues in her run for the presidency because there are
"a lot of white people with disabilities."[18] In fairness, Mizrahi's point was
related to the fact that Donald Trump was leading in polls with white
voters, but the words stung many disabled people of Color and suggest
deeper systemic issues at play. What's more, Mizrahi and her team are
accused of parroting blog posts from the Harriet Tubman Collective, a
group of primarily Black and Brown disabled and/or D/deaf "organizers, community builders, activists, dreamers, lovers," as its motto goes,
who strive for what's referred to as "radical inclusion"; Mizrahi, a white
woman with dyslexia and ADHD, hasn't shared credit—or the spotlight—with the disabled people of Color she claims to want to ally with.
When RespectAbility received a grant from the Ford Foundation in 2016
to fund a program to promote young disabled leaders, Mizrahi and team
named it the Harriet Tubman Fellowships[19]—a blatant example of cultural appropriation, critics charge. "Harriet Tubman and her legacy belong to us," reads a statement from the collective.[20]

Another example of white privilege in mainstream disability circles arose when the Ruderman Family Foundation released its study of police violence against disabled people[21]—the same study that found that one-third to one-half of those killed by law enforcement are disabled. Written by two white men, the report neglected to examine "the impact of race" on how law enforcement tactics are meted out, says a critique by Lydia Brown, Leroy Moore of Krip-Hop Nation, and Talila A. Lewis, the attorney and activist—all of whom are disabled people of Color. It failed to "mention or acknowledge the work of countless disabled and disability-adjacent activists of Color on police violence, even though those most affected and most engaged in this work are Disabled/Deaf Black, Brown, and Indigenous people."[22]

At the same time, disabled queer and trans people of Color have been vital participants in disability activism, often without recognition from the disability establishment. For example, Marsha P. Johnson, a Black trans woman who became known as one of the first people to resist the police during the Stonewall uprising that galvanized the gay rights movement, lived most of her life with psychiatric and physical disabilities. Born in Elizabeth, New Jersey, in 1945, she left her abusive home after graduating from high school and fled to New York City, where she earned money as an occasional sex worker and became one of the first drag queens to go to the Stonewall Inn in Greenwich Village, a bar that had been exclusively for gay men. After a series of police raids—since it was still illegal to be gay—virulent and sometimes violent protest marches and demonstrations broke out over the next week to assert gay pride. Johnson later denied being instrumental in the rebellion, but David Carter's *Stonewall: The Riots That Sparked the Gay Revolution* identifies her as one of a handful of people "in the vanguard" of the opposition.[23] She remained active in gay and trans rights in and around New York, facing frequent clashes with the police. From those encounters, and from her early life on the streets, she endured countless physical and psychological injuries. In 1970, at twenty-five, she had her first mental breakdown (as she called it) and from then on was in and out of psychiatric institutions. For the rest of her life she depended on antipsychotic medication, whenever she could get it. According to disabled trans blogger J. M. Ellison, Johnson cofounded Street Transvestite Action Revolutionaries (STAR), an organization by and for young trans people who lived on the streets, many of whom were women of Color and/or disabled. "Disability justice was at the center of STAR's political analysis," Ellison writes, though the group didn't call it that at the time. "They demanded that transgender people who were subjected to non-consensual psychiatric treatment be released from hospitals, calling them prisoners."[24] Johnson also demanded that people have free access to the therapies and other medical resources they want, not what was forced upon them. She lived much of her life on the streets before her death in 1992 at age forty-six, when her body was found in the Hudson River. Though her death was deemed a suicide at first, some of her colleagues were doubtful and the case remains open.[25]

Another case of erasure within the disability rights movement is Jazzie Collins, an African American trans woman, activist, and community organizer. She was born in Memphis, Tennessee, in 1958, to a strict Baptist family. Her mother was a teenager, so Collins grew up mostly in foster care. At thirty, she moved to San Francisco and soon transitioned to female. HIV-positive, she became an ardent advocate for a variety of marginalized groups; she was active in tenants' rights, labor rights, transgender rights, disability rights, and aging and health issues. She worked with Senior and Disability Action, an organization dedicated to seniors and disabled people, and served as vice chair of San Francisco's Lesbian Gay Transgender Senior Disabled Housing Task Force. A month before her death in 2013, at fifty-four, she was honored at the California state capitol for her service to social justice and equality.[26] In 2015, the nation's first homeless shelter for LGBTQIA+ adults opened in San Francisco's Mission District; it was named "Jazzie's Place."[27]

The disabled queer and trans poet, performer, educator, and activist Kay Ulanday Barrett is another iconoclast who deserves a place in the narrative. Born in Michigan to working-class parents, Barrett identifies as a gender nonconforming Pilipinx Amerikan who often uses a cane for mobility when their chronic pain allows. Currently based in the New York area, they have published two poetry collections, *When the Chant Comes* and *More Than Organs*; been featured as a poetry fellow at the *Lambda Literary Review*; spoken at major universities and cultural centers; and been featured in a variety of publications. Barrett started at open mic nights, inspired by spoken-word art and the slam poetry movement. They soon specialized in work that delves into race, disability, poverty, and their intersections. In poetry and spoken-word pieces, Barrett lays bare how systems of oppression are interconnected and embolden one another, while celebrating the resilience of the several communities to which Barrett belongs. On a mission to promote equal access and justice for queer, trans, and disabled people of Color, Barrett has addressed groups at Princeton University, the United Nations, and many other academic, corporate, and nonprofit organizations that seek to make their environments and their cultures truly inclusive.

Each of these examples is a testament to the need for and importance of Disability Justice, activists say. The old disability rights perspective, as valuable as it's been and continues to be, just doesn't cut it.

～

Disability Justice is fundamentally connected to the concept of intersectionality. In 1989, a UCLA School of Law professor named Kimberlé Crenshaw introduced the term "intersectionality."[28] She used it to address the multiple oppressions facing African American women, the overlaps between racial justice and feminism, between identity politics and economic discrimination. A graduate of Cornell University and Harvard Law, Crenshaw went on to tenure at both UCLA and Columbia Law, specializing in social policy, race, and gender issues. Crenshaw's ideas quickly spread. Activists embraced the concept of interlinked, multilayered, multifaceted oppression. Imagine a Venn diagram in which each circle represents a piece of one's identity: color, religion, ethnic background, language, gender, location, socioeconomic background, and so forth—all the parts that make you *you*, and all the challenges, prejudices, and privileges you live with as a result of being in these groups.

Intersectionality soon became part and parcel of disability culture and a necessary framework for disability activism. The interrelationships of race, gender, and disability—or rather the interrelationships of misunderstandings, even bigotry, based on them—is at the center of work by Disability Justice advocates such as Keri Gray. She is a Washington, DC–based twenty-nine-year-old Black woman with a prosthetic leg due to childhood cancer. She is also a diversity and inclusion consultant. Her work centers on the impact of race, gender, and disability, particularly as they relate to young Black professionals. She works to empower them and other marginalized communities using a framework of intersectionality. "I want people to see my Blackness, my womanhood, my disability, my spirituality. You know what I'm saying? I want people to see those different components," she says on *The Heumann Perspective* podcast.[29]

Recognizing these parts of herself and reclaiming them proudly is both her message and her mission. On Twitter, she uses the hashtag #BlackDisabledLivesMatter with a silhouette of an upward thrusting black fist and the slogan "Melanin + Curves + Scars," which refers to a collection of images and profiles she's put together that "address societal and workplace expectations around body image, performance, and mental health." She encourages online visitors to think critically about the "myths behind these standards" and work with her to help "empower Black culture, leadership, and wellness."[30]

Since February 2019, Gray has also served as senior director of stakeholder engagement and strategic communications at the American Association of People with Disabilities, a grassroots coalition of disability activists. She tells the *Black Women Radicals* blog that she firmly believes in speaking the truth and simultaneously finding opportunities to do better in life and uplift our communities. "If we do not recognize who we are on an internal level," she says, "we will significantly sell ourselves short over and over again."[31]

The lack of homogeneity among disabled people applies to every aspect of our lives, from functionality to race, gender identity, nationality, sexual orientation, socioeconomic status, and all other conceivable demographic markers. If anecdotal evidence isn't enough, the statistics bear this out. According to the Centers for Disease Control and Prevention, disabilities are more commonly found among Americans of Color. That may be because communities of Color tend to have less access to prenatal and maternal care, medical care, and nutritional resources. It may be due to poverty and everyday violence. It may have to do with systemic prejudice and fewer opportunities in general. Overall, roughly 30 percent of Indigenous Americans and 25 percent of Black Americans have a disability, whereas non-Hispanic white Americans clock in at 20 percent.[32]

In addition, there are disabilities that stem directly from trauma—PTSD, other psychosocial disabilities, and physical injuries. Impoverishment itself can cause disabilities. So can famine and genocide and natural disasters and wars and military service. These atrocities impact communities of Color at a greater rate than white communities. Racist systems that made people of Color more vulnerable in the first place are, in a sense, directly responsible for the disability oppression they endure. These racial inequities are due to circumstances that are not beyond society's control—and recognizing this is part of Disability Justice, too.

Poverty is linked to high incidences of every disability type. It's a bit of a chicken-and-egg relationship, though, in that disability can be both a cause and consequence of poverty. "It is a cause because it can lead to job loss and reduced earnings, barriers to education and skills development, significant additional expenses, and many other challenges that can lead to economic hardship," says a report from the Center for American Progress. "It is also a consequence because poverty can limit access to health care and preventive services, and increase the likelihood that a person lives and works in an environment that may adversely affect health."[33]

These intersectional realities are influencing disability activists far and wide. For instance, in 2015, while enrolled in a disability studies PhD program at the University of Illinois in Chicago, Katherine (Kat) Pérez helped launch the National Coalition for Latinxs with Disabilities. She wanted to bring together discrete, isolated disabled Latinx activists. Pérez, a queer disabled Latinx attorney in her mid-thirties, is now the director of the Coelho Center for Disability Law, Policy, and Innovation at Loyola Law School, in Los Angeles. Pérez's disabilities aren't apparent; you wouldn't know by looking at her that she has multiple psychiatric disabilities. You also wouldn't know she has an autistic sister, Cindy, who has psychiatric and intellectual disabilities. Growing up, Pérez watched Cindy come home from special ed crying because bullies threw things at her and called her the R-word. Pérez's sense of the need for Disability Justice—justice that goes beyond what the law covers—was born from those early memories. But it wasn't until she was twenty-six and entering law school that she understood how Disability Justice applies to *her*, too. "I suddenly realized, 'Oh my God—it's not just people like my sister! I am part of this community!'"[34]

She knows too many disabled people fall through the cracks, people like her sister for whom there are no therapies, no housing options, no employment possibilities, people who are utterly locked out of the system through no fault of their own. Pérez is in a position to shine a light on system failures, with particular attention on the intersections of immigration and disabilities. (Pérez isn't an immigrant, but her grandparents came from Mexico.) "Beefing up and enforcing disability law is necessary, but not sufficient," she says. "You can't legislate people's hearts and minds. That happens at another level. You've got to tell these human stories, bring them out into the open."

For Pérez and other allies of Disability Justice, there is almost a resounding chorus of *Hear our authentic stories. Don't ignore us. Don't put us at the back of the line. Don't assume you know what's best for us. Don't speak for us. Don't steal from us. Don't judge us.* It's not enough to pass legislation or "celebrate differences." What's needed is radical action that dismantles mass systems of oppression.

"It's not that everyone has to be always on the same page, because there are certain issues that have to be taken up by certain groups. No one person can speak for all communities," says Sachin Pavithran of Utah State University.[35] He runs a program that, in part, helps disabled Utahns receive the technology they require. Now in his early forties, Pavithran has been blind since childhood. He was born in India, grew up in Dubai, and came to the US at seventeen to further his education. He holds a doctorate in disability studies, with emphasis on disability policy, from Utah State, and he serves on the US Access Board and the Commission on Civil Rights.

Pavithran didn't know about disability rights or Disability Justice when he came to this country. He'd never had much exposure to other disabled people growing up. His parents were his chief advocates. The US gave him a different perspective. "I was kind of in awe at first—the *wow* stage, when everything is cool," he says with a chuckle. Then he began wondering why there are still so many roadblocks for blind people. Gradually, he became interested in policy and systems change.

To him, part of the reason for the slow pace of progress is that certain people in charge think they've got the problems licked already. They know about the ADA, follow it as best they can—so what more is needed? "Most legislators don't come from a disability perspective," he says. "Few understand why [accessibility] should be a priority." You have to go beyond the letter of the law, he says. At the same time, many disability advocates are nearly as frustrating. "So many activists and activist groups are compartmentalized, working in isolation on their own agendas," he says. "We need to collaborate."

That, in part, is what Disability Justice is about—bringing the marginalized people out into the open.

For a 2007 Sins Invalid show in San Francisco, a poster gives a shorthand definition of what was then a relatively new crusade: "All bodies are unique and essential," it says. "All bodies are whole. All bodies have strengths and needs that must be met. We are powerful not despite the complexities of our bodies, but because of them. We move together, with no body left behind. This is Disability Justice."

Nomy Lamm was at that show. She is now Sins Invalid's creative director. She describes herself as a "superfat white, genderqueer, Jewish woman with a lifelong physical disability and PTSD" who, in the audience that day, felt "an urgency, a current in my body saying 'This is the moment, step into it, this is where it's happening.' I wanted in," she writes in a blog post.[36]

Disability organizations she'd known before were "dominated by whiteness, straightness, and maleness [and] concerned primarily with mobility impairments," she explains. "Meanwhile, the radical spaces I had felt more drawn to—anti-capitalist, feminist, anarchist spaces, for example—had little awareness of disability, and often relied on high levels of physical and mental exertion without acknowledging limitations or access needs, inevitably leading to burnout and alienation."

Disability Justice, her post continues, challenges the notion that worth is tied to productivity or to producing something of value to others. Rather, Disability Justice holds that our worth is tied to nothing more than our being human. "Like transformative justice, reproductive justice, and environmental justice, it implies a movement-building strategy and an anti-capitalist critique."

In recent years, Lamm notes, the term "Disability Justice" has been appropriated and misused, or at best misunderstood. She quotes Patty Berne as saying that many people are "using DJ as a stand-in for intersectionality, referencing Brown crips only in language, but not centering actual disabled people of color and queer and gender non-conforming people. It is a movement-building framework—a practice, not an academic theory."

A lot of white disabled people bandy about the term without knowing exactly what it means, Lamm laments. "In fact," she says, "they are often using it to advance their careers as academics and consultants, instead of listening to and amplifying the voices of people of color in the movement."

This kind of talk may alienate some white cisgender disabled people, but it seems a necessary exclusion to help create safe spaces for those who have been ignored or trod upon for too long. Listening to and amplifying those voices is key to understanding Disability Justice—and, ultimately, to making society more accessible for all.

CHAPTER 7

VISIBILITY, COMMUNITY, AND CONTEXT

You could argue that no single event was as important and life-altering to the disability community in the aftermath of the ADA as the development of the Internet. The online world is especially accessible and liberating for many disabled people. Perhaps that wasn't so at first, but as technology was created to enable hands-free inputting and text-to-speech screen readers and other ways of interacting with cyber reality, people with a variety of disabilities felt a new kind of freedom, an ease of interaction, that many had never known before. Besides, you could hide your disability if you wanted to—though, in time, many chose to do the opposite, leveraging the Internet to flaunt their disabilities and their opinions about ableism and accessibility to a degree that was hitherto impossible.

Make no mistake: Activists still cluster in anonymous, noisy masses to protest inaccessible business establishments or movie theaters that show films with offensive stereotypes or government offices that threaten to cut essential benefits or services. But it's a lot easier—and for many, a lot more accessible—to express grievances and camaraderie in the virtual public square.

One champion of using computers to rally disability activism and amplify disability perspectives is Alice Wong, a woman in her early forties who was born with spinal muscular atrophy. She uses a motorized wheelchair and wears a Bi-Pap mask over her nose that's connected to a ventilator device. The image of her partially covered face has become a kind of emblem for the open and affirming worldview she envisions and fights for. Growing up in Indianapolis, Wong graduated from high school two years after the ADA passed—an event that, she says, inspired her to dream big. "Learning about disability history and realizing I was a member of a protected class encouraged me to imagine and create the life that I want," she writes in the *New York Times* in 2017.[1]

Wong went on to earn a master's in medical sociology and worked for more than a decade as a research associate at the University of California, San Francisco, where she served as vice chair of the Chancellor's Advisory Committee on Disability. In 2013, not yet forty, Wong was appointed by President Obama to the National Council on Disability. But her career as a semi-public figure really began in 2014, when Wong launched the Disability Visibility Project, a series of recorded interviews with a broad variety of disabled folks. Originally an ambitious partnership with NPR's StoryCorps, intended to recognize and build "an online community dedicated to creating, sharing and amplifying disability media and culture," according to the website, the project soon became a multimedia powerhouse. From there, her activism spread almost nonstop. "With the disability community," she writes, "I share our stories and speak out against threats to our future by using my privilege and tools such as social media."[2]

In 2015, for a White House celebration marking the twenty-fifth anniversary of the ADA, Wong met Obama remotely via an Internet-powered robot (flying to the event was inaccessible for her), an occasion that itself became a media sensation.[3] She was the first person to attend a White House event in this way. In 2016, she partnered with Andrew Pulrang, a disabled blogger and *Forbes* contributor, and Gregg Beratan, a disabled writer and activist with the Center for Disability Rights, to launch a nonpartisan online campaign called #CripTheVote, to encourage political participation by and for disabled people and make candidates pay attention to their disabled constituents. In 2017, the Disability Visibility Project was adapted into a podcast. In 2018, Wong edited and published *Resistance and Hope: Essays by Disabled People*, a collection of provocative pieces by a cross section of disability activists, many of whom were people of Color, lambasting the Trump administration and generally targeting enemies of fair play and equality. Around that time, with fellow disabled authors and activists Vilissa Thompson and s. e. smith (not to be confused with S. E. Smith, the science fiction writer),

she started DisabledWriters.com to promote disabled authors and jour-
nalists and to help editors connect with them. With novelist Nicola Grif-
fith, she created #CripLit, a series of Twitter chats for disabled writers.
In 2019, Wong cofounded Access Is Love, a campaign to "build a world
where accessibility is understood as an act of love instead of a burden
or an afterthought," according to promotional material. Her partners in
the project were Mia Mingus, the Disability Justice writer and organizer
mentioned in chapter 6, and Sandy Ho, a research associate with the
Lurie Institute for Disability Policy at Brandeis University, an instructor
of disability studies at Lesley University, and a community organizer focused on Disability Justice and intersectionality. In February 2020, *Time*
magazine named Wong one of sixteen standout people or organizations
that were "fighting for a more equal America."[4] Later that year, *Disability
Visibility: First-Person Stories from the Twenty-First Century* was published—a consummately curated collection of short pieces Wong introduced and edited, some familiar and others new. Later that year, at the
height of the COVID pandemic, she launched the hashtag #HighRisk-
Covid19 to draw attention to the particular concerns of many disabled
or chronically ill folks. In 2022, she published a memoir, *Year of the Ti-
ger: An Activist's Life.*

But the goals she'd originally set out to achieve proved harder than
expected. "When you are disabled and rely on public services and programs, you face vulnerability every day," she writes. "This vulnerability is
felt in my bones and my relationship with the state. Fluctuations in the
economy and politics determine whether my attendants will receive a
living wage and whether I'll have enough services to subsist rather than
thrive. The fragility and weakness of my body, I can handle. The fragility
of the safety net is something I fear and worry about constantly."[5]

Connecting with others online provides some degree of comfort, as
well as access to resources, but that isn't true for everyone. In September 2021, the Pew Research Center released a study that concluded that
many disabled Americans cannot or do not access the Internet. They
don't have the equipment or the money or the education to do it. "The
digital divide between those who have a disability and those who don't
remains," writes the Pew Research Center's Andrew Perrin and Sara
Atske. "Roughly a quarter of Americans with disabilities (26%) say they
have high-speed internet at home, a smartphone, a desktop or laptop

computer *and* a tablet, compared with 44% of those who report not having a disability. . . . Americans with disabilities are three times as likely as those without a disability to say they never go online."[6]

The reasons for this digital divide are many. Part of it has to do with money. Disabled people are twice as likely as their nondisabled counterparts to live in poverty, according to a 2009 report from the Center for Economic and Policy Research in Washington, DC.[7] Computers and, especially, adaptive computer input equipment such as voice-recognition systems and adaptive output devices such as screen readers are expensive, as are monthly Internet access fees. "For digital generations like mine," wrote s. e. smith in the blog *Rooted in Rights*, "many things online feel like second nature, but innovations happen so fast that even I often feel several steps behind. For some disabled people, that gap is even more severe, with roots in this nation's segregated approach to education."[8]

In the article, smith goes on to say that disabled students are rarely given the level of personalized computer instruction they need to keep up with their nondisabled peers. "For many disabled people, economic inequality and inaccessibility—the two primary obstacles to internet access—are solvable problems, not intrinsic barriers," observes smith.[9] Moreover, many websites are inaccessible; they have pictures and graphics that aren't tagged with text descriptions for blind people's screen-reading devices to interpret, or they include video clips without closed captioning for D/deaf people. For visually disabled folks, too, links and forms should be labeled as such, and users should be able to "increase or decrease the text size with an on-site tool or browser setting," smith tells *Vox* media.[10] For neurodivergent users, links must be maintained so they don't break or fail; sites shouldn't timeout too fast, either. For those who need them, trigger warnings should be employed for sensitive or violent material.

Many of these solutions are so simple, says smith, that there's no excuse for companies not to employ them. An accessibility consultant should be standard in setting up and maintaining corporate sites and apps.

Still, for those privileged enough to be able to use the Internet, it's proved a great consciousness raiser. "I grew up with the Internet, and while I didn't necessarily initially use it to connect with the disability community, I did find it a convenient way to connect with people who understood me and didn't judge me because of my disability—and a lot of those people were actually disabled," says Nell Koneczny at the Arlington, Virginia–based American Anthropological Association.[11] Nell (she prefers to use her first name) is in her late twenties, a self-described "white woman with short black hair [and] thick, black-rimmed glasses" who was born with hip dysplasia and has psychiatric and learning disabilities. "There was absolutely a sense of empowerment [when I learned] online that other people get hip replacements at a young age, too, and I'm not some weird freak," she recalls.

Nell went on to earn a master's in disability and human development from the University of Illinois at Chicago, and her work today is dedicated to creating more accessible materials for educators and others involved in anthropology. She's particularly attuned to people who are protected under the ADA but may not "own that disability identity," she says. Her immigrant parents "didn't have the generational knowledge" to explore their daughter's rights as a disabled person. The Internet helped her do that. Connecting with others like her also enabled her to feel more comfortable in her own skin. Society often fails to provide what people with nonstandard minds and bodies need, she muses. "As multiply marginalized groups utilize the Internet to connect with each other, there's an opportunity for people to recognize shared experiences that may not have been shared before," she says. "Communities are being built, and a lot of young adults feel safer being themselves online because people are less likely to be judged on appearance—or by their disabilities."

Nowadays she almost feels sorry for the girl she used to be, the girl who was embarrassed to struggle with walking and who beamed at hearing she could pass for nondisabled. "It pains me to look back at that internalized ableism," she says.

~

Filmmaker and activist Dominick Lawniczak Evans loves online gaming. More than a hobby, it's almost an obsession. He's a forty-year-old wheelchair user with SMA, and he's trans—or as he puts it: "a trans masculine non-binary queer disabled person originally from the Midwest."

Using services such as Twitch to stream interactive games, he occasionally makes money at it by accumulating subscribers. For him, though, streaming games is about more than money; it's a way of life. He can play with or against any number of other players anywhere in the world, and he can pause or pick up a game on any number of devices that are accessible to him. Over the years, he's made many friends this way. For him, it's a means of building community.

But the collegiality doesn't always come easily. "There is a lot of discrimination in the streaming community," he says. "I started asking why people weren't using their cameras—not that you should have to, but why were so few of us showing ourselves? People would say, 'Because I play games with one hand and I might get made fun of.' I'd say, 'Well, I play games lying down and, yes, people make fun of me. But so what?'"[12]

Evans started playing lying down when he was sick for a long time. It kept him preoccupied. It staved off boredom and loneliness. "I learned that it's much more comfortable than doing it while sitting in my wheelchair," he says, his voice rising with oxygenated excitement and obvious pleasure. Lying down, he can play for hours. Sometimes other players tease him about it, but he ignores them. "I started seeing other severely disabled people playing games lying down, too, and we've become supportive of each other," he says. "It's like, who cares?"

An element of successful game streaming is building an audience. Some participants are not so much players as spectators. Disabled players, he says, often struggle to gain audience support. "It can be very isolating." He's tried to form clubs to support disabled gamers, but it was frustratingly difficult to get people to stick together. He tells about one group that practically kicked out a disabled member for being too depressing. "This person wanted to hurt themselves because they were facing so much discrimination—they were really looking for someone to talk to, some advice—and the moderator said, 'We don't talk about depressing stuff. We are all about positivity,'" Evans relates. "It was terrible! That person could kill themselves! I left the group."

Then he says something profound. Disability doesn't have to be positive or negative. The reality, he says, is some of both. "It can just be a descriptor, a term, a part of who you are," he adds. We try to put too much positive spin on it sometimes—to be happy and inspiring—to dispel the negative spin, the stereotypes of pity and pathos, he says. Disabled people can do amazing things, and they can also feel sad and dejected at times.

Finding a supporting community in the streaming world he loves is important to Evans. Growing up, he faced a lot of bullying and discrimination that led him to self-harm. His own mother couldn't accept his disability; she insisted he'd get cured someday, either through medicine or exercise or prayer or a combination of these approaches. Coming out as queer at sixteen didn't exactly help. There were times when his mother would punish him for disobedience by locking him in the middle of his room and turning off his power wheelchair so he couldn't move or do anything; his father was mostly silent. Meeting other disabled kids in college, at Wright State University in central Ohio, helped him gain self-confidence.

Better visibility of disabled people, says Evans—truthful, meaningful portrayals of the lives they actually live—might've salved his wounded self-esteem growing up, and it would help him still. He is acutely aware that, for many people, TV and movie (and computer) screens are almost aspirational mirrors; people look for reflections of what they would like to be. Besides seeking entertainment, audiences scan for signals about where to place their allegiances, whom to believe, what's right and wrong. Often without thinking about it, they suss out aspects of the familiar, hoping for a sign of themselves in a better world. But for many disabled people, finding representation that's fair, accurate, and diverse is an uphill battle.

Evans would like that to change. Besides being a gamer, he's directed two short films—2015's *Nance + Sydney*, an ironic romance, and 2014's *Trip*, a drama about a teenage mother—and two episodes of a 2012 TV comedy called *FaceSpace*. In 2021, he directed the music video for "Spaces," a song written and performed by James Ian, who also has SMA. The media, he says, shapes and reflects our society's views, and better media images will make for a better society. With his life partner, Ashtyn, who has multiple disabilities herself, Evans completed a massive study of nearly two hundred TV shows on networks, cable channels, and streaming services, cataloging every portrayal of disability during the 2018–19 season (updated in 2021). The results were not good. At last count, though there were more characters with disabilities than there used to be, the overwhelming majority—69 percent—were cisgender white, and only 10 percent of them were portrayed by actors identified as disabled.[13] Almost all were written by nondisabled screenwriters.

Poor representations of disabilities aren't new, of course. Warped portrayals that use disabilities to connote calamity, immorality, or evil have been common since time immemorial. They are rooted in the classics. In Greek mythology, as famously dramatized by Sophocles, Oedipus pokes out his own eyes, blinding himself, after learning he'd inadvertently had sex with his mother, Jocasta, who subsequently commits suicide. That's disability as tragedy, a mark of depravity. Shakespeare's villainous Richard III is hunchbacked, which conveys his mendacity inside and out. The Phantom of the Opera and the Hunchback of Notre Dame are deformed and considered monstrous, if misunderstood. The evil Captain Hook is an amputee. Witches, ogres . . . we grow up with these images. The trope lives on in the modern day, too, in any number of disfigured, snarling, misshapen, limping, or scarred baddies—the mottled-faced, razor-fingered Freddy Krueger, for instance, or wheezing, masked Darth Vader.

When not evil, disabled characters are invariably pitiful or broken; at best, they may exhibit a humble nobility and strength of character that are nothing short of inspiring. Think of Tiny Tim from Charles Dickens's *A Christmas Carol* or the poster children of medical charities, such as the Muscular Dystrophy Association's "Jerry's kids."

"Every story that's written from this nondisabled lens is not a story of disability; it's a story of *fear* of disability," says Evans. "Until the media starts showing us as full, robust, living human beings, nothing will change."

To describe much of modern disability representation, the late comedian and journalist Stella Young, a wheelchair user with dwarfism, coined the term "inspiration porn." In a TED Talk in Sydney, Australia, in 2014, she explains, "We have been lied to about disability. We've been sold the lie that disability is a bad thing . . . and to live with disability makes you exceptional." Portraying disabled people as heroic for living ordinary lives is like pornography, she says, in that it objectifies one group of people for the benefit of another group. It effectively communicates that disabled people only exist—or are only worth photographing or writing about—to inspire or motivate nondisabled people and get them to think, *However bad my life is, it could be worse. I could be that person.*

"But what if you *are* that person?" she asks.[14]

The misinformation and community-busting isolation that have been prevalent in so many popular depictions of disability may seem so ingrained as to be unbreakable. They provide the context for much of our perceptions of and expectations for people with disabilities. Nevertheless, in the decades since the ADA, the explosion of public disability on social media and elsewhere *from disabled people themselves* speaks to how they have been repositioning, recasting, redefining, and reclaiming what it means to live with a disability—and, in particular, how our culture should view and treat them.

As an expression of activism, maintaining an Internet presence might seem a bit more egocentric than the protest marches of old. But often just being out there, being visible, is an act of defiance. Disabled people are no longer merely filling the streets and stores and theaters and stadiums with wheelchairs, crutches, canes, prosthetic limbs, and service dogs; they're inundating blogs and social media. The Instagram group @DisabilityFashionStylist has more than thirteen thousand followers, @Disabled_Fashion has more than forty-six thousand fans, and the YouTube channel Squirmy and Grubs—about the exploits of an interabled couple—is closing in on a million subscribers. The Internet is a megaphone. It's branding. It has become a way to demonstrate to the world that disabled people really can do and be anything. It's a two-pronged approach to taking on injustice, one that can be both angry and joyous all at once. For many participants, that *is* activism; it's fueled by a desire to dismantle the system, even while celebrating the glorious possibilities for disabled people and maybe rocking a new outfit or hairstyle.

Rosemarie Garland-Thomson, a professor of English and bioethics at Atlanta's Emory University and author of *Extraordinary Bodies: Figuring Physical Disability in American Culture and Literature*, has written extensively about disability identity and its social constructs. "All of the identity movements, starting in the mid-twentieth century with the women's movement and the Black Nationalist movement, were trying to destigmatize the identity for which they were seeking justice," she says.[15] She's a white woman in her early seventies, with round black-framed glasses and silver hair that sways as she speaks. At first glance, you might not notice that her right hand has four fingers, and her left arm ends at about elbow level with a sort of two-fingered hand. That's her disability. In a *New York Times* op-ed essay, she describes herself as "born with six fingers altogether and one quite short arm."[16]

In the Black Nationalist movement, she says, there was the slogan "Black Is Beautiful"; big "natural" Afros were prominent, as opposed to the slicked-down white-style hairdos sported by the previous generation of African Americans. Afrocentric clothing was trendy, too—colorful dashikis and kente cloth. "These were ways of bringing forward the idea of being proud to be part of a stigmatized identity group," she says. "And in the women's movement, the idea of women wearing pants instead of dresses or skirts seemed radically defiant at one time."[17]

These styles of dress and comportment sent a message that the way someone looks or acts may have been denigrated and stigmatized, but "we are claiming those aspects that have been devalued *as our own*," says Garland-Thomson.

Similarly, in the early 1980s, a paraplegic athlete named Marilyn Hamilton committed a small act of reclamation and insurrection when she launched Quickie brand wheelchairs. She told reporters she was frustrated by the boxy, cumbersome cold metal wheelchairs available then, so she had friends design and build her a customized lightweight neon-blue racing wheelchair. Soon, all her disabled friends wanted one. Demand soared, and Quickie became a bestseller. Before the end of the decade, Quickie was taking in some $40 million a year—and wheelchairs have never looked the same since. New aerodynamic wheelchair designs, from Quickie and other manufacturers, continue to be introduced. Current brands and models of power wheelchairs sound more like race cars than mobility aids: Quickie Q500, Permobil K450 MX, Invacare Storm, Jazzy Air. They boast about gearhead things such as torque, maneuverability, speed, and turning radius. There are front-wheel, mid-wheel, and rear-wheel drive configurations. There are pneumatic tires and solid rubber tires, knobby tread or smooth tread. Today's chairs feature functions that allow for not just reclining and tilting but raising the seat height up and down, which are therapeutic but also useful for active lifestyles. You can plug in a cell phone or ventilator. You can connect the joystick control (choose your type of joystick) to a computer mouse. You can decorate your wheels with flashing lights and reflectors. A current catalog of colors includes hues and tones such as "electric red," "tangerine red," "bubblegum pink," "grape madness," "prism black," and "wet black."[18]

But Quickie was the first to design wheelchairs with pizzazz—both aesthetically pleasing and ruggedly functional. "You could say that Quickie wheelchairs were a kind of equivalent to the Afro or miniskirt," Garland-Thomson observes.

The reclamation of individual identity is aided, though, by a reclamation of the group identity. If you're going to have enough pride to demand respect from others, it helps to know and believe that the community to which you belong is one you can feel proud of, too, as opposed to one with limits and few prospects. Better representation—in history books, on TV, on social media—can reinforce this idea, this reclamation of community identity, says Garland-Thomson. Again, she draws a comparison to other social justice movements. The feminist historian Gerda Lerner, an Austrian-born intellectual who died in 2013 at ninety-three, taught that women can be proud of their heritage even though many of their contributions to society have gone unrecognized or been erased from the established canon. "Disabled people have always been making culture, but we haven't had it in the knowledge record," says Garland-Thomson. "We're only now beginning to discover who they were."

There's a practical, functional benefit to all this, she says. Taking charge of how you feel about yourself, how you present yourself, even if it's only in small ways, enables you to wrest a degree of control over your interactions with the world. It can also influence how other people treat you. It's a kind of social finesse, Garland-Thomson clarifies, that's familiar to many disabled people. Back in 1970, English author James Partridge was in a car fire that severely and permanently scarred his face at age eighteen. Twenty years later, he wrote a book called *Changing Faces*, and in 1992 he founded an organization of the same name to support people with facial disfigurements. "He taught them they didn't need to cover their faces or try to conceal themselves, but rather to develop certain social skills so other people would be less afraid of them," says Garland-Thomson. It's a kind of empowerment model, she adds. "If someone is treating you badly, by all means call them out on it. But if you want meaningful interchanges with other human beings, it's in your own best interests to find ways to get them to take you seriously, to not let them demean you, not reduce your humanity." It's akin to the modern notion of emotional intelligence, she says—knowing how to work *with* others, not compete against them.

Some disabled trailblazers exercise that stigma management on social media, while other folks do so in person. Both forms are, in a sense, revolutionary acts by those who are intent on changing people's minds about what it means—what it looks and feels like—to be disabled.

CHAPTER 8

THE POLITICS OF BEAUTY

O n the website for IMG Models, an international agency headquartered in New York, there used to be a page about the disabled fashion model and actor Jillian Mercado, before she switched agencies. It quoted her as saying, "Disability doesn't have to be ugly."

It's a simple yet profound pronouncement. Presenting herself this way was wise and pointed and historically significant. Throughout history, disabilities *were* seen as ugly—so ugly as to be unwelcome (even legally prohibited) on the streets of certain cities. As recently as fifty years ago, it was illegal in some parts of the US for a visibly disabled person to be in public at all. The so-called "ugly laws" started in nineteenth-century San Francisco, today a bastion of progressive diversity.[1] It was shortly after the gold rush, which had brought a spate of desperate prospectors, many of whom ended up destitute. This in turn caused a steep rise in the number of beggars clogging the streets of this bustling western metropolis. City officials passed the nation's first ugly law ostensibly to remove beggars from the streets (much the way some politicians and demagogues want to do now with our unhoused population). Unsightliness was tantamount to an assault on public propriety and serenity, a disturbance of the peace. Similar statutes rose up across the country.

The longest lasting of the ugly laws was in Chicago. According to historian Paul Longmore, Chicago enacted its version of an ugly law in 1881, "a city ordinance [that] warned: 'No person who is diseased, maimed, mutilated, or in any way deformed so as to be an unsightly or disgusting object . . . shall therein or thereon expose himself to public view."[2] It's unknown how many arrests or citations were actually made as a result, but Chicago's decree wasn't repealed until 1974, the last of its kind on the books.

Even if you weren't arrested, the late nineteenth and early twentieth centuries were especially difficult times to be considered unprepossessing. The prominent social critic and pacifist intellectual Randolph Bourne (1886–1918), whose head was deformed from a birth accident and whose spine was bent from childhood tuberculosis, was judged so unattractive that he was barred from entering New York's exclusive Century Club, though a member—his editor at either the *Atlantic Monthly* or the *New Republic*; it's not clear which—had invited him there for lunch. No one at the Century Club, so far as we know, apologized or made excuses. Explanations were unnecessary. The reason was obvious. He was that repulsive. It didn't matter how widely he was published or how well connected he'd become. He wasn't put in jail, as far as the historical record shows, but he was repeatedly ostracized because of how he looked, which needless to say was beyond his control.

Today, of course, we know better. (Don't we?)

In 2019, disabled essayist Melissa Blake became so annoyed at online "trolls" who said she was too unattractive to post selfies that she took a radical step. Blake, who was born with Freeman-Sheldon Syndrome, a bone and muscle disability, and who was then in her late thirties, decided to post a different selfie every day for a year with the hashtag #MyBestSelfie. "With each selfie," she recounts later, "I felt more comfortable in my own body and discovered a freedom I'd never really felt before as a disabled woman."[3]

Blake, a white woman with dark-red hair and glasses, did not post selfies to be vain, she insists. Rather, they were a kind of political messaging. The more people saw her and got used to how she looks, the less stigmatizing it became. "I posted selfies to unapologetically take up space and demand to be seen as a disabled woman," says Blake, who now has more than a 117,000 followers and counting. It was a way of "taking back my power. . . . People actually need to see disabled people."

If they see more real disabled people, particularly disabled people who look different from nondisabled people, the general public may assimilate disabled body types into their views of what's normal, what's welcome, even what's pleasing to the eye. Disabled people shouldn't have to emulate nondisabled standards of beauty; they should be able to center their representation on their authentic experiences of difference.

Beauty—or the politics of beauty—isn't always about physical appearance. Sometimes other traits are represented as appealing/desirable or unappealing/grotesque in ways that can have repercussions for the disability community. In 2019, Oscar winner Lupita Nyong'o told a reporter that she'd found inspiration for the voice of her murderous character in Jordan Peele's Us by listening to the speech of Robert F. Kennedy Jr.; Kennedy, an environmental activist and notorious conspiracy theorist and anti-vaxxer, has spasmodic dysphonia, a neurological disorder that causes involuntary spasms of the larynx. "In the film, Nyong'o's hair-raising performance is defined by a haunting amplification of the disorder, which sounds like what might happen if you swallowed a cheese grater," the New York Times reported.[4]

Equating the sounds of a disability with something eerie, something designed to strike terror in the hearts of listeners, was so patently offensive that it didn't take long for Nyong'o to apologize. "The thought that I would, in a way, offend was not my intention," she told ABC's The View a few days later. "I say sorry to anyone that I may have offended."[5]

~

Jillian Mercado isn't the first disabled model to be photographed in glossy magazines. In 1987, a quadriplegic college student named Ellen Stohl posed for Playboy. Her pictorial was considered newsworthy. The New York Times headline read "DISABLED MODEL DEFIES SEXUAL STEREOTYPES."[6] She may go down in history as the first visibly disabled woman to do a high-gloss nude photo shoot—though the Times reported that, a few years earlier, Hustler magazine had printed photos of amputees "in aggressive sexual poses," which had largely been dismissed as being in poor taste. Stohl's photos were comparatively refined. They were, in all, eight pages of soft-focus shots of a twenty-three-year-old woman in her wheelchair and little else. Her lower half was draped, either for reasons of modesty or to disguise a degree of atrophy. That is, the pictures didn't display her most emaciated or disfigured parts; in fact, what was revealed didn't look particularly disabled. In that regard, she didn't go as far as some models today, who show their catheters or colostomy pouches. (In 2015, the paraplegic blogger Rachelle Friedman Chapman won media attention for posting photos in her underwear, with catheter and leg bag clearly visible.)[7] But there were shots of Stohl in her wheelchair; she certainly wasn't hiding it.

Stohl was a student at California State University, Fullerton, at the time. She'd grown up in Portland, Oregon, and had survived what she refers to as a "neck-crushing" (as opposed to "backbreaking") car accident some four years earlier, at eighteen. An aspiring actor, she attracted *Playboy*'s editors by sending, uninvited, a portfolio of photos. "Sexuality is the hardest thing for a disabled person to hold onto," she wrote in her accompanying letter. "This is not to say that they are not capable, but rather that society's emphasis on perfection puts a definite damper on self-esteem." She was offered a contract for an exclusive pictorial. Then, between 1987 and 1988, the magazine sent her on a publicity tour of the US and Australia; afterward, she toured England and Brazil on a lecture circuit. There were many articles about her, in many different languages.

Fast-forward thirty-two years. Now a wife, a mother, an actor, and a professor of educational psychology and counseling at Cal State, Northridge, Stohl recalls her photographic unveiling with unabashed pride. "No one had a layout like mine," she says, beaming. "I planted a seed. There were definitely trailblazers before me, but I was the first to really forge a sexual identity for women with visible disabilities."[8] It was never her intention to be a spokesperson, she says. For her, posing was just a way to express her sexuality, something she feared she'd lost in her accident. She'd felt neutered by it. But her choice garnered considerable flak. *Playboy* wasn't exactly feminist. Didn't her pictures reinforce sexist ideals and the objectification of women?

"Sure, I succumbed to the stereotypical constructs of beauty," she says, "but I also blew apart the definition of sexy by having a disability." Too often, she says, disabled people weren't seen as sexual; she likes to think she helped change that a little. Magazines such as *Playboy* that objectify women do contribute to patriarchal oppression, she concedes, but she had to fight to be seen as a woman first, before she could fight for women's rights. Her photos enabled women to embrace their "perceived imperfections," she says, and find beauty in themselves as they are. "When people treat you differently, you think you *are* different," she says.

At fifty-five, Stohl still struggles occasionally with self-esteem. She wishes more disabled actors and models had been around when she was newly disabled. They might have helped with her adjustment. "It's still hard for someone like me to get an audition for anything that doesn't specifically say *disabled*," she groans. The media, she says, needs to show more "disabled parents and coworkers, disabled lawyers and doctors, even disabled murderers and detectives. We need to be included without being special or unusual."

After Stohl, there was a prolonged gap in disability representation in the beauty industry. Then, one Tuesday evening in April 2012, there was a big leap: the Sundance channel debuted a new reality show called *Push Girls*. It was about four young paralyzed women—Tiphany Adams, Auti Angel, Mia Schaikewitz, and Angela Rockwood. They were, respectively, a model, a dancer/choreographer, a dancer/graphic designer, and a model/actor. They were all dynamic personalities and bombshell gorgeous. There was a lot of glamour posing to accentuate their gorgeousness, but mostly the show followed them in their daily lives as they did their makeup, tooled around the LA area, prepared for work, went out to lunch, and so forth. There were interviews about their sex lives and other activities and desires. The first season's fourteen half-hour episodes were popular enough to generate a second season of ten episodes a year later, with additional cast member Chelsie Hill, another paralyzed dancer.

The program was the brainchild of executive producer Gay Rosenthal, the force behind an earlier documentary series about people with dwarfism called *Little People, Big World*, a somewhat voyeuristic, no-holds-barred look at the lives of some disabled families, which ran for six seasons on TLC. In an interview with the *Wall Street Journal*, Rosenthal explains her inspiration for *Push Girls* in rather mundane terms: "If I find a character that I really spark to, it's very organic." She admits she isn't a disability advocate per se; her motivations were more about finding a market niche. She tells the *Los Angeles Times* that she's proud "to make a difference, shattering stereotypes and changing perceptions."[9] The Sundance Channel's general manager Sarah Barnett, who effectively bought the show from Rosenthal, tells *The Daily Beast* it was an opportunity to "shed some stereotypes."[10]

Push Girls scored important points for disability empowerment. In one episode, for instance, Rockwood declares, "I can't hold in my little belly, and I have these noodle arms, but I feel sexy." That a disabled person could feel sexy, let alone look sexy, was eye-opening for some viewers. But perhaps most importantly, the episodes weren't just about these women's disabilities. They were about everything else in their lives as well. In NPR's *Pop Culture Happy Hour* blog, writer Linda Holmes observes: "Popular television is bad at lots of things, and one of them is representations of people with disabilities." *Push Girls*, she writes, showed these women having worries other people don't, yet without "even a whiff of pity." This did not make them heroic, she stresses; each woman had narratives that were only partially related to their disabilities. "They seem to have the right balance here of stuff that is about the wheelchairs, which is interesting and helpful to share with an audience, and stuff that isn't about the wheelchairs, which is important to avoiding making the women seem precious or one-dimensional."[11]

Push Girls never raised strong political points, though. It scarcely addressed broader social issues or disability activism. Watching it, you might almost think these five women were the only wheelchair users in the world. And try as it might to portray them as three-dimensional characters, their disabilities were central to the point of the show. It's also worth noting there wasn't much diversity. They were all spinal cord–injured wheelchair users; although one of the women, Angela Rockwood, was partly of Asian descent, the others all identified as white.

As an industry, the beauty business is predominantly concerned with female beauty, of course. But there are a handful of disabled male models starting to pop up. In 2015, Jack Eyers—ruggedly handsome, his cream-toned skin rippling with muscles—became the first male amputee to appear on the runway at New York Fashion Week, wearing outfits by Italian designer Antonio Urzi. Two years later he was on the catwalk at London Fashion Week, modeling for London-based designer Teatum Jones.[12] Eyers was born in Glastonbury, Somerset, England, with proximal femoral focal deficiency in his right leg, meaning part of the femur was malformed, causing the leg to be shorter than the other. He had to wear a brace that made his knee unbendable. When he was about ten, the stigma of his leg began to bother him even more than the fact that it interfered with his playing rugby and soccer. "I became very ashamed of my leg and very unconfident," he says. He refused to wear shorts or swim trunks in public; in fact, he often wore two pairs of pants at the same time to try to hide the difference between his legs. "The only disability figures in the media were Captain Hook or villains in James Bond. So I felt like a villain. I felt very vulnerable, ugly," he says.[13]

One day, at a routine appointment to get his leg brace refitted, he met Louis Brownsell, an amputee stunt performer and actor who had played an injured soldier in the movie *Saving Private Ryan*. Inspired by this example, Eyers decided at age sixteen to have his leg amputated above the knee—just like Brownsell.[14] "Before my amputation, I considered myself as disabled and restricted by my condition," Eyers says on his website. "However, since my amputation, my so-called disability has actually opened many doors."[15] In an interview with *Ability* magazine, he adds that as soon as his leg was gone he felt "freer, lighter."[16]

A fitness nut whose day job is being a freelance personal trainer, Eyers performed at the opening ceremony of the 2012 Paralympic Games in London and had hoped to compete in the 2020 Paralympics in Tokyo, but the games were postponed by the COVID pandemic; he would have represented Britain in canoeing, a sport for which he's traveled the world. As a model, he was sponsored by NRGFuel Sports Nutrition, a British dietary supplement company; appeared on the cover of the British edition of *Men's Health* magazine; and did a photo shoot for Boohoo.com, an online clothing line. Now in his late twenties, he's represented by VisABLE, an agency that specializes in disabled models and actors.

A curious thing can happen when disability and beauty collide. In 2007, the actor Selma Blair—who had starred in a host of hit movies, including 1999's *Cruel Intentions*, 2001's *Legally Blonde*, and 2004's *Hellboy*—was named one of *People* magazine's "world's most beautiful people." Then, in October 2018, she told *Variety*, the entertainment industry news source, that she'd been diagnosed with multiple sclerosis.[17] "I am disabled. I fall sometimes. I drop things. My memory is foggy. . . . But we are doing it," she posted on social media afterward, adding that she'd probably had MS for fifteen years, but it had gone undiagnosed.

In the past, when stars known for their pulchritude as much as anything else suddenly became disabled, their luminescence seemed to dim; they became personae non gratae, unbankable. But lately, people are asking why that should be. Was Christopher Reeve, the *Superman* star, any less handsome after his backbreaking equestrian accident in May 1995?

There was a pause in this career, sure, but he did manage to make a few movies after becoming quadriplegic. Likewise, Michael J. Fox continued to appear on TV for a time after announcing in November 1998 that he'd had Parkinson's disease for seven years and it was getting worse.

A year after announcing her MS, Blair appeared at the Oscars red carpet, walking in an elegant gown with the aid of a cane. This prompted a photo spread and feature in the March 2019 issue of *Vanity Fair*, in which she says, "There's no tragedy for me. . . . A cane, I think, can be a great accessory."[18]

Canes may have once been a stylish accessory for an urban gentleman dandy, but never before for a glamorous woman—and certainly not if it was a needed, crutch-like tool. It could have been a dramatic reclamation of what constitutes "beauty," yet the media didn't see it that way. "I really appreciate [Blair's] talking about living with MS and relate strongly to many parts of her experience," writes Katie Tastrom, a disability lawyer, writer, and activist, in the blog *Rooted in Rights*. "However, the media coverage and what interviewers have seemed to focus on [are] the same old disability tropes of: inspiration porn, being lauded for being a 'good sick person,' and using atypical examples to generalize about what it is like to be disabled."[19]

Disabled people do amazing things every day, Tastrom continues. They take care of their children and sometimes each other. They write and paint and sing. They are politically active. They survive all manner of abuse. None of this is necessarily "brave" or "inspiring"; it's just what people do in the course of living their lives. So if Selma Blair is living her life and trying to continue her career, why is that especially gutsy? Why shouldn't she try to go on with her life and career? Why is going to the Oscars with a cane—which she needed—touching? For her, it was either that or not go at all.[20]

Still, if a mobility aid such as a cane can be considered not just a neutral, functional tool but a *beauty enhancement*, a fashionable accoutrement, that's saying something. As with the tricked-out, brightly colored, aerodynamic wheelchairs that burst on the scene in the 1980s, other items for people with disabilities should be as cosmetically pleasing as they are practical.

Clothing is a good example. If past generations wanted apparel that was designed for disabled bodies, they had little choice but to look through catalogs of dull, shapeless, utilitarian garments designed to make life easier for "caregivers" and hospital staff. These postsurgical recovery and rehabilitation outfits might have been comfortable, but they were hardly stylish. To meet the vanity needs of disabled people, perhaps especially younger disabled people, a whole industry of "adaptive apparel" began springing up in the early 2000s. These togs were both functional and appealing. Authored Apparel, for instance, based in Greer, South Carolina, makes a dress that can be pulled on from the feet, without standing up.[21] Toronto-based IZ Adaptive manufactures a full wardrobe, including outfits for those who sit all day—jeans, say, with zippers on both sides, an elastic waistband at the back, no back pockets or rivets, an extra-long zipper fly, a wider cut across the lap and thighs, flat seams to avoid skin irritation, and concealed zippers at the ankles for easy on and off and access to a leg bag.[22]

It's not just specialty retailers that are in on the act of creating accessible clothing. In 2016, Target launched a special line of its Cat & Jack brand with soft fabrics and no tags or pockets, among other modifications. The same year, the designer brand Tommy Hilfiger debuted Tommy Adaptive.[23] Online retailer Zappos also sells similar fashion products, including Nike FlyEase sneakers, which have zippers and Velcro closures.[24] Such easy-to-put-on and properly fitting clothes "increase confidence and independence," says Alette Coble-Temple, a wheelchair-using psychology professor and disability rights activist at John F. Kennedy University in Pleasant Hill, California.[25]

A more customizable specialized option is Rebirth Garments, a clothing maker in Chicago that aims to create gender nonconforming "wearables and accessories for people on the full spectrum of gender, size, and ability," according to company literature. The brainchild of Sky Cubacub, a nonbinary queer and disabled Filipinx person with lifelong anxiety and panic disorders, the line is both practical and political. Garments have no tags and can be made with seams on the outside, for those with sensitive skin; most are made of colorful stretchy fabrics such as spandex, and all can be made to individual specifications. That's the practical side. Politically, the brand is about expressing individuality and identity, especially queer and disabled identity. "Trans and disabled communities have very particular clothing needs that are not adequately served by mainstream clothing designers," Cubacub says. Rebirth Garments, on the other hand, opposes beauty standards that are "sizeist, ableist, and conform to the gender binary. Instead, we maintain the notion of Radical Visibility, a movement based on claiming our bodies and, through the use of bright colors, exuberant fabrics, and innovative designs, highlighting the parts of us that society typically shuns." The brand is dedicated to what the website refers to as a "QueerCrip dress reform movement."[26]

Overall, the fashion choices are varied enough that Los Angeles–based Stephanie Thomas has built a career as a professional disability fashion stylist. In 2003, the former Chicago Bulls cheerleader, who is a congenital amputee with missing digits on her right hand and feet, began contacting fashion designers about making clothes for people with disabilities. At the time, she found little interest. The next year she launched *Cur8able*, a disability fashion and lifestyle blog, and trade-marked her Disability Fashion Styling System, which, she says, is based on more than a decade's worth of research. In 2015, Cur8able became a company that's dedicated to "pulling together disability-friendly clothing [and] disseminating advice," says the website. "I use my Disability Fashion Styling System to curate looks for people with disabilities and consult fashion industry professionals on how to better meet the styling needs of people with disabilities," Thomas explains.[27] She also lectures in fashion marketing.

~

The future of disability in the beauty industry rests with the up-and-comers. Each new success story seems to pave the way for the next one, at least until the business is saturated with disability beauty, which won't happen for a long time. Still, though opportunities may remain scarce, they're no longer impossible. You can imagine yourself in that world; it will never again be unattainable.

That's partly because of Aaron Rose Philip. Before she was twenty years old, Philip—a transgender woman with CP who uses a motorized wheelchair and who's originally from Antigua and Barbuda—had appeared in fashion and beauty ads, in a music video, and on national TV. Her accomplishments are even more amazing when you consider how she and her family were once unhoused in New York. But they managed. As a kid, she started a sort of comic/sci-fi blog called *Aaronverse* about a fictional land where disabilities were normal and the nondisabled minority struggled to fit in. Her blog was so clever and popular that, at the age of twelve or thirteen, she was invited to address the executives at Tumblr headquarters to explain how she'd learned to leverage their online platform so creatively.

The Internet also played an important role in her budding modeling career. One day in the summer of 2017, when she was sixteen and visiting her mother in the Caribbean, Philip announced her obsession with fashion. "I really *loved* it, more than I ever thought I did," says Philip with unabashed enthusiasm.[28] (She speaks with a New Yorker's passionate rapidity.) But she never saw anyone like herself in the magazines she enjoyed. "I had to ask myself, why is that? There was no good reason. So I said, let's give it a try! That's when I decided to try to be a model."

At the beginning, she realized she couldn't just go to an agency and get signed. She couldn't go to open calls "like everyone else does," she says. So she went on the Internet. She took selfies and composed blogs and posted on social media about her dream. To her surprise, her pictures and writings started gaining attention. "It was a slow start, but then things began piling up. I knew this was a long shot, I really did, but somehow the stars aligned. People wanted to see me and understand where I came from."

Soon she was getting nibbles from fast-fashion brands such as H&M and American Eagle. It wasn't long before she signed with Elite Model Management, which represents many well-known supermodels. (As of this writing, she's moved representation to Community New York.)

Philip acknowledges she's had to make adjustments to show the modeling world she's as good as anybody else. Some people weren't ready for what she had to offer. "They had to think outside of themselves. It wasn't like I made a big protest. I'd just show up for work, and that made people *think*," she says. "I mean, really, why *can't* someone who can't walk exhibit fashion? It doesn't make sense."

At photo shoots, there's generally someone on hand to help her change clothes and do her face and hair. That's usual for models, but Philip requires extra hands-on assistance with dressing. At home, her dad helps her get up in the morning. But he doesn't usually accompany her to work.

Philip does not consider herself a disability activist, but she has become an advocate—if only by virtue of insisting on being able to do what she sets her mind to. She has learned about the issues disabled people—especially Black trans disabled people—face from personal, lived experience. And her agents promise she will go on to do "amazing things," she says, though as "a new face, a new concept," she'll have to work at least twice as hard as anyone else. She figures she's young and there's time. "Fashion kind of views me as 'more than a model' in the sense that my presence as a girl with a disability is valued beyond modeling," she muses.

In 2019, she made her runway debut for Willie Norris Workshop, followed during the COVID pandemic by a digital runway for Collina Strada; in the fall of 2021, she sashayed down the catwalk in her wheelchair for Moschino at New York Fashion Week. "My disability will not stop me," Philip declares, reluctantly adding that sometimes people don't know what to do with something they haven't encountered before. The thought passes quickly. "When people start to hate on you, that means you're challenging them," she says. "It means you're having impact."

CHAPTER 9

CASTING AND MISCASTING

One Sunday evening in June 2019, wearing a bright yellow off-the-shoulder gown custom-made by designer Rachel Antonoff, singer and actor Ali Stroker raised her muscular arms in triumph after winning the Tony for *Oklahoma!* To thunderous cheers, she told the audience, "This award is for every kid watching tonight who has a disability, who has a limitation or a challenge, who has been waiting to see themselves represented in this arena."[1] She was aware of the import of her moment in the spotlight. She wasn't the first disabled performer to win a Tony, but she was the first one in a wheelchair. "When Ali Stroker rolled onstage in her wheelchair to accept the Tony Award for featured actress in a musical, audiences at home went bananas," the *Los Angeles Times* reported. It quoted several social media posts, including one from Twitter user @Meaghandances, who said: "Ali Stroker just became the first actor in a wheelchair to win a Tony Award and I'm legit sobbing. As a woman with a disability, this means everything."[2]

Stroker knows she is a role model to many people. "I am making change every day in the world," she says, aware that she's "representing women and people with disabilities."[3] Because she's been paraplegic since her spinal cord injury at age two, she says she's very comfortable with her disability; it's all she's ever known. But her disability experience still isn't always comfortable. She's drawn to live theater, she says, because people are always staring at her anyway. On stage, though, it's "a different kind of attention," she says. "It feels much more powerful. I feel like I am in control."[4]

When she was training at New York University's Tisch School of the Arts—in 2009, she became the first actor in a wheelchair to graduate from its drama program—she had to negotiate with administrators and instructors to ensure her access requirements were met. Some of the curriculum had to be adapted, and there was a lot of trial and error. For instance, in a musical theater course there was an exercise called *type-ing* to help identify the sorts of roles for which performers were best suited. The young woman in the wheelchair didn't fit any of the available types, she says, so she had to create her own; she had to make roles that suited her personality, talents, and look. Since her graduation, the program has instituted several permanent changes to accommodate disabled students. She's received thank-you notes from some of them. "To know that my experiences have helped and inspired others is the greatest feeling in the world," she says.[5]

Still, after graduation, frustrated that she couldn't land an audition anywhere, she began writing her own one-woman show. Once again, she felt she had to create openings for herself. Gradually, however, she began to get offers. Her first big break was in 2012 on *The Glee Project*, a realty television series that auditioned performers for the musical comedy *Glee*. Though she didn't win the talent competition, it brought a lot of attention and more opportunities. In 2015, she garnered glowing notices as Anna, the kindhearted best friend who's attuned to injustice, in a Broadway revival of the rock musical *Spring Awakening*. In 2018, she played disability rights activist Judy Heumann in Comedy Central's reenactment of the Section 504 sit-ins for the program *Drunk History*. Then *Oklahoma!* came calling.

Since winning the Tony, Stroker became part of the #AerieREAL Role Model campaign, modeling the lingerie brand's garments, and in December 2020 she made headlines anew by starring in a Hallmark Channel romance, *Christmas Ever After*—the first to be headlined by a visibly disabled actor. She says it's "a little shocking" how few disabled people are represented in media, considering how many disabled people there are. "It has a little bit to do with people not really wanting to look disability in the eye," she says, "because it makes them uncomfortable." It shouldn't, she goes on, because disability of one sort or another is something most people will have to face sooner or later.[6]

Back in 1980, when D/deaf actor Phyllis Frelich won the Best Actress Tony Award for Mark Medoff's *Children of a Lesser God* (the same role for which Marlee Matlin would receive an Oscar six years later), it mattered, too. But that victory was different. Medoff wrote the part specifically for her. Anyone else who has ever played the role has been D/deaf; it's intended for a D/deaf actor. Stroker's achievement, on the other hand, was for a part—Ado Annie, the "girl who cain't say no"—that did not call for a disabled actor. It's never been performed by a visibly disabled person before, at least not on Broadway.

~

Acting is a tough career choice for a disabled person. Disabled characters have long appeared on stage and screen, though typically not realistically or constructively. Disabled actors, however, have not.

The list of roles that have been played in "crip face" is long and goes on to the present day. Arguably one of the best—and most realistic, to some disabled viewers—was Daniel Day Lewis's turn as Irish painter and writer Christy Brown in 1989's *My Left Foot*. Brown painted and wrote with his left foot, the only limb he could control because of his severe CP. The actor is not disabled, but he won an Oscar for the depiction the following year, mere months before passage of the ADA. Many disability activists at the time forgave the casting because the portrayal felt true and sympathetic without pity-mongering. Disability historian Paul Longmore praised the film's depiction of Brown's "glorious rage. . . . At last a movie hero utterly true to our experience as disabled people."[7] But the disability community's acclaim was quelled when Joan Collins, star of the prime-time soap opera *Dynasty*, told a reporter that she admired the handsome British actor's masterful ability to "make himself look so ugly." Calling CP *ugly* was blatantly insulting and offensive. Activist Lillibeth Navarro, then executive director of the Southern California chapter of ADAPT, wrote in the *Los Angeles Times* that Collins's remark was a slap in the face. "This is Hollywood; this is where images are made," she said. "Society must change its negative image of persons with disabilities, [and] this is where it ought to start."[8]

Even post-ADA, accurate and fair renditions of disability in media remain few and far between. Not long after *My Left Foot*, everyone seemed to love Forrest Gump, the multiply disabled protagonist played by nondisabled Tom Hanks in the 1994 film of the same name—everyone except certain disabled viewers, who felt the portrayal was hammy and preposterous. To them, it milked the character's unspecified disabilities for symbolic and artificially uplifting effect.[9] Then *Million Dollar Baby*, the hit 2004 movie starring Clint Eastwood and Hilary Swank—about a young boxer who becomes quadriplegic and ultimately decides that suicide is her best option—was swiftly judged a "cheap shot at disabled [people]," in the words of disability activist Mary Johnson.[10] Swank, who is not disabled, played the tragic quadriplegic. "Many people with disabilities, including the National Spinal Cord Injury Association, a national advocacy group with 13,000 members, see the film as one that uncritically advocates euthanasia for quadriplegics," reported the *Chicago Tribune*.[11] The 2016 romantic melodrama *Me Before You* evoked a similar morbid theme and mordant protest. In it, a quadriplegic man (played by Sam Claflin, who is nondisabled) chooses suicide to spare his lover/caregiver the burden of caring for and about him.

There were high hopes for Guillermo del Toro's *The Shape of Water*, winner of the Oscar for Best Picture of 2017. It was touted to be an artistic look at a D/deaf woman's sexual arousal. Unfortunately, the D/deaf woman—portrayed by non-D/deaf Sally Hawkins—has an affair with an amphibious subhuman creature that's been captured in a laboratory. For some viewers, this translated to "she deserves a freak like her," as D/deaf-blind writer and critic Elsa Sjunneson scoffs.[12] Toward the end, there's a song-and-dance dream sequence in which Hawkins sings "You'll Never Know." The effect, says Sjunneson, author of *Being Seen: One Deafblind Woman's Fight to End Ableism*, is to reassure the audience that the actor doesn't really need sign language. "Undercutting her disability broke the flow of sign language, the believability of disability, and indeed, the power of her words through sign," she says. Finally (spoiler alert), the woman dies—like so many other disabled characters before her—only to be resurrected under water to join her ichthyic lover. "Society would rather imagine a disabled woman living under water with the only creature that has ever loved her . . . than [see] her above the waves, being loved and desired by the other humans," says Sjunneson.

The problem doesn't end with these strange fantasy pictures. Even relatively recent, more true-to-life depictions invariably cast nondisabled actors in roles that could have and arguably should have gone to disabled performers—a snub that seems to say disabled actors aren't presentable or desirable. Examples include Jamie Foxx as Ray Charles in the 2004 biopic *Ray*, Eddie Redmayne as Stephen Hawking in 2014's *The Theory of Everything*, Bryan Cranston in 2017's *The Upside* (a fictional story about the believable relationship between a quadriplegic man and his personal-care assistant), and Joaquin Phoenix as the late quadriplegic cartoonist John Callahan in 2018's *Don't Worry, He Won't Get Far on Foot*. No matter how fine the performances may be, many disabled people see them as mimicking or lampooning the way actual disabled people live. They come off as phony or insulting impersonations or even crude caricatures.

According to research by the Ruderman Family Foundation, some 80 percent of disabled characters on the small screen in 2018 were portrayed by nondisabled actors.[13] The study, which covered about 280 network and streaming shows, found that roughly half featured characters with physical, cognitive, or mental health disabilities. That's a surprising number. The report went on to say that even when disability *is* present, it is "almost always portrayed as an undesired, depressing and limiting state." If people want stories with disabled characters, why not make them good ones? Why not hire more disabled talent to ensure fairness and simultaneously differentiate these programs from the clichéd fare?

Hollywood has long defended the practice of casting nondisabled stars on purely practical (read: mercenary) grounds. Studios need well-known and popular names to anchor projects and guarantee an audience; besides, they claim, it's hard to find good disabled talent. True as that may seem, the reasoning is a little circular. How can disabled actors become box office stars if they're never given a chance? How can they even get a start if they can't get into workshops and training courses? How can casting directors claim it's hard to find disabled talent if they've scarcely made an effort to look?

To be fair, actors—nondisabled actors, that is—weigh in that their craft is all about pretending to be something they're not. That's part of the job description. They don't have to be a detective or a murderer to play one, so why should they have to be disabled to play a disabled person? It's make-believe, after all, and disabled people are part of the mix of society, fair game for impersonation.

It's a reasonable point, or it would be in a just world. Nondisabled actors might be appropriate for disabled characters *if* more disabled actors were getting tapped for parts, say advocates. But if they can't play "regular" parts that don't call for a disability, and they're also barred from disabled roles because they're not famous enough, then they are truly locked out. "Access needs to be a component of the art," says Cheryl Green, a documentary filmmaker who has disabilities, writing for an entertainment industry website.[14]

Including more disabled talent might even attract more viewers. "These are critical voices with stories that are never going to be told [unless things change]," contends disabled sound editor and Oscar-nominated documentarian Jim LeBrecht. Disabled people, he says, "contribute to society," and getting their stories out in the open would improve "how people perceive people with disabilities."[15]

It would be a mistake, however, to say there are no actors with disabilities working today—in fact, their numbers seem to be growing. In the 1980s and '90s, prime-time TV viewers could see Geri Jewell, who has CP, in NBC's *The Facts of Life*; Chris Burke, who has Down syndrome, in ABC's *Life Goes On*; Danny Woodburn, who has dwarfism, in seven episodes of *Seinfeld*; and Nancy Becker-Kennedy, who is quadriplegic, in a half-dozen episodes of CBS's *The Louie Show*. That was about it. But between 2008 and 2013, R. J. Mitte, who has CP, was on AMC's *Breaking Bad*. From 2017 to 2021, Netflix's *Atypical* featured autistic young adults. In 2018 and 2019, Sundance TV's *This Close* portrayed besties who are D/deaf, one of whom is gay. Model Jillian Mercado has been in Showtime's *The L Word: Generation Q* since 2019. Also in 2019, Zack Gottsagen, who has Down syndrome, starred in *The Peanut Butter Falcon*. In 2020, Kiera Allen, a wheelchair user, made her debut in the Hulu suspense film *Run*. From 2020 to 2021, Freeform TV's *Everything's Gonna Be Okay* included autistic actor Kayla Cromer. And in 2022, D/deaf actor Troy Kotsur won the best supporting actor Oscar for Apple TV's *CODA*, which also won best picture.

Perhaps no disabled actor has logged more on-screen appearances in recent years than Robert David Hall. From 2000 to 2015, he was Doc Robbins, the medical examiner in the hit CBS series *CSI*. It may not have been a leading role, but he kept it throughout the entire run of the series, even as other actors left. After the first few seasons, his name appeared in the opening credits—it was a big enough role for that. Hall was already in his fifties; decades earlier, in his early thirties, he'd lost both legs in an auto accident. Between then and *CSI*, he'd worked mostly in radio and had voice roles in cartoons, landing only the occasional live-action part. He played a judge, for instance, in three episodes of *L.A. Law* and another judge in four episodes of *The Practice*, roles for which he could mostly stay seated behind a bench in a big black robe, thus hiding his disability. Then came *CSI*.

To date, Hall is the longest-running recurring disabled actor in a major series, clocking in at some 328 *CSI* episodes. In that regard, he far surpasses Peter Dinklage, the actor with dwarfism whose Tyrion Lannister appeared in all sixty-seven episodes of HBO's *Game of Thrones* between 2011 and 2019, its entire lifespan (though perhaps Dinklage had more total minutes on screen than Hall). After a decade in films, Dinklage won four Emmys for the role. He stands less than four and a half feet tall. Performers with dwarfism—sometimes called People of Short Stature, or Little People—have a long history in entertainment, often playing elves, munchkins, or sidekicks. Dinklage is rare in that he's played major parts in a broad spectrum of movies and TV series, in dramatic, romantic, and comedic turns. His credits include 2003's *Elf* (in which he was not an elf but rather the yuppie Miles Finch), 2017's *Three Billboards Outside Ebbing, Missouri*, 2018's *Avengers: Infinity Wars*, and 2021's *Cyrano*. In other words, he's played many roles that did not require his particular disability.

Closing in on the record for recurring TV appearances is Daryl "Chill" Mitchell, the comedic actor and former hip-hop artist (and one of the few nonwhite performers on this list) who debuted the role of tech specialist Patton Plame in CBS's hit spinoff series, *NCIS: New Orleans*, in 2014. Through the program's final episode in 2021, Mitchell appeared in 138 episodes. Thirteen years before that role, he became paralyzed from the waist down in a motorcycle accident. He was already a viable star, having appeared in several popular TV programs, including *The John Larroquette Show* and *Veronica's Closet*, both for NBC. His accident would've ended his career once upon a time. But it barely paused his. Within about a year of becoming disabled, he starred in a short-lived NBC sitcom called *Ed*.

A big step for disabled actors and the depiction of disabilities in general occurred in the fall of 2016, when ABC rolled out a provocative sitcom called *Speechless*. It focused on the lives of a "typical" middle-class TV family—frenetic but passionate mom (played by Minnie Driver), hilariously incompetent dad (John Ross Bowie), superior know-it-all tween daughter

(Kyla Kenedy), sarcastic and nerdy teenage son (Mason Cook), and, finally, the high-school–age son who happened to be a nonverbal wheelchair user with cerebral palsy (Micah Fowler, who actually *is* a wheelchair user with CP, though in real life he speaks). Add to this clan a trusty-but-irreverent helper named Kenneth (Cedric Yarbrough).

With this motley crew, prime time seemed to recognize disability as a worthwhile commodity and a central theme, the linchpin for a show that wasn't sentimental or maudlin. It proved to be sitcom gold. Its first season averaged 6.23 million viewers per episode.[16] It won a Television Critics Association award in 2017 for outstanding achievement in youth programming. To the network, it was about a "special needs family," but to disabled viewers the depiction was about as authentic, or at least as relatable, as you could hope for on television; it sparked a deep sense of connection. Scott Silveri, its creator and executive producer, told reporters the series was inspired by his own childhood; he grew up with a brother with CP. "We don't want the character to be defined by the disabilities," he told the press, "the same way that people with disabilities don't want to be defined by their disabilities." The disabled kid, J.J. DiMeo, behaved like a normal high schooler. "Just because J.J. is in a wheelchair doesn't mean he's not going to fight," Silveri said. "It doesn't mean he doesn't want things. And it doesn't mean he's not a jerk sometimes. . . . We keep saying to ourselves, 'Is this a character we would write even if he didn't have a disability?' And if it was all about the wheelchair, then—not interested."[17]

As the series progressed, not all episodes rang true. But others felt dead-on. There were bits about the foibles of fighting for access to equal education. There were bits about affording an accessible van. There were bits about playing the "disability card" to gain unfair advantages. Perhaps best of all, J.J. felt true and relatable because the actor wasn't faking it.

The show lasted for three seasons, or sixty-three half-hour episodes. That was successful enough to encourage executives to consider other disability-centered sitcoms. In 2019, Netflix released a series called *Special.* Told in fifteen-minute episodic segments, it was about the exploits of a gay young man with CP. He walks jerkily and has some mild spasticity—so mild, in fact, that he tries beyond all reason to pass for nondisabled. He makes up some excuse about recovering from an auto accident, rather than admit his disability is inborn. It was a very different type of comedy from *Speechless*. Where *Speechless* was made for prime time, *Special* was edgy and progressive. It dealt with this young man's sexual awakening. It dealt with his struggle to become independent of his overprotective mother. It dealt more with his struggle to combat his own internalized ableism than his struggle to come out as gay, though there was that, too.

The program starred and was created and written by Ryan O'Connell, who really is a gay young man with CP, just like his character. It was based on his 2015 memoir *I'm Special: And Other Lies We Tell Ourselves*. In an interview in *IndieWire*, O'Connell says, "I wrote the book when I was twenty-six, so I was just kind of a dumb-dumb and I had just come out about my disability. I didn't understand anything about disability or things like internalized ableism. I was so in my infancy with my disabled journey. I couldn't talk about all the things that I want to talk about now, which is why *Special* was so incredible, because I feel like I've grown up so much and have become woke to my own damage, and the damage of living in an ableist society."[18]

In time, as part of his coming-of-age, his character comes to see that his primary battle for identity and independence has to do with facing down that ableism. For him, ableism is worse than homophobia because it's less well recognized. This is a heavy concept for a sitcom. Now in his early thirties, O'Connell understands that his program is an attempt to bridge two worlds. Growing up, he tells disabled writer Keah Brown, "there was my disabled life—surgeries, physical therapy, leg braces—and then my life at school, where I was the only disabled person. My parents were well-intentioned and just wanted to immerse me in 'regular life,' but I think in doing so I had limited exposure to other disabled people, which created this discomfort in my disabled identity. Also, from an early age, I realized disability was not really understood or talked about in society. So I tried to stuff it down as much as I could."[19]

This kind of comedy—the comedy of searching for disability pride in the midst of rampant ableism—is new in its specifics, yet universal in its appeal. It humanizes the disability experience, or at least one important aspect of it, for those who are uninitiated. It gives the nondisabled a perspective on disabled lives—and maybe helps other disabled people feel not quite so alone. If nothing else, it speaks to the growing cultural acceptance of disabled people as a minority, and—in the gentlest terms—of ableism as a menace not unlike racism, sexism, homophobia, transphobia, and other forms of bigotry.

Almost as if in recognition of a growing trend toward more authentic disability representation—or at least the need for it—the Ruderman Family Foundation secured a first of its kind pledge from CBS in June 2019 to "audition actors with disabilities with each new production picked up to series."[20] That means a promise to seek out more disabled talent for *all* future programs. In January 2021, NBC Universal made similar assurances, pledging to pursue disabled actors for its TV and movie projects going forward.[21] Of course, similar pledges have been made for better representation of other minorities, with mixed results. How well will the media giants live up to these assurances? Will other studios follow suit? And to what extent will such opportunities actually lead to better and more varied representations of disabilities?

For Keah Brown, a twentysomething African American bi woman with CP and a self-avowed TV junkie, changes can't happen fast enough. She's fed up with "the monolithic view of disability" she sees in the popular culture she adores. In 2017, partly in reaction to the whitewashing of disability in major media, she started a viral hashtag on Twitter—#DisabledAndCute. Brown, the author of *The Pretty One: On Life, Pop Culture, Disability, and Other Reasons to Fall in Love with Me* and *Sam's Super Seats*, shares that she started the hashtag as an act of rebellion and self-reclamation.

"So often when you see stories about disabled people, they're disabled white men," she says.[22] "People have no grasp that our community is full of people of Color! It's full of women! It's full of people in the LGBTQ community! It's full of people who run across multiple intersections."

As a child, with little framework for basing self-esteem as a disabled bi Black girl, she tried to pass for nondisabled—and sometimes succeeded. Whenever she felt winded walking with friends at the mall, she would make some excuse for sitting down on a bench till she felt better. If that didn't work—if there wasn't a bench handy or she needed more time than her friends would allow—she would just grin and bear it, never wanting anybody to view her as needy. This changed one day in her early twenties when she looked in the mirror and decided to say four nice things about her appearance. It felt good, put her in a good mood, and she repeated it the next day. And the next. After a few weeks, it became a self-reinforcing habit. She started feeling better about herself and feeling better able to be upfront and honest about her limitations, too. It helped remove any sense of shame over her body, over being disabled, over not looking like the celebrities she so admired. It helped her feel proud.

She has both visible and invisible disabilities. She can walk but has difficulty with long distances, and she has "mental health issues." If people like her hadn't been erased from mainstream media—let alone from disability narratives—it would've made a world of difference. She'd like to see more different types of people in front of and behind the camera—people with every manner of disability and complexion and gender identity. "That's why I fight so hard to expand the idea of who is disabled, because it's very white male centered right now. I want to bust up that theme and tell people there are people like me in the world. People who have CP but aren't wheelchair users, or who have any disability and are people of Color."

You can't blame her impatience. At times the battle for better representation in Hollywood can seem hopeless. Back in 1979, the Media Access Office was formed to help promote actors with disabilities. "Our mission, our message, is to get the media to respond to the burgeoning civil rights movement for people with disabilities," Alan Toy, a disabled actor (*Beverly Hills 90210*, *In the Line of Fire*, *The Aviator*, and *Annie Live!*, among other film and TV credits) who was then president of the Media Access board of directors, told an interviewer in 1989.[23] While the office no longer exists, it started a tradition of presenting annual Media Access Awards for the best portrayals of disability. The awards continue to this day, now funded by Easterseals, but their impact on the industry is debatable.

Nevertheless, examples of disability casting keep making headlines. In the fall of 2021, for example, Marvel's *The Eternals* included the first D/deaf superhero in a movie, Makkari, played by Lauren Ridloff, who is D/deaf and a person of Color.[24] Marvel has had disabled superheroes before—notably, Professor X and Daredevil—but never a visibly disabled actor. "It is so important to showcase people with disabilities with intersectional identities," Ridloff tells Lauren Applebaum, a disabled reporter, "because that allows viewers to see beyond disability. People with disabilities are multilayered—we are complex breathing human beings."[25] Ridloff, who was born D/deaf, in 1978, to a Black American mother and a father of Mexican descent, says she'd had doubts about pursuing acting because she never saw people like her on screen. She tells *Variety* that when she got the part of Makkari, "It felt like it was [after] a lifetime of waiting."[26]

In the comic books, Makkari is a non-D/deaf, beefy, white, blond-haired cisgender male. Marvel's decision to recast the character reveals what Ridloff calls a growing awareness of "the need to tell new, fresh stories. We've seen so many stories out there with the same tropes, with the same characters, and we're getting restless. . . . Hollywood sees the importance of bringing more representation on the screen."[27] *The Eternals*, she says, shows diversity "without actually having that become the point of the story. It just is. It's just like the real world."

Ridloff understands the power of her position, at least as far as other disabled people are concerned. She gets what it means to represent. She could hide—or at least minimize—her disability, since it doesn't show, but she doesn't. In fact, she made sure her character's sign language was accurate—unlike, say, Sally Hawkins's crude impersonation of sign language in *The Shape of Water*. In interviews, Ridloff even highlights "D/deaf gain," pointing out how she didn't need earplugs during loud sound effects while other cast and crew did; she also says she never minds sitting next to crying babies on airplanes. "There are times that we're just lucky to be Deaf," she tells the *Hollywood Reporter*.[28]

She's not shy about Hollywood's shortcomings, urging "more opportunities for other Deaf people [and] for people with other disabilities, not only in front of the camera, but also behind the camera. We need more people in the writers room. We need more people involved with pre-production. We need people who are Deaf or have disabilities."[29]

Within weeks of that interview, as if on cue, Marvel introduced another disabled superhero of Color, Echo—aka Maya Lopez—to viewers of its *Hawkeye* series. She is portrayed by Alaqua Cox, a D/deaf actor and amputee with a prosthetic leg who is a member of the Menominee and Mohican Nations. "What could be better than two deaf superheroes?" blogs Mineli Goswami, an India-based writer with unilateral hearing loss.[30]

And then it did get better. Echo/Lopez is slated to return in her own series.

CHAPTER 10

WHAT'S SO FUNNY ABOUT DISABILITY?

The YouTube sensation Zach Anner, who has cerebral palsy—"the sexiest of the palsies," as he puts it in one of his most famous bits—has gained an unusual degree of star power. In 2010, when Anner was twenty-five, he entered a contest to become Oprah's "Next TV Star" for her cable network. He won. The resulting program, *Rollin' with Zach*, came with a $100,000 award. But the show was canceled after six episodes, ostensibly over creative differences. The producers wanted uplifting, inspiring stories of heroic disability victories; Anner just wanted to make people laugh.

After Oprah, he created a weekly YouTube series called "Workout Wednesday," featuring his unique klutzy and haphazard exercise routine. Before turning thirty, Anner landed a contract with the online entertainment company SoulPancake for a series called "Have a Little Faith," a look at Anner's idiosyncratic take on organized religions. By that time he'd moved to LA. When the ABC sitcom *Speechless* debuted, Anner was hired as a writer and story editor. He even appeared in a few episodes.

In his hilarious 2016 memoir, *If at Birth You Don't Succeed: My Adventures with Disaster and Destiny*, Anner explains that he started making videos in college at the University of Texas, Austin—a series of short, often scatological interviews with local personalities that aired on the university's public access channel. With boyish enthusiasm, Anner—who uses a wheelchair—says that his disability has been a mixed bag professionally. It's closed some doors but also given him oodles of material. His career only took off, and life became easier, when he stopped "trying to do things the able-bodied way, and doing them poorly."[1] He learned to harness his disability experience without entirely relying on cringe-inducing self-abasement. A good example occurred by accident at his first stand-up gig at Carolines, a New York City comedy club. Toward the end of his set, his wheelchair abruptly broke apart. "Two bolts had shot out from the sides of the chair, causing it to slump awkwardly and stopping me in mid-sentence," he recounts. "It was an unplanned disaster. *Hallelujah!* I looked around the audience, shrugged my shoulders, and said, 'Ummmm . . . that's new!' They laughed. 'I really don't have any more material, but it looks like I'm going to be here awhile, so . . . how are you guys doin'?' They went wild."[2]

It was an I-meant-to-do-that kind of insouciance, an easy-going acceptance of life's absurdities that some might say is the epitome of disability cool. *We won't let the foibles of our bodies or our equipment cramp our style. Nothing can stop us!*

Anner's mission, if that's the word, is to dispel common myths about disabled lives. They're neither the saddest, most tragic existences imaginable nor the happiest, most inspiring ones either. "Folks with disabilities are human beings just going through normal shit," is how he puts it.[3] But he only learned about disability rights when he appeared in the 2018 Comedy Central *Drunk History* episode about the Section 504 sit-ins. (Anner played "man in wheelchair.") In retrospect, he regrets snubbing the disability community when younger; he didn't want to identify as one of *them*. "A terrible way to think! A huge mistake!" he says now. "My disabled friends today enrich my life so much. Having someone who understands what it's like to be patted on the head by strangers—to have people mistake you for a dog and think that petting you is okay—does something good for your soul."

Since the cancellation of *Speechless*, Anner has been pitching new TV shows with disabled characters. But he may be a victim of his own success. "A few producers are like, 'What's the point of *another* CP show?'" Anner says. "Of course, it's not another CP show—it's a show with characters who happen to have CP. I mean, the human experience is much wider than a diagnosis."

When a character has CP, or any other disability, and it's not the headline, he stresses, we'll know we've made progress.

~

isabled people seem to know, almost instinctively, that there's no better tool for shaking up the status quo, no better mechanism for up-ending the zeitgeist, than a good, enduring, eye-opening laugh. Ask any disabled person if there's anything funny about their life, and chances are you'll get an emphatic *yes!* Living with a disability can be rough. It can be maddening, enraging, depressing—sometimes all of the above. Disabled people face constant access barriers—even decades after the ADA made them illegal—and myriad other forms of exclusion. They deal with undependable technology, unreliable help staff, and endless government bureaucracy. They cope with poverty and isolation and loneliness. They wrestle with their own internal demons.

Yet through all this, their lives can be hilarious.

On any ordinary day they may experience riotous bodily mishaps, usually without meaning to, or quirks of fate that seem to prove the amateur theologian's assertion that God has a sense of humor. And if they're being honest, sometimes there is nothing quite so uproarious as the mealymouthed ways nondisabled people react to what disabled people call "normal." They're hysterical in their foot-in-mouth awkwardness.

So, yes, disabled people can be funny, their lives are funny, and they are often acute observers of other folks' funny fears and faux pas.

The practice of laughing in the face of disability has a long lineage, but not always in a good way. "Too often and for too long, people with disabilities have been objectified as a source of amusement," writes Michael Rock, an autistic journalist and blogger. "Since ancient times, they have frequently appeared in such fields of entertainment as circuses. In medieval and Renaissance Europe, little people were highly coveted as court jesters."[4]

But there is a difference between laughing *at* disabled people and laughing *with* them. Today, in its diversity of expression, technique, and subject matter, crip comedy knows few bounds. The humor may be visual or verbal or both. It may be revelatory, scatological, observational, self-deprecating, or offensive. Have you heard the one about the dyslexic agnostic who stayed up nights wondering if there really is a dog?

The modern idea of using disability consciousness for comedic effect—as opposed to fake disability buffoonery, à la Jerry Lewis's klutzy faux spasticity—can arguably be traced back to the cartoonist John Callahan. In the 1980s and '90s, his primitive drawings and caustic captions were making people laugh and feel uncomfortable, usually at the same time. At its height, his work was syndicated in more than two hundred newspapers around the world.[5]

Perhaps no one was more surprised by this success than Callahan himself. He'd had a rough childhood. He was adopted at six months old by a blue-collar family in a suburb of Portland, Oregon, and he struggled from an early age with issues of abandonment and belonging. When he was eight, he was sexually molested by a nun at the Catholic school he attended.[6] At twelve he began drinking—heavily, he says—and he struggled with alcoholism thereafter. In 1972, at twenty-one, Callahan was in a car accident that severed his spine and paralyzed him from the diaphragm down. He wasn't driving; he was passed out in the passenger seat. The driver, who was also drunk, was someone he'd just met.[7]

In time, he relearned to hold a pen and guide it across the page with his other hand. That's why his drawings have an awkward, childlike quality. After the accident, his cartoons began gaining attention at a local paper, before achieving widespread syndication.

His humor was unusual. In one classic cartoon, an instructor at an aerobics class for quadriplegics commands, "O.K., let's get those eyeballs moving." Another shows two disembodied human heads resting on wheeled boards at a street corner, begging cups on either side of them. One of the heads wears an eyepatch, and the other one tells him, "People like you are a real inspiration to me!" A third cartoon depicts a blind beggar with an odd haircut carrying a sign that reads, "Please help me, I'm blind and I think I may have a MULLET!"

Some may consider his work in poor taste, but Callahan himself called his style "survivor humor."[8] He wasn't just referring to surviving his car accident. He struggled with psychological issues throughout his life. Still, it was his quadriplegia that seemed to jump-start his career. He went on to publish more than a dozen collections of cartoons and two memoirs, and his work was adapted into two animated TV series: *Pelswick*, about the adventures of an ordinary boy in a wheelchair, and *John Callahan's Quads!*, an adult cartoon with a variety of foulmouthed disabled characters who live together in a mansion.

In a *New York Times* interview in 1992, just as the ADA went into effect, Callahan said he wished the law protected disabled people's freedom to laugh at themselves. "I'm sick and tired of people who presume to speak for the disabled," he added. "My only compass for whether I've gone too far is the reaction I get from people in wheelchairs, or with hooks for hands. Like me, they are fed up with people who presume to speak for the disabled. All the pity and the patronizing—that's what is truly detestable."[9]

On the whole, disabled people loved his work, his chutzpah. In that 1992 *Times* article, Royce Hamrick, a wheelchair user who was then president of the San Diego chapter of the National Spinal Cord Injury Association, said, "In the disabled community, we make a lot of jokes that stay within that community. What John is doing is bringing those out to everyone else."[10]

It's impossible to say which of his comics were the community's favorites. Was it the blind man and his guide dog being escorted onto a plane as the helpful flight attendant says, "We've arranged a window seat for your dog so you can enjoy the view"? Or the two cowboys squaring off in a classic Western shootout—except one of them has no arms. "Don't be a fool, Billy!" shouts an onlooker.

When he died in 2010, at fifty-nine, Callahan's obituary in the *Los Angeles Times* called him a "politically incorrect cartoonist."[11] To disabled fans, that missed the point. He was politically dead-on.

A completely opposite persona elevated Kathy Buckley—who bills herself as "America's first hearing-impaired comedienne"—to national prominence in the early 1990s. Her stand-up routines were unabashedly inspirational. She talked about her troubled life, which was almost unbelievably brimming with pathos. As an infant she had a blood disorder that required an emergency transfusion. At five she developed meningitis. At eight she was diagnosed with hearing loss, which may or may not have been caused by the blood disorder or the meningitis. She was teased, labeled "simple," sexually abused, and, at twenty, run over by a Jeep while sunbathing on the shores of Lake Erie. A few years later she was diagnosed with cervical cancer. After surviving all that, she got a job as a massage therapist, where she often told clients jokes as a form of psychological medicine. One of her customers was Geri Jewel, an actor with CP who played "Cousin Geri" on a dozen episodes of *The Facts of Life* in the early 1980s and "Jewel" in *Deadwood* from 2004 through 2006. Jewel suggested Buckley join her in a comedy fundraiser for cerebral palsy. She did so well that she soon got gigs at comedy clubs. Appearances on *The Tonight Show*, *The Today Show*, and many other variety and talk shows followed.

Adhering to the "oralism" tradition that some D/deaf activists reject, which discourages learning sign language, Buckley wears hearing aids, reads lips, and speaks rather than signs. "I spent about thirteen years with some of the top speech therapists in this country just learning how to talk so people would understand me," she says in one routine, "and now they all think I'm from *New Yawk*."

In recent years, she's transitioned from comedy to motivational speaking. She claims to inspire thousands of people annually by sharing her story of "overcoming adversity." It's a message that flies in stark contrast to the anti-inspirational thrust of most disability activism today, and certainly is a far cry from Callahan's outrageous form of empowerment.

Closer to Callahan's legacy is a stand-up comedian with a brash attitude who burst on the scene in August 2006—a scruffy young doofus named Josh Blue, who won an NBC reality show competition called *Last Comic Standing*. He was an unlikely winner, since he very obviously has CP. He's lanky, with wild curly brown hair and a shaggy beard to match, and he skulks across the stage with a stoner's lazy-looking gait (or is it just his CP?), decked out in a loose-fitting bowling shirt and jeans. Yet his hippie-dippie patter is unexpectedly sharp and intelligent, a contrast to his loopy singsong CP-inflected cadence. He uses his spasmodic movements and uneven modulations to great comic effect. Some of it is self-deprecating—in one performance, he jokes about his inability to make air quotes, for instance—but a lot of his shtick pokes fun at the audience, at how foolishly, how painfully and self-consciously politely, other people react to him.

"People ask me if I get nervous before coming up on stage," he deadpans to the studio and TV audience. "I say, 'Heck no. I get this many people staring at me all day!'" A roar of guffaws ripples through the crowd, and he smiles appreciatively before continuing, as if drinking in their laughter, as if it fuels him: "I was walking downtown, and the drunk tank stopped and picked me up." More laughter. "I was like, 'Uh oh.' I was like, 'Wait a minute here, fellas, there's a misunderstanding.' . . . I was in [jail] for seven days. They're like, 'Damn, buddy, what did you drink?'" The boisterous bursts grow louder, and he delivers his punchline: "I'd like to inform you that you're all going to hell for laughing at me."[12]

Blue was born in 1978 in Cameroon, West Africa, where his father taught American literature at a local university. (He calls himself "a white African American.") He grew up in St. Paul, Minnesota, but it was while he was a student at Evergreen State College in Olympia, Washington, that he ventured into stand-up at a local open mic night. He did well enough to get the bug. Competition after competition eventually led him to reality TV. But he certainly wasn't immune to the barriers of ableist prejudice. "In elementary school, I had a buddy who had palsy, too, and we were the first kids with disabilities to go to public school in Minnesota," he says. "So we definitely had a lot to educate the world on, even at a young age."[13]

He had lots of "hang-ups" about his disability in those days, he says. When he was fifteen, his parents moved the family back to West Africa for a year, so his father could resume teaching there. (This time it was Senegal.) The experience changed his perspective. "Being fifteen in a Third World country—talk about an eye-opener!" he says. "Who gives a shit about cerebral palsy when other people are so much less fortunate? They have use of their bodies, but they don't have clean water!"

He laughs about it, but Blue sincerely feels fortunate. He's through worrying about how others judge his disability and has no time for folks with preconceived notions. Does that make him a champion of disability rights? Yes and no. Blue certainly embraces disability pride; people have asked him if he'd take a cure if one were available, and he says he probably wouldn't. This is the only life he's ever known. Plus, having CP pays dividends. "It's what got me to this point, and I'm not struggling, you know?" he says. "Obviously it would be nice to tie my shoes sometimes without having a conniption fit, but other than that I'm more than okay as I am. In fact, I'm so happy with myself and my disability that, well, if you have a problem with it, that's *your* fuckin' problem. You don't like how I look, just turn away."

Yet he's always been more focused on making people laugh than on challenging the system. He knew some of the old-time activists in Denver, where he's lived for years. Beginning in July 1978—before Blue was born—people from Denver's Atlantis Community, a local independent living center, took to blocking intersections and lying in the street in front of inaccessible city buses. The Gang of 19, as they came to be known, inspired protesters for many years and formed the basis of the national grassroots group ADAPT. Denver's Rapid Transit District ultimately became the first in the nation to install wheelchair lifts on buses.[14] "That whole gang that was jumping out of their wheelchairs in front of the buses—that was amazing," Blue reflects. "But it was the spirit of the times, you know? Nowadays you have to do something else to get attention. We don't need to demand ramps anymore, not like we did. Now it's more about asking the world to treat us like fellow humans even though we move differently. Which is a weird thing to rally for."

Instead, he prefers to push the point through his stand-up. He never gets in your face to demand respect. That's not his style. "Telling people, 'Listen to me! This is important!' is not a convincing, compelling way to educate," he says. "They're not going to click to it. Know what I mean?" By spotlighting the unspoken, though, he makes ableist bigotry look oblivious and absurd. His friend termed it "reverse teasing," he says—a subtle technique for steering people to recognize their own prejudices. Comedy has always been key to this kind of consciousness raising. It's not unlike how Redd Foxx, Dick Gregory, and Richard Pryor opened white people's eyes to racism, or how Joan Rivers and Phyllis Diller satirized a certain kind of sexism—via people's funny bones.

Blue knew he was having an effect when, one evening a few months after his *Last Comic Standing* win, he wandered into a bar that happened to be having an open mic comedy showcase, and, to his amazement, three other comics there also had CP. "I was like, 'Oh my God! I've created a monster!'" he recalls.

He hadn't created them so much as inspired them. Funny people with CP had always existed; they tend to learn early on to grin and roll their eyes at the disconnect between their lives and others' perceptions of them, Blue theorizes. Only now, because of his example, they had the courage to get on stage, and the club gatekeepers had the inclination to let them. But Blue believes his influence goes beyond the CP community. "If I'm out there and I'm funny as shit, you're going to come to the conclusion that disabled people are just another brand of human being—without my having to force it down your throat."

He pauses a moment.

"I'm still forcing it down your throat, but it's coated in humor."

Still, comedy can be a solemn business. Scholars have long pondered how and why it works. "Comedy enacted by disabled comedians is potentially a powerful tool through which hegemonic norms around disability can be challenged and renegotiated," concludes a 2015 paper by British academic Sharon Lockyer. Her study was based on the realization that a growing number of comedians with disabilities had transformed the comedy landscape.[15]

Yet disabled comedians may still face a hard time being taken seriously, so to speak. "Why should there be a preconception that those with disabilities are worse at telling jokes than those who aren't?" writes Ted Shiress, a comedian and blogger with CP. He theorizes it may be that people are still uncomfortable laughing around someone who is disabled. It "isn't thought of as a nice thing to do," he says. His disability causes him to speak slowly if he wants to be understood, so he says he often has to compensate by getting to his punchlines as quickly as possible. He can't let a comedy bit drag out or he'll lose his crowd. He's learned to use his instrument, as singers say.

But are disabled comedians doing disability comedy, or are they just doing comedy? Shiress says that if a disabled comic's spiel is only about disability, it'll be boring and unimaginative. That doesn't mean, however, that the disability should be or even could be off-limits. "The issues that come with a disability can be great comedy fodder, but it shouldn't define you entirely," he says.[16]

Charles Walden, a longtime Philadelphia-based comic with CP, might agree. His impressive résumé includes appearances on BET's *Comic View*, *Apollo Comedy Hour*, *Russell Simmon's Def Comedy Jam All-Stars*, and Martin Lawrence's *First Amendment*, as well as in the 2017 movie *Holy Hustle* (as "Man with Tumor"). His subjects are far-reaching, touching on race and movies and current events. But sometimes he uses his slight spasticity for comedic inspiration. For instance, he jokes as Josh Blue does about appearing to be drunk, but his take is a little different. "I don't drink," he tells one crowd, "because I'm afraid if I started drinking I might start walking straight. And I know if I start walking straight, I'll lose my benefits."[17]

Another approach comes from Will Marfori, an Orlando, Florida–based stand-up comedian with CP, too, who has been on TV's *Late, Late*

Show with Craig Ferguson and on Sirius/XM Satellite radio. He jests just as much about his Irish-Filipino heritage as about his CP, which isn't all that visible. But his hands appear somewhat twisted and clumsy, which leads him to quip that *cerebral palsy* means "I really suck at building model airplanes." But it's not so bad, he adds; friends never ask him to help them move.

The stand-up comic Christopher Crespo takes a slightly different tack. Just a year old when the ADA passed, he was born in North Bergen, New Jersey, with complicated syndactyly, meaning his arms end at about his elbows and his fingers are somewhat fused together. One of his early stand-up routines was to start off grabbing the microphone with one arm—squeezing it between a partial hand and elbow—and then, with his other deformed arm, slowly picking up the mic stand and placing it behind him. This would take a while, typically to dead silence. Once done, he would intone, "Don't worry, I'm just like you guys. . . . I put my pants on one hour at a time."[18]

Crespo wasn't always sure about using his disability in his act. At the beginning, he didn't want to talk about it at all. He wanted to prove he had merit for his wit and timing, not garner attention out of pity. "I always feared that I'd be booked on a show to fulfill some diversity bullshit," he says. "I don't want to be on a show because they need a cripple; I want to be there because people want to see me perform."

A teacher at a comedy class told him he'd better address his disability because it was noticeable and people would wonder about it. He later realized that he was full of ideas related to his disability; it was an endless source of comedic invention—or, as he puts it, "I always go back to making fun of myself."

Danielle Perez has an alternative perspective. She identifies as a Latina "bilateral below-the-knee amputee." She uses a wheelchair. In 2004, when she was twenty years old and in college at San Francisco State University, the Los Angeles–raised Perez was run over by a streetcar. Both feet had to be amputated. She told CNN that she found healing at comedy clubs. When she's on stage, she's not concerned about what people think of her disability. "I'm just worried about *Are these jokes funny?*" she said.[19]

Perez went to her first open mic night at "this crappy little Hollywood coffeeshop," and she discovered how much she likes making people laugh. Most stand-up venues, however, are not very accommodating to disabled people. She often has to put on kneepads and crawl into basements or up flights of stairs to enter a club, or go in through a back alley, and then be lifted on and off stage; she can rarely get into the green rooms where comics warm up and practice—and network. "It's not fair that I miss out on that," she says.[20]

These access barriers could be a career killer. In the comedy scene, she explains, if you don't go out every night to an open mic showcase, you're quickly forgotten. "No one's gonna book you," she told the *Disability Visibility Project* podcast. "There's so many people doing comedy . . . that if you don't put yourself into people's faces and spaces, they're not gonna remember you, you know?" It's not just architectural barriers that impede her exposure. She tells of a comedy club in New York that had booked her but then called the day of her performance to say the manager was "not okay" with her wheelchair. Even if she didn't need assistance getting on stage, she wasn't welcome. "And it's like, what the fuck is that? . . . I can't do a free, unpaid comedy show in an improv theater? It's just kind of ridiculous," she said.[21]

In 2015, she went on *The Price Is Right,* the TV game show, in her wheelchair—and won a treadmill and walk-in sauna. You couldn't write a better springboard for comedy. She posted the clip on Twitter, it went viral, and she was invited to appear on *Jimmy Kimmel Live!* The exposure got her more club dates and fans.

Perez often uses her personal experiences as raw material. "My jokes are about me and my body and my life and what I'm going through, and it's all from my perspective," she says. She talks about her accident, her battles with depression, her abortion, her rape—stuff that might not sound funny. But everyone has emotional baggage, which gives her routines a kind of relatability—especially for women and gay men, she says in that podcast. "It's more than just telling jokes, you know? You're actually touching people."

She avoids being preachy, but she's aware of her potential for political impact. "I am a Latina. I'm a woman of Color. I'm in a wheelchair. I'm disabled—and I'm onstage, but I'm telling you fucking pussy jokes? Like, hey, that's freedom! . . . When was the last time you saw a woman that looked like me have the floor and be able to say whatever she wants and own a room and make people laugh?"[22]

For some, just being out there and being bold is a kind of political activism in itself. For other disabled humorists, though, a less direct approach is a better fit. Jessica and Lianna Oddi, Canadian sisters with SMA, follow in cartoonist John Callahan's . . . tire prints . . . with an Instagram and web comic series called "The Disabled Life." It started as a Twitter feed—all words, no pictures—but the fan base kept growing. The Oddi sisters love to draw as well as wax sarcastic, so a graphic version evolved as a kind of natural outgrowth. "It seemed the perfect way to merge the two things we love—drawing and sarcasm," Jessica told the e-magazine *Mashable*.[23]

One typical drawing shows three people at a casino table. The central figure is a woman in a wheelchair. To her right is a woman standing with one hand casually resting on the wheelchair's push handle; on the other side is a seated guy with his elbow on the wheelchair armrest. The ironic caption reads, "Personal space." Another is titled "Online Dating"; it has two panels, the first showing a woman in a wheelchair smiling at her dating app when it says "you matched: Some Hot Guy." But in the second panel she's puzzled and angry; the app reads, "Some Hot Guy said: 'Hey, you're pretty 4 some 1 in a chair though. lol. Can u have sex, babe?'"

The sisters say they have always used sardonic humor to cope with awkward interactions, particularly those involving strangers who get nervous or unnatural around their disabilities. It's the comedy of mismatch, a disparity between how they view themselves and how others react to them. Feelings of awkwardness—of being out of step with what the world seems to expect—are universal, apparently, because the comic strip has both disabled and nondisabled fans. "To find out that people can completely relate to us and our stories is just amazing," says Jessica.[24]

Laughter is the sisters' main objective, but if the material helps audiences learn something new, that's even better. The website contains a caveat, though: "Other people with disabilities may or may not agree with our views. And that's cool! Because us disabled folks are people too, with a wide range of opinions."[25]

If the Oddi sisters' comics skewer the disabled-nondisabled disconnect, Shannon DeVido's videos shatter it. DeVido, who has SMA, was in the 2020 romantic comedy film *Best Summer Ever* and appeared on Comedy Central's *The Nightly Show with Larry Wilmore*, among other venues. But when the New York–based comedian, actor, singer, and writer is not on mainstream media, she creates video clips for social media. She writes and stars in a YouTube channel called "Stare at Shannon," and in 2020 she cofounded a production company, King Friday Productions.

Disability, she says, is a "hot, weird topic" because it can break down barriers while also making people uncomfortable.[26] Nondisabled people don't know what is and is not okay to say and do around disabled people. "I'm never offended by that," she says, but she finds that using comedy to bust open supposedly taboo conversations is valuable. For her, that often means relying on self-abnegating visual pranks. For instance, in one YouTube clip she pretends to be auditioning for a Power Rangers movie by doing stunts such as driving her motorized wheelchair in circles—until the control mechanism gets stuck and she can't stop spinning.

She says she generates her own material because there weren't enough traditional job opportunities for someone like her. Her goal, she says, is to produce work that "circumvents what society thinks you should be doing as a disabled woman."[27]

If you're lucky and talented, having others laugh with you can weave a kind of magic spell. The court jesters of old could leverage this sort of beguilement to speak truth to power; disabled comedians often seem to wield a similar influence. Yet few of them dive very deeply into political controversies.

Maysoon Zayid, a Palestinian American actor, writer, and comedian with CP, is an exception. She demonstrates the jester-as-activist concept as well as anyone. Zayid bowls over audiences and her thirty-two thousand Twitter followers with her articulate, funny, and truthful observations and opinions. In one essay, Zayid writes of Donald Trump, "[He told] his friends at Fox: 'I spent millions of dollars making buildings good for people that are disabled.' He seems to want a Cheeto for complying with federal law, even when it takes being repeatedly sued for him to adhere."[28]

In her top-rated 2014 TED Talk, she explains her CP this way: "I shake all the time. Look, it's exhausting. I'm like Shakira! . . . It's not a birth defect. You can't catch it. No one put a curse on my mother's uterus, and I didn't get it because my parents are first cousins, which they are."[29]

In a way, Zayid *is* as dynamic as Shakira. Her delivery is rapid-fire and no-holds-barred. Born in New Jersey to immigrant parents, Zayid earned a bachelor of arts in acting from Arizona State University. But her choice of roles was limited, to say the least. "When I started auditioning, it was really the reaction of people in the room that told me [it wasn't going to happen]," she told cohosts Kallen Blair and Alie B. Gorrie in the 2019 Amazon interview series *Ability*. She recalls an audition in which the casting director didn't say anything to her, just stared blankly, but the message was clear: because of her disability, Zayid had no chance of ever getting cast. Instead, she was told to write her own one-woman show, something like Nia Vardalos's *My Big Fat Greek Wedding*, which had started as a one-woman play in Los Angeles in 1997 before becoming a hit indie movie in 2002. A similar monologue, she figured, would showcase her talents.[30]

But one Thanksgiving, before she'd completed writing her script, she had her friends rolling on the floor hysterically when she was trying to tell them "heart-wrenching stories," she says. "I was like, 'Oh? I have a gift for this?'" From then on, she knew what she wanted to do. "I'm going to become like Richard Pryor. He's Brown, he shakes, he's a comic, *and* he's in movies. I'm totally going to do this!"[31]

She signed up for a comedy class that concluded with a showcase at Carolines. She was instantly hired and started touring. By 2003, she'd cofounded the New York Arab-American Comedy Festival, an annual variety showcase. In 2008, she appeared in the Adam Sandler comedy *You Don't Mess with the Zohan* and more recently has been on the ABC soap opera *General Hospital*. She sold a semi-autobiographical comedy series that never got made and is now developing a new comedy series called *Sanctuary* about a Wall Street lawyer who gets sucked into the gritty world of immigration. If it ever gets made, Zayid will play the lawyer—a character who's not written as disabled but, of course, will be because Zayid is.

Despite her success, she says, the entertainment business remains maddeningly discriminatory. "Comedy clubs remain inaccessible, which means breaking in is a huge challenge," she says, adding that she doesn't usually use a wheelchair, though she does use one in airports, amusement parks, and other large venues. "Intersectionality also plays a huge role. It is easier to get stage time if you are a man than a woman and if you are white rather than a minority."[32]

For her, the ideal would be to have disabled people and other minorities appear in all entertainment venues, particularly when they aren't necessarily the point of the show. Not that she doesn't firmly believe in being loud and proud about disability. The more disabled people who embrace the identity—who don't try to pass for nondisabled—the better it will be for everyone, she says. She goes on to stress that it's vital for a full range of disability stories to be heard and seen—provided they "are told *by* us, not about us."

Zayid is a stickler for that authenticity. It is, in a sense, her brand of activism, filtered through her sharp sense of humor. She makes no attempt to be artificially upbeat or make light of her disability, as some other disabled comedians do. She allows negative feelings to show, something that might not have been possible before the ADA—when disabled public figures tended to adopt a grin-and-bear-it stance or be self-deprecating. Zayid's powder-keg mix of acerbic wit and righteous anger can be as enlightening as it is provocative, yet it is fundamentally fueled by the same kind of energy and outrage that propels all social justice movements. Her style and content may be unconventional and pathbreaking, but the issues she targets—bigotry, inequity, and oppression—are as old as our civilization.

PART III

THE CONTINUING EVOLUTION OF DISABILITY ACTIVISM

CHAPTER 11

HEALTH-CARE DISPARITIES

Lessons of COVID-19

From the earliest days of the COVID pandemic, it became glaringly evident that disabled people aren't treated fairly by the health-care system. To some nondisabled people, that was surprising. The health-care world is where you might think disabled folks would find the best access and feel most welcome. But nothing could be further from the truth, and when the infrastructure of the medical establishment—the rush of the clinical delivery apparatus—is stressed, as it was with COVID, disabled folks become the most threatened. Not only were they at risk from and vulnerable to the ravages of the coronavirus, but they were up against another wholly unnecessary and preventable adversary: the negligence and outright prejudice of a system designed to give aid. During the worst of the pandemic, the disparities and injustices imposed on the disabled population were so egregious that some policymakers were forced to acknowledge it and change course.

Mainstream awareness of health-care inequities began surfacing in March 2020, when some state and medical authorities were considering rationing vital resources such as ventilators, which were in drastically short supply. The fancy word for rationing is "triage"; hospital workers evaluate who has the greatest need and who will receive attention first, prioritizing patients based on expected outcomes. In the face of draconian scarcities, disabled and elderly people were considered the most expendable, or at least the least likely to benefit from emergency care. In

Alabama, for instance, people with intellectual or cognitive disabilities were specifically deemed "unlikely candidates" to receive ventilators;[1] Kansas and Tennessee,[2] referring to previously established "standards of care," singled out people with "advanced untreatable neuromuscular diseases" in their "exclusion criteria" for denying critical care during a crisis. The Washington State Department of Health issued guidelines telling doctors and hospitals to provide ventilators and other critical treatments to younger and healthier patients before giving them to others who may need them just as much.[3] Arizona, Louisiana, Maryland, Michigan, New York, Pennsylvania, and Utah had similar exclusions.

It was a cold calculation, a brutal metric of who was most and least entitled to receive treatment. The University of Washington Medical Center issued a statement that the goal of its emergency protocol was maximizing "healthy, long-term survival" of the greatest number of people, defined as "weighting the survival of young otherwise healthy patients more heavily than that of older, chronically debilitated patients. Such weighting has general support in medicine and society-at-large."[4]

But to disabled people, it was unfair, discriminatory, and illegal. Across the country they sprang into action. Before the end of March, online petitions were widely circulated. In Massachusetts, Colin Killick, executive director of the Disability Policy Consortium in Malden, and Marlene Sallo, head of Boston's Disability Law Center, said in a March 17 letter to the editor of the Boston Globe, "Should hospitals prioritize those with the least resource-intensive needs or exclude from access to life-sustaining care those with lower survival probabilities, they would be engaging in discrimination. The disability community will aggressively push back against any attempt to ration care against the disabled, through advocacy and, where necessary, legal action."[5]

On March 24, David Carlson, director of advocacy for Disability Rights Washington (state), one of many groups that filed a complaint with the federal government, told a reporter, "In these times, we need to be committed to our civil rights, and not adopt other methods of determining value in people." If resources are scarce, Carlson suggested, patients should be treated on a first-come, first-served basis or by a random lottery.[6] Soon after, on April 16, the Berkeley, California–based Disability Rights Education and Defense Fund (DREDF) posted the following warning: "DREDF reminds health care providers that longstanding federal and state nondiscrimination laws . . . prohibit such rationing measures when they result in the denial of care on the basis of disability. . . . No one should face discrimination in the provision of life-saving care. The rationing of health care services away from people with disabilities or chronic conditions during this time of crisis is not only ethically wrong, it is illegal."[7]

Then an additional panic shot through the disability community: There was alarming discussion that pandemic-strapped hospitals could actually *take breathing devices away* from people who used them regularly, so others could have them. As a result, many disabled people who already had ventilators at home said they wouldn't go to the hospital even if they needed to, for fear of having their equipment confiscated so someone else—someone younger or nondisabled—could use it.

The mainstream press got wind of the story. A March 23 op-ed in the *New York Times* was promptly followed by articles in *The Atlantic* on April 3, the *Washington Post* on April 9, *Time* on April 24, and elsewhere.[8] It wasn't long before the federal government had to react, though perhaps not as decisively as some might have hoped. As early as March 23, NPR reported that Neil Romano, chair of the National Council on Disability, had asked the Department of Health and Human Services to take action.[9] On the afternoon of Saturday, March 28—when, presumably, there was less media scrutiny—Roger Severino, director of the Office for Civil Rights, issued a press release stating his office would open a series of civil rights investigations to ensure that states did not allow medical providers to discriminate. The office would not, however, tell states how to allocate care; it simply put "entities on notice that they need to start considering the civil rights implications of any crisis standards of care plans they may be putting into effect."[10]

The official guidance Severino offered included statements such as "We're concerned that stereotypes about what life is like living with a disability can be improperly used to exclude people from needed care."[11] But the federal agency also provided immunity from legal liability, including civil rights claims, for "activities related to medical countermeasures against COVID-19."[12] That was in keeping with another outdated standard, one that had the force of law—the Public Readiness and Emergency Preparedness Act of 2005, passed after Hurricane Katrina, which stipulated "liability immunity" related to emergency measures . . . except in matters of "willful misconduct." The act had nothing to do with coronavirus; it was simply an example of how the federal government protects itself from accountability. In other words, if you were discriminated against by COVID protocols, you probably couldn't sue.

Medical rationing and redistribution were not new. New York State, for example, had published "ventilator allocation guidelines" back in 2007 that not only allowed but encouraged the removal of ventilators from people who depended on them regularly if there was a shortage.[13] Those guidelines were drafted in the aftermaths of Hurricane Katrina in 2005 and the SARS epidemic of 2003, shocking events that caught the health-care system by surprise and "highlighted the need for preparedness plans," as one New York State document says.[14]

By April 10, 2020, Severino's office did step up somewhat. According to the autistic activist and scholar Ari Ne'eman, the Office of Civil Rights had required Alabama to "fully rescind guidance excluding people with intellectual disabilities, dementia, and others from ventilator access and commit to not 'include similar provisions singling out certain disabilities for unfavorable treatment or use categorical age cutoffs' in future guidelines."[15] That was just a starting point. Pennsylvania, Colorado, and Massachusetts preemptively canceled all exclusions from care. "Though many state plans still have categorical exclusions based on particular disability diagnoses, the tide is clearly turning," Ne'eman wrote. "But more work remains to be done."[16]

Separately, Ne'eman told the press, "Our civil rights laws don't go away in the midst of a pandemic. We don't suddenly replace the ADA or other civil rights laws with generalized utilitarianism the moment things get difficult."[17]

After the Office for Civil Rights warning to health-care providers, disabled people's worries were far from over. Many faced a conundrum related to their home-care attendants. Because people with underlying medical vulnerabilities were at greater risk of contracting the disease, they self-isolated as much as possible. But many disabled folks still needed outside help to get in and out of bed, and to be washed and fed, which put them at risk if their helpers were asymptomatically carrying the virus. The workers themselves, who don't typically have medical insurance or receive paid sick leave, were afraid of contracting it, too. Many of them preferred to stay sheltered at home.

On top of that, Medicaid budgets were stretched extra thin. Many disabled and chronically ill folks rely on Medicaid—the joint federal-state program that provides medical assistance to low-income elderly and disabled people—to pay for their daily care. States were facing an unusual fiscal crunch. Unemployment rolls had soared as businesses closed or put employees on furlough, sales tax coffers were drained since no one was shopping, and there was an urgent need to offer free, widespread COVID testing. On March 27, Congress passed the $2 trillion Coronavirus Aid, Relief, and Economic Security (CARES) Act, which not only doled out emergency cash to businesses, individuals, and states but also increased federal Medicaid matching funds to help states respond to the pandemic. But to receive this bump up in the federal Medicaid matching rate, states could not alter their Medicaid programs in any way. The extra money was intended for unusual pandemic-related expenses and could not be "spent on solving problems that [the states] created for themselves," as then Senate Majority Leader Mitch McConnell put it—a proviso that some governors found intrusive.[18]

In New York, site of the largest virus outbreak early in the pandemic, then governor Andrew Cuomo swiftly rejected the $6.7 billion in extra Medicaid dollars offered to his state because it would prevent him from executing a planned overhaul of New York's Medicaid system, an overhaul that included slashing $2.5 billion from the cash-strapped program.[19] For disabled New Yorkers, Cuomo's Medicaid cuts and his refusal to take the federal aid made no sense. The benefits program needed more money, not less, so people could find and retain safe, reliable caregivers. In addition, before anyone on Medicaid can receive long-term home care, there's a host of worker screenings and vaccinations to schedule and approve. Ordinarily, that's a sound safeguard, but at that point many supposedly nonessential medical offices were closed because of a combination of fiscal belt-tightening and pandemic-related safety considerations. Just when people needed help the most, they were stalemated.

"All our normal stresses are exacerbated and amplified tenfold under these conditions," said Bryan O'Malley, executive director of the Consumer Directed Personal Assistance Association of New York, an Albany-based independent group that facilitates in-home personal-care services throughout the state.[20] "Look, whatever disparities exist in health care—and there are many—are exponentially worse in the long-term care sphere. That's just how it is," said O'Malley.

A primary fear among many in the disability community was exacerbated at that point: the dread of being forced into an institution. In the early months of the pandemic, nursing homes and other institutions were death traps. A disproportionate number of those who contracted COVID, as well as those who died from it, were living or working in crowded long-term care facilities. In such places, social distancing is impossible. For a time, the facilities also couldn't secure an adequate supply of masks and other personal protective equipment due to a combination of excessive demand, lack of foresight from government agencies tasked with preparing for emergencies, and competition from hospitals. Nursing homes were "not the initial focus of the federal coronavirus response, which prioritized hospitals," said Elaine Ryan, vice president of government affairs for state advocacy at AARP.[21]

If the disability community was alarmed by potential medical rationing and Medicaid cuts, the most marginalized within the community were even more afraid because they were at the greatest risk. Poor people and people of Color—disabled or not—were becoming infected with and dying from COVID at a disproportionately high rate.[22] There were two primary explanations for this: First, these people tended to have less access to vital health-care information and resources. Second, a large number of them lived or worked in prisons and institutions such as nursing homes, where the disease spread rapidly. Anita Cameron, the Black autistic lesbian activist mentioned in chapter 5, wrote a blog post in 2020 cautioning that federal guidance from Severino and the US Office for Civil Rights—the gentle warning against health-care discrimination—lacked clarity. It "won't stop medical personnel steeped in their own biases from doing as they wish," she wrote. Cameron called the pandemic a "wake-up call for people to see what the results of racial bias, discrimination and disparities in health care look like," and went on to say, "Of the major organizations working on the issue of medical rationing and discrimination, few, if any, have Black staff or Black management, so we're not thought of. As yet, none have reached out to Black activists and organizations in a meaningful way."[23]

In Detroit, Dawn Gibson—an African American activist, blogger, organizer, and consultant who advocates for more research into how people of Color are impacted by diseases and health-care disparities—also raised her voice. Gibson has ankylosing spondylitis, a type of severe arthritis, and other chronic conditions that limit her diet; she's also the founder and host of Spoonie Chat, a weekly Twitter discussion for anybody living with an invisible illness or disability (the title is a riff on the notion of *spoons* as a stand-in for energy). Gibson told a reporter, "There is a systemic resistance to the pain of Black people."[24]

Additional obstacles were outraging hard-of-hearing people, who are estimated to number some 11.5 million Americans.[25] According to the National Association of the Deaf's chief executive officer, Howard Rosenblum, government and medical updates and guidelines related to the pandemic rarely included sign language accompaniment, especially in the smaller TV markets (and closed-captioning technology to spell out spoken words was dangerously inadequate). The worst offender: then president Trump. "Months into the coronavirus pandemic, the White House still does not have American Sign Language interpreters at its televised public health press briefings," CNN reported in late April. "Many in the Deaf community say they are growing wary [sic] of not having important information disseminated to them through qualified sign language interpreters."[26]

Making matters worse, the face masks that were recommended to slow the spread of the disease impeded lipreading and sign language interpretation. "They hinder speechreading and present barriers for D/deaf and hard-of-hearing individuals who use American Sign Language (ASL) or Cued American English via Cued Speech (CS)," wrote Sarah Katz in *Business Insider*. Both ASL and CS are visual communication methods that rely on not just finger actions and hand gestures but facial expressions and mouth movements. She said accessible masks with transparent panels do exist but are almost never used, even in hospitals. That's not surprising, perhaps, because hospitals are frequently inaccessible to D/deaf people, she said. "Many medical professionals are treating patients from behind a barrier and not allowing in-person interpreters," wrote Katz.[27]

Rebecca Cokley, the activist mentioned in chapter 1, told *Time* magazine, "You're really increasing the risks to disabled people's health when they don't have access to these basic services. This is really life or death for our community."[28]

Nevertheless, for many disabled people, a strong, stubborn vein of tenacity and even good humor ran through the wrenching sense of menace. Increased use of telecommuting was seen as a boon for those who find leaving home—let alone going to an office—to be onerous. If this trend continues, some said, it could help reduce the high disability unemployment rate. The expanded availability of education and entertainment online also made life more accessible for many disabled people; schools put their coursework online, museums opened their exhibits to virtual views, and studios released more first-run movies to pay-per-view and streaming services.

"The COVID-19 pandemic has allowed the online disability community to demonstrate its seemingly boundless collective capacity to care, listen, and inform," wrote Amy Gaeta, a disability activist and PhD candidate in the Literary Studies and Visual Cultures programs at the University of Wisconsin, Madison, on the blog of the *Disability Visibility Project*.[29] "Unsurprisingly, disabled people, as well as many adjacent communities (people of color, trans, and queer folks), have been at the frontlines of coordinating COVID-19 mutual aid groups all over the world. Amid this pandemic . . . I see how much nondisabled people need the disabled community. We are experts when it comes to isolation and pandemics. . . . We know how to live vulnerably, which is to live together. We know all this because for many of us, it's our daily reality."

In a way, fear of and reaction to COVID policies unified the disability community with a new and urgent sense of purpose. It created mutual aid groups, or "pods," where disabled people would provide essential services to their peers. "Many disabled, elderly, fat, immunocompromised, and vulnerable people went to heroic measures to defend our communities and ourselves," says Leah Lakshmi Piepzna-Samarasinha, in an essay for the *Disability Visibility Project*.[30] They cite the Disability Justice Culture Club, which used the Internet to create infographics about COVID safety strategies; the Nobody Is Disposable Coalition, which put out patient advocacy guides; Fat Rose, which created and shared crowd-sourced information to help guide people who were terrified about medical rationing; and the Crip Fund, an ad hoc group of disabled friends, mostly queer and people of Color, who raised money to give to other disabled Black, Indigenous, and people of Color who were in dire need. Not to mention "organizing that was more private—all the everyday, word of mouth, not so public efforts to spread information, tools, scripts, and safety strategies, spread crip to crip, in texts, phone calls, voice memos and online messages," they add.[31]

"Mutual aid can appear in many forms, whether through the distribution of funds for communities, donating to help fulfill the needs of an individual in a marginalized community, or organizing and sharing resources for members of said communities," says Teighlor McGee, the disabled activist of Color who started the Black Disability Collective.[32] For example, they say, a mutual aid program sprung up in Minneapolis in March 2020, offering $200 stipends to women, transgender, and non-binary folks in need, prioritizing Black and Indigenous applicants. Another, the Trans Disabled Care Fund in the Minneapolis–St. Paul area, used Patreon—a membership platform for content creators—to collect funds for deserving disabled trans people, giving out $100 payments over the course of six months or one lump sum of $600. "Accessibility and dignity are key components of mutual aid when disabled folks have the opportunity to be both the organizers and recipients," says Mc-Gee. Much of the aid happens virtually, because "digital organizing and virtual events work to eliminate many of the accessibility barriers that disabled community members face in traditional movement spaces." McGee, whose work focuses on racial justice and creating a "culture of access," adds that mutual aid work, most of which is on a volunteer basis, enables the disability community to "navigate through conflict and return our focus back toward fighting to dismantle oppressive systems."[33]

Even before COVID, health-care discrimination was a constant threat. A global health group called the Missing Billion reported in July 2019 that disabled people were three times more likely than their nondisabled counterparts to be denied health care and four times more likely to be "treated badly" by their local health-care systems, though the researchers didn't specify in what way they were treated badly. Led by Hannah Kuper of the London School of Hygiene and Tropical Medicine and Phyllis Heydt, an official at the World Health Organization, the group highlighted the stigma disabled people often face from health-care workers. Disabled people "have worse health access and poorer health outcomes," the report says. The organization, which puts out an occasional newsletter about how to fix these problems, seeks to be a catalyst for "inclusive health," its website explains. Change, the site argues, must come from a multipronged approach of political, social, economic, and educational efforts.[34]

One alleged culprit is the for-profit insurance industry. A case in point: In February 2019, the disability rights activist Carrie Ann Lucas—a champion of disabled parenting, among other things, who had a form of muscular dystrophy and diabetes—died in Loveland, Colorado, at forty-seven, because of complications from an illness that her insurer refused to cover adequately. As a Facebook tribute put it, "a shero of our community was murdered in the name of cost containment."

Disabled people often have expensive health-care needs. Only a broad-based strategy has any hope of working, considering how health-care disparities come in many forms. "People with severe intellectual, developmental disabilities get denied organ transplants, purely on the basis of their having a disability," says Teresa Nguyen, a public health expert in Denver who was born with the genetic brittle bone condition osteogenesis imperfecta not long after her parents emigrated from Vietnam.[35] She cites a September 2019 report from the National Council on Disability, which warned about people with autism, intellectual disabilities, mental illnesses, or HIV being refused organ transplants, despite scientific evidence that their prognoses were no worse than anyone else's. The NCD study said, "These denials are frequently based on discriminatory assumptions that the lives of people with disabilities are of poorer quality than those of people without disabilities, and on misperceptions about the ability of people with disabilities to comply with postoperative care . . . despite the existence of studies debunking those misconceptions." The NCD further highlighted problems such as doctors and insurance companies that use incorrect, misinformed assumptions about quality of life to score disabled patients' feasibility for a range of other necessary medical treatments.[36]

"It's as if the value of somebody's life with a disability is considered less," stresses Nguyen, who has repeatedly called for doctors, insurers, and hospitals to create guidelines for *not* basing medical decisions on a patient's disability. Before returning to the Mile High City, where she was born and earned a bachelor's and master's in public health, Nguyen was a policy analyst at the Department of Health and Human Services in Washington, DC, working to improve community integration of people with developmental disabilities. While there, she led an initiative with the Federal Emergency Management Agency to compile protocols related to medical ethics issues for people with disabilities. She'd like to see the project completed by her successors. Meanwhile, she's now employed by Colorado's Employment First Advisory Partnership, addressing disabled Coloradans' work requirements by providing a range of practical supports, including aligning state health policies, such as those under Medicaid, with employment goals set by the Department of Labor.[37]

Growing up as the daughter of immigrant parents, Nguyen experienced firsthand how difficult it can be to navigate the system. "For us, it involved a lot of interpreters," she recalls, meaning literal translators and, figuratively, those who attempt to interpret educational and health policies for immigrants who aren't accustomed to them. Her Vietnamese parents weren't at all aware of what she and they were entitled to—and their interpreters and case managers weren't always up to the task either. They might have helped with securing material objects such as wheelchairs and advancing Nguyen's educational pursuits, but beyond that their knowledge of disability rights was frustratingly limited. "We as a society are only starting to catch on to the multicultural aspects of disability," she says. "Whenever legislation is passed, I always think, *How do we ensure it gets interpreted for those who need to connect with it?* That should be a priority going forward."

She says it's high time for medical-delivery systems to catch up with the advances in medicine and technology that have enabled disabled people to live longer and more active lives. "We need sustainable policies that block disability discrimination in all aspects of health care," she says.[38]

Perhaps the most astonishing aspect of that discrimination is the plethora of inaccessible doctors' offices.[39] The ADA requires medical facilities to accommodate all manner of impairments, but many facilities are not quite so obliging. For instance, very few physicians' offices have exam tables that move up and down or have grab bars or, alternatively, have sufficient staff to help with transfers from a wheelchair or to interpret sign language. "Health-care services remain deeply inaccessible," says Silvia Yee, an attorney with the Disability Rights Education and Defense Fund, speaking at a disability law symposium in April 2012.[40] The situation has scarcely improved since then, if at all. She cites clinic restrooms that don't have grab bars or reachable faucets, health plans and facilities that don't provide essential information in braille or other alternate formats such as written descriptions of visual imagery, and providers who refuse to assist patients with speech impairments or developmental disabilities in making appointments or understanding directions. As a consequence, necessary tests and scans may get delayed, get short shrift, or be skipped altogether, unless patients really insist on them.

June Isaacson Kailes, associate director of the Center for Disability and Health Policy at Western University of Health Sciences in Pomona, California, has compiled a checklist for medical offices to help them comply with the ADA. Even the most competent doctors, she says, "are missing half the body if they only look at patients who are sitting in a chair."[41]

Yet lawsuits against medical offices have been few and far between. In a 2010 interview with the website Disaboom, Kailes ponders why medical offices have been able to skirt ADA regulations when restaurants, movie theaters, and stores have been taken to court for similar infractions. "People talk about suing inaccessible movie theaters or stores, but they never think about their doctors' offices," she observes.[42]

Advocates say quiet acceptance of ADA infractions in medical facilities might be the worst problem of all. Disabled people could be depriving themselves of complete medical care out of sheer exhaustion from fighting the system. Kailes says hopeless complacency is so common she calls it the "Four F experience: frustration, fatigue, fear, and failure. For some people, the effort of seeking health care is just too exhausting and/or degrading," she says.

This disregard for implementing ADA regulations, she adds, diminishes opportunities for disabled people to have longer, healthier, more productive lives.

～

The solution to health-care disparities and discrimination is almost too big and multilayered to contemplate. It has to do with systemic, structural biases, of course, but whether the shortsightedness and narrow-mindedness should be addressed from the top down (starting with state health departments, hospital groups, and insurance carriers) or from the bottom up (looking first to doctors to alter their attitudes and habits) is hard to say. Probably a combination approach is needed. One might almost expect the medical establishment to be steeped in stodgy and arrogant bureaucracies. One might expect Big Pharma and the insurance companies that control the purse strings to be so laser-focused on their bottom lines that they're prone to forget about the lives they are affecting. But doctors and nurses themselves? They may not be the root of the problem, but they're certainly a big part of it. They are the ones who directly connect with patients and are responsible for how their patients are treated. Ultimately, whatever plan of attack for fixing health-care discrimination one contemplates, fairness and safety come down to the behavior of individual practitioners. The system can't change its conduct toward disabled people if the frontline workers who implement the system, who ply the trade, don't recognize their own shortcomings and work to repair them.

Dr. Lisa Iezzoni, a Harvard Medical School professor and health policy researcher at Massachusetts General Hospital's Mongan Institute, has been investigating health-policy issues related to disabled people since 1996. She's a wheelchair user who was diagnosed with multiple sclerosis in 1980 while a medical student. "The vast majority of doctors view quality of life for people with disabilities as less than that for people without disabilities," she says. Most disabled people, however, "don't view their lives as tragic. They've figured out how to get around in a world that wasn't designed for them and view their lives as good quality."[43]

In February 2021, she released the results of a twenty-year survey of 714 practicing physicians in multiple specialties and locations across the US; the survey results confirmed and quantified her assertions. More than 82 percent of the doctors said people with significant disabilities have a lower quality of life than their nondisabled peers, an attitude that not only contradicts what disabled people themselves report but likely contributes to the health-care disparities disabled people experience. Only 56.5 percent of the physicians in the study said they "welcome" disabled patients in their practices, and a mere 40.7 percent felt "very confident" about their ability to provide them with the same quality of care as other patients.[44]

"That physicians have negative attitudes about patients with disability wasn't surprising," says Iezzoni. "But the magnitude of physicians' stigmatizing views was very disturbing. [It] shows the erroneous assumptions and a lack of understanding of the lives of people with disability."

That bias, she says, can affect treatment decisions. Iezzoni notes that most medical education doesn't include disability topics. She recommends improvements in medical school curricula and ongoing in-services for practicing physicians to train doctors about disabled people's lives and attitudes.

Adding to the problem, she observes, is that most clinical trials exclude disabled people because they're not considered typical or average enough. So drug interactions with certain neurological conditions such as muscular dystrophy or autoimmune diagnoses such as lupus haven't been tested. Among other consequences of this omission: many physicians' first professional contact with disabled people occurs when they come in seeking help. "That is inevitably going to affect how doctors approach a person with disability," she says.

That can be not only awkward but dangerous. The study cites examples of surgeons who assume that wheelchair-using women with early-stage breast cancer want a mastectomy instead of breast-conserving surgery—whereas these doctors assume the opposite of nondisabled women—because they believe disabled women don't care as much about their appearance. "Potentially biased views among physicians could contribute to persistent health care disparities affecting people with disability," Iezzoni's paper concludes.

Her survey may have been the most authoritative of its kind, but it wasn't the first to shed light on this problem. In 2012, the National Disability Rights Network and Disability Rights Washington documented multiple cases of physicians' withholding care from disabled patients without their consent. The doctors felt the treatments—everything from hydration and nutrition to transplants—weren't appropriate given the patients' prospects in life.[45] In 2020, the Council on Quality and Leadership—a Towson, Maryland–based organization dedicated to quality-of-life issues for people with disabilities and chronic illnesses—studied the attitudes of more than twenty-five thousand health-care providers, including physical and occupational therapists, physicians and dentists, clinical technicians, and nurses and home-health assistants. The research revealed that although most of these professionals say they're not prejudiced against disabled people, they nevertheless have implicit anti-disability biases that "can contribute to inequitable healthcare access and health outcomes for people with disabilities."[46]

In addition to better training of doctors, quadriplegic attorney Andrés J. Gallegos at the National Council on Disability advocates for a series of legislative changes. "If physicians' hearts cannot be changed, then let them be tamed by aggressive countermeasures in education, policy changes, and civil rights enforcement," he says.[47] For instance, he calls for overturning state laws that allow doctors to arbitrarily remove life-sustaining interventions from patients before transferring them to a different hospital or facility—a common procedure in some places and sometimes performed regardless of the patient's previously stated wishes. Such practices stem from disdain for disabled lives, he says. "State legislators should enact or amend legislation to require facilities to use an independent due process mechanism for mediating and deciding medical futility disputes," Gallegos contends.

Many disabled people report feeling pressured to sign do not resuscitate orders, especially when entering the hospital. These documents essentially tell medical professionals not to take every reasonable measure to preserve their lives in a crisis. Disabled folks doubt other patients' lives are treated so cavalierly.[48]

It's not an exaggeration to say that the consequences of health-care prejudice can be deadly. In June 2020, a forty-six-year-old quadriplegic man named Michael Hickson was hospitalized in Austin, Texas, for a urinary tract infection, sepsis, pneumonia, and COVID symptoms. Though the hospital was not then overrun with COVID cases, his doctors withdrew all life-sustaining treatment, including artificial nutrition and hydration. When the patient's wife, Melissa Hickson, objected, a doctor told her matter-of-factly that the decision was based on an assessment of Michael's poor quality of life as a paralyzed man. She recorded the conversation (you can hear it on YouTube).[49] Six days later, Michael died.

Afterward, Melissa told the media that their being Black might have contributed to the denial of care, but "the main reason was because of his disabilities."[50]

CHAPTER 12

NOT DEAD YET VS. THE RIGHT TO DIE

(Content note: This chapter contains information about suicide.)

In the summer of 2013, the world was introduced to Brittany Maynard. A twenty-nine-year-old California newlywed, she had moved to Oregon to end her life. Oregon had legalized assisted suicide, and Maynard had a malignant brain tumor. Her story made her a *People* magazine cover girl.[1] "A TERMINAL CANCER PATIENT'S CONTROVERSIAL CHOICE," the cover said. Maynard's story was politicized and sensationalized. She became a kind of poster child for Compassion and Choices, the right-to-die organization, formerly known as the Hemlock Society and the Final Exit Network, which was founded by British-born Derek Humphry, who'd published in 1991 a suicide handbook with recipes for poison, called *Final Exit: The Practicalities of Self-Deliverance and Assisted Suicide for the Dying.*

In November 2014, Maynard's wish was fulfilled; she died by self-directed causes in Portland, Oregon. Nearly a year later, in October 2015, her name resurfaced as her home state of California pushed through its own Oregon-like assisted-suicide law.[2] California became the fifth state to authorize medical aid in dying. Besides Oregon, which established the nation's first right-to-die law back in 1997, Washington State passed similar legislation in 2008; Montana legalized it by court decree, not legislative action, in 2009; and Vermont's version came in 2013. But after California, more places followed like dominoes in a row: Colorado in 2016, DC in 2017, Hawaii in 2018, New Jersey and Maine in 2019, and New Mexico in 2021.

Why this relatively sudden wave of support for assisted suicide is hard to say. Certainly public opinion had shifted. Back in 1947 and 1950, less than 40 percent of respondents to a Gallup poll favored "legally and painlessly" ending a terminally ill person's life. By 1973, support had grown to 53 percent. Since 2013, the figure has never dipped below 69 percent. At last count, in 2018, Gallup found that 72 percent of Americans felt doctors should be able to help terminally ill people die, though only 54 percent thought it was "morally acceptable"—a difference that can be explained by Americans' "general tendency . . . to be hesitant to ban behaviors even if they think they are morally wrong," writes Gallup's Megan Brenan.[3]

A diverse coalition of disability leaders and organizations has struggled to stanch this trend. Their dogged opposition began decades before Maynard's passing, in reaction to a series of earlier judicial decisions that seemed to favor the right to die. In April 1996, a disabled attorney named Diane Coleman launched Not Dead Yet, a grassroots activist group dedicated to opposing the legalization of doctor-assisted suicide. The practice, she argued (and still argues today), is discriminatory against disabled people. If a doctor or anyone else helps someone die, it's illegal; why should it be legal if the person has a disability or medical condition? Assisted-suicide measures, which seem to be about personal liberty, effectively deprive ill and disabled people of their right to equal protection, she argues. The ADA established that people with disabilities and medical conditions are a protected class of citizens; if the ADA enshrines our rights in life, she says, shouldn't it do the same in protecting us from death?[4]

Coleman, a longtime member of ADAPT, admitted in April 2020 that the cheeky name for the group she started wasn't her idea. "I was at a national disability rights conference in Dallas," she explains in an online post. "ADAPT organizer Bob Kafka called out to me and said, 'I've got a name for your group,' a group that increasingly seemed to be needed to combat the growing public sentiment that disabled people are better off dead (and society is better off without us)."[5] Kafka and Coleman are fans of the movie *Monty Python and the Holy Grail*, in which the line "I'm not dead yet" is a running gag.

Two days after naming her group, Coleman gave testimony at a Congressional subcommittee hearing on a proposed bill, the Assisted

Suicide Funding Restriction Act of 1996, to prohibit using federal funds for euthanasia, mercy killing, or related types of suicide. Emboldened by endorsements from more than forty disability leaders, Coleman told the legislators there is a widespread misperception that disabled people's lives are tragic and hopeless. The public is given little realistic information about how they cope or how those who become ill or disabled *could* cope. No wonder people who acquire disabilities often see death as the only viable solution, she said.[6]

The proposed act never passed, but Not Dead Yet is still active today. It's grown to an international crusade with chapters and allies around the globe. Its objection to permitting medically enabled suicide has nothing to do with morality or religion; it is purely a disability rights cause. Not all disability activists agree on this issue. Some say assisted suicide is about freedom of choice at the end of life and has nothing to do with disabilities. Yet Coleman and her crew's resolve has only intensified, even as state after state passed versions of right-to-die legislation.

The impetus to legalize assisted suicide seems founded on a deep-seated fear of decrepitude—an understandable yet often misinformed dread. Most people don't seek a poison prescription as a solution to unbearable pain, research shows.[7] Rather, it's the anxiety about what's to come, the panic over losing autonomy and burdening loved ones, which cause them to consider ending their lives. "In surveys and conversations with counselors, many patients say that what they want most is a choice about how their lives will end, a finger on the remote control, as it were," the *New York Times* reported in 2004.[8]

Some two months after Maynard's death, in January 2015, her widower, Dan Diaz, told the media, "Her decision to pursue that simply as a last resort kind of came early on."[9] To reiterate: It was, for her, *a last resort*—chosen in the initial stages of her illness, sparked by fear of what she thought was to come.

Decisions made in a panic—when newly diagnosed, perhaps, certainly before you learn to adjust to a new disability or chronic condition—shouldn't necessarily be adhered to. They are made with incomplete or inaccurate information about the possibilities for a good post-diagnosis life, contend Not Dead Yet members. Maynard may have been in her right mind, and her decision rational and fully cognizant, but the potential for coercion when people are worried and vulnerable is too great.

The coercion may be subtle, or it may be downright abusive. "At less than $300, assisted suicide is, to put it bluntly, the cheapest treatment for a terminal illness," said the late Marilyn Golden, then senior policy analyst at the Disability Rights Education and Defense Fund. "This means that in places where assisted suicide is legal, coercion is not even necessary. If life-sustaining expensive treatment is denied or even merely delayed, patients will be steered toward assisted suicide."[10]

Even if the intent is not venal, missteps can occur. Nearly half of the assisted suicides in Oregon to date "did not have a health provider present at the time of death," writes Coleman in an open letter to then California governor Jerry Brown in September 2015, urging him to veto that state's assisted-suicide bill (he didn't). "With no independent witness required, there is no evidence that they self-administered the lethal drugs, or even that they consented at the time of death. . . . These laws grant blanket immunity and effectively foreclose investigation of wrongdoing."[11]

The laws may not name nonterminal disabled people as such, but they have real-world implications for marginalized populations such as the disabled, the poor, the uninsured, even the profoundly misunderstood. These folks may easily feel pressure—psychological or financial—to get out of the way, to unburden others. Governmental approval of physician-aided death signals that any suicidal ideations disabled or chronically ill people feel may be rational and reasonable. *If the government says it's okay, then it must be.* That can be a blow to any tenuous attempt at maintaining self-esteem and pride, if not outright encouragement to penny-pinching managed-care providers or stressed-out caregivers to expedite the end of their obligations to those who draw a disproportionate share of vital resources. "For every case such as this," says Golden, referring to Brittany Maynard, "there are hundreds—or thousands—more people who could be significantly harmed."

Harmed, perhaps, or even killed.

～

Legally speaking, these cases started with the right to refuse treatment, and who exactly has that right—questions that precede the ADA.

In 1975, Karen Ann Quinlan, a twenty-one-year-old New Jersey woman, passed out after a night of partying—she'd had too much to drink, presumably—and fell into what's termed a "persistent vegetative state," meaning she was kept alive but was largely unresponsive. Doctors said she had no chance of recovering. In 1976, her father won approval from the state Supreme Court to remove her ventilator. She was still unresponsive but continued to breathe on her own for nine years, ultimately succumbing to pneumonia in 1985.

In 1983, a twenty-six-year-old social worker with cerebral palsy named Elizabeth Bouvia lobbied to end her own lifesaving treatment. She was not vegetative. In fact, she had recently had a miscarriage and her marriage had broken up. Financial troubles had also impelled her to withdraw from graduate school, and she was grieving the recent loss of her brother. But a California judge overlooked all these factors, which might have been treatable with psychotherapy or antidepressants, and granted her request to die. To everyone's surprise, however, she never followed through. As of this writing, she's still alive, in her early sixties.

In the same year, a twenty-five-year-old Missouri woman named Nancy Cruzan had a bad car accident that left her in a vegetative state similar to Quinlan's. After five years, her parents asked to have her feeding tube removed. The hospital refused. In the end, the Cruzan case became the first right-to-die decision brought before the US Supreme Court. The high court ruled that a competent person had the right to refuse treatment; the only question was, was Cruzan competent? The parents subsequently convinced a lower court that this would have been their daughter's wish, and the feeding tube was removed in December 1990. It took more than a week for Nancy Cruzan to die.

The right to refuse treatment was again cited in the 1989 case of David Rivlin, a fully aware, awake, and responsive quadriplegic man of thirty-eight who petitioned a judge to have someone switch off his ventilator. Rivlin's fiancée had left him, his parents had died, and poverty forced him to live in a nursing home. But this time, refusing treatment was too scary and would have made for a painful death. So with the judge's okay, Rivlin found a physician to inject him with Valium and morphine as well as disconnect the respirator. He was gone in a half hour[12] and became the first known recipient of physician-assisted suicide—that is, someone who had sought medically induced death, as opposed to simply refusing lifesaving treatment.

Also in 1989, a thirty-four-year-old quadriplegic named Larry McAfee appealed to the Georgia State Supreme Court for the right to turn off his ventilator and receive painkillers to ease his hasty demise; he also wanted legal immunity for anyone who helped him achieve this goal. He won his case, but once he had control over his own life-and-death decision, he no longer wanted to die. Like Elizabeth Bouvia before him, it was that sense of control he wanted most. McAfee was quoted in the news complaining, "I'm fed up. I have no control over what's done to me, how it's done or by whom."[13] He died of pneumonia in 1995.[14]

These cases—Cruzan's and Quinlan's in particular—may have inspired Terri Schiavo's husband to petition for removal of her life support in 2005. She was a young woman in St. Petersburg, Florida, who fifteen years earlier had abruptly collapsed one day in her home at age twenty-six. It remains unclear why. Whatever the cause, her breathing was impacted, and her brain was deprived of oxygen for too long. She spent the next decade and a half in a hospital bed, nourished through a feeding tube and nonverbal. She could've gone on that way for many more years, but her husband, who in the interim had found a new fiancée, went to court to have her feeding tube removed, saying she would never have wanted to live this way. Her parents, however, insisted she was responsive to stimuli. They could tell by her eyes and a furtive smile that occasionally snaked across her lips.

Not Dead Yet and other disability rights groups filed a friend-of-the-court (also called an *amicus curiae*) brief in support of Mary and Robert Schindler, Terri Schiavo's parents. They argued that "persistent vegetative state" was hard to define and often inaccurate. They obtained testimony from disabled people who had recovered from such a state. They fought for more careful scrutiny of situations in which people push to remove life support from those who can't give consent. Relying on technology to survive does not mean your life has no value, they insisted— something many disabled people know from personal experience.

Their cause went all the way to Capitol Hill, an effort that received front-page attention. Diane Coleman told a reporter, "We very much wish that Congress would intervene on a broader level and create meaningful protections for people who are in guardianship."[15] The case was lost. Terri Schiavo's plug was pulled in March 2005, and she died shortly thereafter, at the age of thirty-nine.

More than a decade later, in 2016, a fourteen-year-old girl in Appleton, Wisconsin, named Jerika Bolen, who was born with spinal muscular atrophy, lobbied to turn off the ventilator that was keeping her alive. News reports said Bolen was motivated by the comforting promise of an afterlife in which she'd be able to move freely and escape her persistent physical pain. Not Dead Yet tried to intervene, to offer alternatives, but the Bolen family was not rich and had few resources or remedies. Bolen had one other last request: She wanted to attend her class prom. She wasn't a senior yet, so a special prom was put on in her honor. Shortly after, Bolen's ventilator was turned off. She died quickly, in September 2016, before her fifteenth birthday.[16]

Three months later, the US Food and Drug Administration approved the world's first treatment for spinal muscular atrophy—Spinraza—which might have helped her.[17]

~

Assisted suicide and its consequences gained a certain national urgency in 1990, when suicide guru Jack Kevorkian entered the scene. To this onetime physician, the right to refuse treatment wasn't enough; he believed in the right to *acquire* death when desired, to purchase it as you would any commodity such as toilet paper or potatoes. At the time of his death, in June 2011, at age eighty-three, from kidney and respiratory failure, the man known as "Doctor Death" claimed to have helped more than 130 people end their lives. Often it was with the aid of the suicide machine he'd built, which—ever the showman—he called either the "Mercitron" or the "Thanatron." Even those who may have found his obsession with death somewhat creepy hailed him as a hero of self-determination. Yet many others accused him of not only playing God but actively targeting people with disabilities or chronic illnesses. All of his victims/clients were disabled or ill, and even a conservative estimate by the Gerontological Society of America says that only a quarter of them were actually terminally ill.[18] He wasn't helping them; he was out to get them—or, at best, he was nurturing and exploiting their depression. In that, he was the opposite of disability pride incarnate.

It would be a mistake to say the disability community was entirely united against Kevorkian. Some bought his "free will" and "self-determination" arguments; some of them said the possibility of being able to end their lives if they couldn't bear them any longer was the only thing that kept them sane. They didn't want to lose that escape route.

But the story behind the escape route that Kevorkian offered was distorted. For one thing, he was no longer a licensed, practicing physician. He *had* been licensed, in Michigan, but in 1976 he moved to California to take up painting and writing. He reportedly lived a simple life there, wore clothes purchased at thrift stores and occasionally took part-time jobs at local hospitals. In 1984, he quietly began a campaign of offering painless suicide to death-row inmates. In 1988, back in Michigan, he took the idea a step further: He advertised in Detroit newspapers a new service he dubbed "bioethics and obiatry," which included "death counseling." Two years later he got his first customer, as far as we know—Janet Adkins, a teacher from Oregon who had Alzheimer's. She was just fifty-four, had a husband and two sons, and died in Kevorkian's Volkswagen van. She reportedly flipped the switch herself, which released sodium pentothal into her veins via an intravenous tube. It effectively put her to sleep. One minute later, once she was fully unconscious, it released into her bloodstream a solution of potassium chloride that stopped her heart.

Kevorkian was charged with murder. The story made the front page of the *New York Times* in June of 1990. Adkins's death, the paper said, "alarmed many experts in medical ethics and confused many legal experts. The case raises the specific legal question of what constitutes assisted suicide and the more general philosophical question of what role, if any, doctors should play in helping their seriously ill patients die."[19] *Vanity Fair* put it this way: "Is he Socrates or Mengele?"[20] But before the end of the year, criminal charges were dropped because, at that point, Michigan had no laws related to assisted suicide. Instead, civil charges were filed; the county prosecutor pursued and won a permanent injunction barring Kevorkian from ever again using his suicide machine in the state of Michigan. The judge also suspended his license to practice medicine in the state.

Kevorkian was undeterred. More patients/victims followed at a rapid clip. It took four more years, and many more deaths, before the American Medical Association effectively disbarred Kevorkian, calling him "reckless" and "a great threat to the public." In 1999, he boasted on TV's *60 Minutes* about the lethal injection he'd given a fifty-two-year-old Detroit man named Thomas Youk, who had amyotrophic lateral sclerosis (ALS), or Lou Gehrig's disease, and even showed a video of the incident. Kevorkian was found guilty of second-degree murder and sentenced to ten to twenty-five years in a maximum-security prison. The judge, Jessica R. Cooper, told him from the bench, "Consider yourself stopped." In 2007, after eight years behind bars, Kevorkian was released on parole, promising never again to counsel or assist anyone in how to die.

Kevorkian may have been stopped, but his actions had repercussions. In 1994, the state of Oregon—home of his first customer, Janet Adkins— passed the nation's first "death with dignity" law. It was challenged in the courts but ultimately reaffirmed in 1997. Then, in 2001, US attorney general John Ashcroft tried to block it, calling assisted suicide "not a legitimate medical purpose." The case went all the way to the US Supreme Court, which, in a 2006 decision known as *Gonzales v. Oregon* ("Gonzales" was Alberto Gonzales, the attorney general who succeeded Ashcroft and continued to pursue the case), ruled that the attorney general had overstepped his authority, thus upholding the Oregon law.[21] This, in turn, opened the door for more states to follow. Which they did.

Some might say these events have had several positive results. There is more awareness of the need for palliative and hospice care—that is, we've gotten better at providing for peaceful, painless transitions to a natural death. And every state that's passed an assisted-suicide bill has put safeguards in place to try to prevent abuse: The laws apply only to those with six months or less to live; more than one physician must agree to the diagnosis in order to prescribe lethal meds, usually barbiturates; the doctors must take into account the possibility of depression; and the deadly dose cannot be forced on a person unwittingly, as in so-called angel of mercy euthanasia killings—it has to be self-administered, though in some cases patients can designate someone else to feed them the poison.

However, though Not Dead Yet and others applaud improvements in palliative and hospice care, they contend that no safeguards are adequate against persistent anti-disability prejudice and the emotional, economic, and practical obstacles to maintaining a good quality of life for anyone with a chronic illness or disability. Those who have not lived with a disability may not fully understand the unnecessary pressures put on those of us who don't fit a certain standard. Yes, some chronically ill and disabled people wish to die, but if asked why, they typically say their life has no meaning or joy. Rather than addressing *those* causes, state after state has rushed to provide poisoning. "When a terminally ill person expresses the wish to die, nearly two-thirds of Americans, including doctors, believe that this wish should be granted and that doctors should be allowed to assist in such a death without risking prosecution," wrote health-care author and columnist Jane E. Brody in June 1997.

> But some researchers and medical personnel who specialize in the care of dying patients say that before accepting at face value the requests of patients for help in dying, the reasons behind their suicidal thoughts warrant a closer look. Recent studies have revealed that most terminally ill patients who contemplate suicide are seriously depressed. . . . The end of life is always sad, but when pain and other problems are controlled, it does not have to be a period of grim despair. That [despair] is usually depression, and even as death nears it can be recognized and treated. When it is, thoughts of suicide can evaporate.[22]

Brody wrote this in anticipation of two Supreme Court decisions related to challenges of state laws that specifically banned physician-assisted suicide. Eight days after her piece was published, the high court found that New York and Washington State *could* prohibit physician-assisted suicide, and no one—including terminally ill people—has a constitutionally protected right to that suicidal assistance. The upshot was that individual states could either bar or allow the practice; it was up to the state authorities.

It may sound reasonable to stipulate "less than six months to live," as the laws do, but Not Dead Yet and others insist that it's impossible to gauge life expectancy with any accuracy. Every year, Oregon's Public Health Division reports on the state's Death with Dignity Act, and in the most recent accounting it estimates that 370 people received prescriptions for a lethal cocktail in 2020 alone, meaning they were medically determined to have six months or less to live. As of January 2021, 60 percent of those people took the poison and died; another 18 percent did not take the dose but died anyway. That seems to show that 22 percent of the Oregonians who were determined to have six months or less to live survived longer than expected, or more than half of those who did not take the poison managed to outlive their prognoses.[23] Granted, there may have been reporting errors; the state's own tally acknowledges "status was unknown for 80 patients." But according to Michael Barnett of the Harvard T.H. Chan School of Public Health, as many as twelve million Americans are misdiagnosed every year—and that's "a very conservative estimate," he said in 2018.[24] Earlier, a 2011 study led by Dr. Debbie Selby, a palliative-care physician at Sunnybrook Health Sciences Centre in Toronto, Canada, found that doctors' predictions for life expectancy are wrong more often than not.[25] Researchers laid odds on the time remaining for 1,622 hospice patients. Only a third of their guesses proved right. Most were overly optimistic, but nevertheless incorrect. "We are not good at being very accurate," Dr. Selby told the *Globe and Mail*, adding that not much can be done to improve doctors' accuracy. "We can't tell the future," she said.[26]

Certainly many disabled people who are active today have already outlasted their prognoses. Even those with progressive disabilities can't forecast the pace of their increasing debility, let alone their lifespan. In addition, biomedical advances keep changing the metric. Assisted-suicide laws ignore these realities. In Oregon, for instance, there is no provision for those who refuse (or don't know about or can't afford) treatment that might extend their lives. Jonathan Modie, lead communications officer at the Oregon Health Division, told a reporter in 2018 that his state's Death with Dignity Act is "silent on whether the patient" must exhaust "all treatment options before the prognosis of less than six months to live is made."[27]

There may indeed be, as supporters maintain, scant evidence of abuse in places like Oregon. Yet no one can deny that other kinds of abuse—spousal, child, or elder—are notoriously underreported, and evidence of such abuse is difficult to come by. Scarier still is the fact that, because self-administered poisoning is considered a private act, none of the state-mandated safeguards require oversight of the actual ingestion of poison. No one has to witness how and when the lethal drug is received. The possibilities for manipulation or mishandling are ghastly.

Such guile or misuse is not all that unlikely. Several of those who obtained physician-assisted death in Oregon were first turned down by their doctors—doctors who knew them and were familiar with their situations. They had to search for a physician who was willing to go along with their suicidal leanings. For instance, in 1999, *The Oregonian* published the story of Kate Cheney, who was eighty-five when she died by assisted suicide under Oregon's law. She was in the early stages of dementia, and her physician had declined to provide the lethal prescription she requested. She found another physician, but the second physician ordered a psychiatric evaluation, which determined Cheney lacked the "capacity required to weigh options about assisted suicide." The request was again denied. Cheney's daughter, Erika—described in the press as "fiery"—reportedly became angry and insisted on another psych evaluation. "Her daughter's assertiveness . . . made the psychiatrist wonder whose agenda this really was," said *The Oregonian*.[28] A related article in the *Weekly Standard* put it this way: "It appeared that her daughter had more of a vested interest in Cheney's assisted suicide than did Cheney herself. The psychiatrist wrote in his report that while the assisted suicide seemed consistent with Cheney's values, 'she does not seem to be explicitly pushing for this.'"[29] In the end, permission was granted by a third opinion, that of a clinical psychologist (not a licensed psychiatrist or physician), who noted that Cheney's request "may be influenced by her family's wishes." Cheney had said she wanted the pills not because she was in irremediable pain but because she feared becoming unable to attend to her personal hygiene and becoming a burden to others. Shortly after, she took the lethal dose and died.

Ten years later, in 2009, a woman named Linda Fleming became Washington State's first person to die under its version of the suicide law. She was sixty-six, divorced with two children, and had stage IV pancreatic cancer. Her life expectancy wasn't good, but she'd also declared bankruptcy two years earlier because she couldn't pay off her credit card debt of just $5,800. A former social worker who had been unable to work because of an unspecified disability, she was living in subsidized housing on $643 in monthly disability checks, according to press coverage. Her life was rough even before the cancer diagnosis. So her doctors were reluctant to provide the poison she'd requested. Frustrated, she sought the aid of Compassion and Choices, the pro-suicide organization. Robb Miller, executive director of the local chapter, obligingly helped Fleming secure the lethal prescription. Afterward, he told a reporter he'd been unaware of her bankruptcy and other personal problems.[30] They didn't matter to him anyway; she wanted to die, and that was all he needed to know. Because of her diagnosis, he didn't look any deeper or further.

Compassion and Choices is not a cult. It's a collection of socially minded, progressive-thinking adults. But the organization's true, unvarnished mission is to enable suicide *for all*. To take one's own life is a God-given right, they maintain. The group's official strategic plan, revised and adopted in 2018, is to make society one that "empowers everyone to chart their end-of-life journey." It aims to gain easy access to medically assisted suicide for half the US population by 2028. "In addition to authorizing more states," the statement goes on, "we are also addressing the many regulatory roadblocks that limit access."[31] In other words, it seeks to remove the scant safeguards that exist.

The former Hemlock Society doesn't target disabled or chronically ill people per se; it merely sees this vulnerable population as a means to an end. Brittany Maynard, the young newlywed with cancer, was a means to an end. It's easier, more palatable, to pass suicide laws that single out disabled and chronically ill people. The group knows there is a double standard. It's betting on the slippery slope the rest of us dread.

What it hasn't figured on, though, is the enduring determination of disability activists.

CHAPTER 13

"EASY TO GET IN [BUT] IMPOSSIBLE TO GET OUT"

The Struggle for Deinstitutionalization and Medicaid Dollars

(Content note: This chapter contains descriptions of abuse.)

In June 2017, social media (and a smattering of conventional media, too) were filled with images of protests against proposed Medicaid cuts. In the biggest demonstration, some sixty activists—mostly people with disabilities—gathered at then Senate Majority Leader Mitch McConnell's DC office. Some of them lay on the floor like corpses, disrupting the space in a "die-in" to signify they would rather perish than be forced into institutions, as the proposed cuts would almost certainly do.[1]

Institutions were known to be terrible, unlivable places. As far back as 1887, the investigative journalist Elizabeth Cochran Seaman—better known by her nom de plume, Nellie Bly—posed as a poor and confused woman to do an exposé of Blackwell's Island Insane Asylum in New York, from the inside. Calling it "a human rat-trap . . . easy to get in [but] impossible to get out," she wrote of spoiled food, freezing temperatures, rodents, and a bath routine that was more about punishment than hygiene.[2] Bly's exposé led to a public outcry, but no major reforms took place. More than a century later, basic hygiene may be better, but abuse, neglect, and a lack of control over one's own life remain all too common at today's institutions. "Even before the pandemic," says Laura Mills, a researcher at Human Rights Watch, "the US government failed to ensure that nursing homes were adequately staffed and regulated."[3]

The 2017 demonstration was led by the grassroots activist group ADAPT, the same one that began decades earlier in Denver by protesting against inaccessible buses; by now it had morphed from American Disabled for Accessible Public Transit to American Disabled for Attendant Programs Today. Thus rebooted, its primary cause became deinstitutionalization.

After the Olmstead-Curtis decision of 1999, which was supposed to make it illegal to force disabled Medicaid recipients into nursing homes and other institutions, the fight to end that practice should have been over. The legislation that followed the decision plainly states that low-income disabled people have the right to receive state-funded supports and services in the community rather than be forced into institutions when (a) community supports are appropriate, (b) the person wishes to live in the community, and (c) community services can be deemed reasonable accommodations as defined by the ADA. Six years after the ruling, to help states meet those demands—to reassure them that they wouldn't lose federal funding by moving recipients out of institutions and into the community—Congress launched the Money Follows the Person (MFP) initiative as part of the Deficit Reduction Act of 2005. MFP, which didn't go into effect until 2008, giving Congress time to organize it, provided states with funding to reduce their reliance on institutional care and develop community-based long-term care options.

The MFP program was mostly successful. From its start through the end of 2019, officials claim it freed nearly 101,600 people with disabilities and chronic health conditions to live autonomously in their own homes or with family.[4] That's the good news. The bad news, however, is that too many people remain stuck in institutions due to Medicaid budget reductions, lack of affordable and accessible housing, and general malfeasance. The US Census Bureau's American Community Survey estimates that roughly 5.1 percent of the 61 million disabled American adults—or some 3.1 million—live in institutions at present.[5] That may be an undercount, considering the figure doesn't include those who live in group homes or other congregate settings. The same survey estimates that some 41 million disabled Americans are *not* living in institutions, which would seem to indicate that the remainder—roughly 20 million disabled Americans—aren't living in their own homes.[6] Some are doubtless living on the streets. Whatever the number of institutionalized disabled

Americans, most of them, though probably not all, would prefer to live elsewhere. Other studies show that the population of institutionalized folks with intellectual disabilities alone plunged 89 percent from its peak in 1967 through 2015, though that still leaves more than 21,000 of them, or 13.5 percent, in a "supervised residential setting" such as a nursing home or hospital, whether or not it's necessary.[7]

As of this writing, the MFP program has not been renewed.

Other attempts to resolve Medicaid's institutional bias have similarly fallen by the wayside. Back in 1997, during the Clinton administration, a bill called the Medicaid Community Attendant Services and Supports Act was introduced in the House of Representatives. Supporters hoped it would fix the problem and enable Medicaid recipients to receive noninstitutional long-term care. It took more than a decade—till 2009—to introduce it in the Senate, where it was renamed the Community Choice Act. By either name, it would require state Medicaid plans to cover home-based personal assistance, fulfilling the promise of Olmstead-Curtis. Critics called it federal overreach, butting into the states' business—and as of this writing, it has not passed.

Also in 2009, when President Obama first proposed the Affordable Care Act, which came to be known as Obamacare, it included provisions for funding ongoing personal-care assistance for everyone who needed it, not just those on Medicaid. That portion of the bill, Title VIII, was dubbed the Community Living Assistance Services and Supports (CLASS) Act. It would have provided funding for in-home or institutional care—the recipient's choice—for what was estimated to be twelve million Americans who require such ongoing support and aren't eligible for Medicaid. Because of its flexibility, CLASS would have made home-based care more feasible; even a family member could be "hired" as personal-care help. Benefits money could also be used for home modifications such as installing a ramp or roll-in shower. Though a voluntary program, it would have encouraged all taxpayers—regardless of age, health, or income—to pay into the system; that is, people had to make premium contributions to insure against their eventual need for long-term care. Anyone who put in money for at least five years could receive benefits.

CLASS received congressional approval, and Obama signed it into law in March 2010. But in the election of November 2010, Republicans took back control of the House of Representatives and gained seven seats in the Senate. Thus emboldened, Republicans in both houses began trying to repeal CLASS (and indeed, all of Obamacare) as too expensive. CLASS was the low-hanging fruit, the easiest provision to attack and cut off. The numbers didn't add up, opponents insisted; it wouldn't draw in enough contributions to be self-sustaining over the long haul. The opposition grew so great that it threatened to upend the entirety of Obamacare. By October 2011, Obama himself announced he would not attempt to implement it. In January 2013, he repealed CLASS (as part of the American Taxpayer Relief Act), sacrificing it so the rest of Obamacare could stand.[8]

Without CLASS, Medicaid remains the only government program that helps foot the bill for long-term care.

Many disabled people require daily—and sometimes round-the-clock—personal-care assistance. They may need help with getting in and out bed, bathing, dressing, being fed, getting to work, receiving treatments, or remembering to do daily tasks. That kind of support can be expensive.

For those who qualify for Medicaid—you have to be low-income, a senior citizen, and/or disabled—it provides a degree of financial assistance with ongoing custodial help. As of January 2021, more than seventy-six million Americans receive Medicaid. But Medicaid is only partially funded by the federal government; most of its funds and management are done at the state level. Every state program is different, and the federal government only has so much power over state-run programs.

If you don't receive enough Medicaid dollars to pay for all the in-home help you need—and sometimes Medicaid's estimates of how much help a person needs or qualifies for are woefully inadequate—and if you don't have family members to voluntarily provide extra help, or aren't independently wealthy, you may end up institutionalized. Medicaid seems to prefer institutionalization, or at least find it easier—born of outmoded ideas or, in some cases, self-dealing officials with ties to hospital administrators. Few recipients, if any, choose institutionalization if they can avoid it. Some folks who really can't manage their own lives might need the 24/7 support of a group home or assisted-living facility, but that's not the same as being forcibly committed to a large institution. Even the safest, most hygienic institutions deprive people of certain liberties. You wake up, go to bed, and eat meals not when you want to but when the staff finds it most convenient. You have so little power, so little agency, over your own life that the potential for abuse seems almost inescapable. "Once you were institutionalized, you were at the mercy of staff," recalled activist Mary Johnson in her 2003 book, *Make Them Go Away*. "Incarcerated for no crime other than disability."[9]

The systemic bias toward institutionalization has roots in age-old prejudices against disabled, ill, and older people—that they should be rounded up and kept out of sight. It's billed as being "for their own good," of course, but the evidence suggests otherwise. "Not only do adults usually enjoy greater choice when they live in their own homes relative to individuals living in congregate care or group home settings, but independent and semi-independent settings are also associated with better outcomes and lower costs," says Florence DiGennaro Reed, a lead researcher at the University of Kansas's Department of Applied Behavioral Science.[10] Similarly, the University of Kentucky conducted a quality-of-life survey of Medicaid recipients both before and after moving from institutions to their own homes. Before, only 49.5 percent of respondents answered yes when asked whether they were able to do "fun things"; after living in the community for a year, 78.2 percent answered in the affirmative. More significantly, when asked "Are you happy with the way you live your life?" just 52.6 percent of institutionalized people said yes, while a whopping 86.9 percent of those who'd lived a year in the community did. "Fundamental to the movement toward full inclusion of people with disabilities in their communities is the belief that people should have the right to choose where they live and receive services," writes lead researcher Christina T. Espinosa.[11]

The benefits of deinstitutionalization apply across the board. A survey by the Association of University Centers on Disabilities, a multicampus academic group headquartered in Silver Spring, Maryland, concluded that the advantages are consistently numerous and varied, even for the most severely intellectually disabled people. "A review of 36 studies of outcomes over time for nearly 5,000 people with intellectual and developmental disabilities moving from large institutions to community living arrangements found highly [sic] consistency in positive change in daily living skills for the movers," the research found. "Altogether 31 studies indicated positive outcomes as compared with five showing negative outcomes."[12] Grading for "skill development" in four key areas—language and communication, self-care and domestic capability, community living ability, and social poise—the study further found that those who showed marked improvement from leaving a large institution surpassed those with negative outcomes by a ratio of nine to one.

Still, certain state legislators resist moving people out of state-run institutions. They say it'll cost too much, and perhaps they've succumbed to pressure from the privately run nursing home industry (an estimated 69 percent of nursing homes have for-profit ownership[13]). They maintain this position despite studies showing that allowing people to live in a community setting instead of an institution not only makes them happier but is actually cost-effective. "Nationally, nursing home care averages about $75,190 per patient each year. Care in the home, through such services as meals-on-wheels and daily visits by a health aide, averages $18,000 a year," according to a 2010 AARP study reported in USA Today.[14]

For many disabled people, the twin fears of institutional bias and governmental tightfistedness are never far away. "I was born a disabled child with spina bifida into a working-class family," says Stephanie Woodward, a wheelchair-using attorney and longtime activist. "I would not be here today if it wasn't for Medicaid."[15] Medicaid, she adds, provides vital funding for 30 percent of adult Americans with disabilities and 60 percent of disabled children. When politicians tinker with its budget, they threaten those people's very lives and liberty.

Disabled people's security always feels tentative, hanging in the balance of political fluctuations. The Biden administration floated a policy initiative to expand Medicaid's budget for home care, but it's been stalled by fiscally conservative legislators and, as of this writing, remains far from a sure thing. "There are currently more than 800,000 adults and children on Medicaid waiting lists" for home- and community-based services, writes Rachael Scarborough King, an associate professor of English at the University of California, Santa Barbara, and wife of the prominent health-care activist Ady Barkan, who has ALS.[16] Barkan advocates for free universal health care, including long-term in-home personal-care assistance; King is one of his primary personal-care providers. For Barkan, as for many disabled people, home-based support is everything. Without it, King says, her husband would have to go into an institution—and that, she says, "would not be livable." Biden's proposed

$400 billion for home care would clear the waiting lists and provide a living wage for caregivers, she adds, but its future remains uncertain.

To some extent, the fate of disabled people depends on where they live. Medicaid rules vary by state. California, the notional birthplace of disability rights, is often considered exemplary in its home- and community-based support system. As early as 1973, following years of demonstrations by disability activists, then governor Ronald Reagan signed into law the state's groundbreaking In-Home Supportive Services (IHSS).[17] It was the first of its kind in the nation, allocating a share of its Medicaid dollars to home-based attendant services.

But Nancy Becker-Kennedy, a quadriplegic actor, writer, therapist, and activist who has lived in California since the 1970s, says IHSS isn't all it once promised to be.[18] Its problems illuminate the impossible binds other state Medicaid recipients face.

From early on, she says, the California system struggled to connect workers with those who needed them. The turnover rate was high. Most workers were paid the minimum wage, and they had no way of organizing to raise their working conditions. In 1977, followers of the farmworker labor leader Cesar Chavez joined with home-care workers to form a committee that would later become a labor union, the United Domestic Workers of America. The new union strengthened personal-care aides' bargaining power, but disparate interests feuded on other fronts. For instance, some unionists wanted private home-nursing registries to serve as their official employers to handle payroll taxes and other logistical details, while others wanted to remain independent contractors. Many "consumers," as the disabled people were called, didn't want to give up their right to hire their own attendants directly; they didn't trust an agency to provide them, preferring the control and autonomy that comes from being an employer.

In 1992, a new network of bureaucracies was created to serve as a registry/agency and facilitate relations between the state, the union, and the end users—a nonprofit consortium called the IHSS Public Authorities.[19] "I had trepidation," Becker-Kennedy recalls. "I'm pro-union all the way, but I began to wonder if the union leadership understood the needs of disabled consumers."

This speaks to the importance of collaboration among social movements. Could the union brass, representing the personal-care laborers, truly comprehend and address the needs of the disabled folks it served—and vice versa? The quandaries were many. If a disabled person goes into the hospital for an extended time, which is not unusual, what happens to the care worker? Under current rules, the home-care worker doesn't get paid during that time and has to find another job, leaving the disabled consumer without assistance upon returning home. Also, IHSS only pays for one caregiver at a time, which discourages using an experienced attendant to train a new one. In addition, some aides work as live-ins for many years; if the disabled client dies, the caregiver—who may not be so young anymore—is out of a job and effectively unhoused. There should at least be some sort of pension system. Moreover, spouses and parents who may spend many years working as caregivers can't earn Social Security credits (though proposed legislation would change this).

To resolve these and other grievances, California's Public Authorities have governing committees—made up of disabled users and home-care workers, among others—which are supposed to guarantee fair representation of the different interests. Yet, inevitably, infighting persists. Some counties conduct strenuous background checks to screen potential workers; others don't. Some have training classes for employees and employers; others don't. In 2019, when new rules were instituted to designate specific tasks expected of home-care workers and the length of time each task should take—intended to ensure efficiency and safety for everyone involved—participants on both sides argued it was an untenable degree of micromanaging. If what you need takes longer than the time allotted, your allowable hours could be cut and your needs left unmet.

In such a dysfunctional system, everyone gets hurt—disabled clients and caregivers alike. Becker-Kennedy wants caregivers to get more money, which will attract better people to the profession and improve retention, but she doesn't want disabled people to get shafted either. She has raised all these issues and others time and time again. "They don't get it," she says. "The leadership isn't disabled and hasn't worked as attendants. They don't seem to understand." She feels betrayed, powerless. It's almost as if her home care has been turned into institutional care. "They're trying to build an industry that's just like the nursing homes," she says, "except using our homes for real estate."

Conceptually, Medicaid dates back to 1937, when US surgeon general Thomas Parran proposed a plan to provide health care for those who were receiving Social Security, which was then just two years old. He didn't necessarily have long-term custodial care in mind, or institutional reform, but it was a lot better idea than his other signature project—the now-notorious Tuskegee syphilis experiment that sacrificed the lives of 128 unsuspecting Black men between 1932 and 1972. His pitch for a public health service didn't last as long, though. By 1939, it had foundered as opponents preferred to let profit-making private insurance handle the nation's health needs.[20]

In the 1950s, Virginia "Gini" Laurie, a St. Louis–based Red Cross volunteer, became an early champion of deinstitutionalization on humanitarian grounds. She wasn't disabled, but after four of her siblings died from polio in the 1930s and '40s, she decided to help in polio wards. The polio vaccine was introduced in 1955, but for years afterward there were still plenty of polio survivors in hospitals and nursing homes. In 1957, the development of a portable, affordable, self-regulating ventilator called the Bird Mark 7 Respirator helped make home care a viable option for many of them. Two years later, Laurie wrote an essay urging that people no longer needed to stay institutionalized, if they ever did. "They need a pair of hands that they can direct. They do not need to be buried alive in a nursing home. They need to continue to live their lives as they choose," she wrote.[21] She kept advocating for the independence of disabled people through her death in 1989 at seventy-six.

The impact of her advocacy rippled through the health-care community in various ways, reaching beyond those with physical disabilities. In 1963, President John F. Kennedy signed the Community Mental Health Act to move people with intellectual disabilities out of big state hospitals. But Kennedy's assassination less than a month later disrupted the initiative. Congress never managed to fully fund what Kennedy had imagined.

In 1965, however, President Lyndon B. Johnson launched Medicaid as part of his Great Society programs. Technically, it was included in Title XIX of that year's Social Security amendments, its stated purpose to provide health care for low-income Americans—"the medically indigent," as the New York Times reported.[22] Nothing was said about ongoing personal care or institutionalization per se. In fact, Medicaid was somewhat overlooked at first, in light of the simultaneous passage of the broader Medicare program, which provides coverage (though not long-term care) for *all* Americans when they turn sixty-five. More than a year after its passage, Dr. Howard Rusk, an authority in rehabilitation medicine, reported on Medicaid as a "little known provision" that was "another step forward in providing our disabled citizens with medical care."[23] Benefits, he explained, would start in "the seventh month of disability" if the disability was expected to last at least a year. In those days, "disability" generally signified an inability to earn a living (it still does under Social Security law), and the emphasis was on helping people get back to work. Medicaid was seen as a temporary fix at that point.

Yet even then, it contained a provision for anyone over age eighteen who'd had a disability since childhood and might never be able to find gainful employment; the majority of these recipients, said Rusk, had intellectual disabilities (only he didn't use that term)—"an increasing number [of those with intellectual disabilities] are outliving the parents on whom they have always been dependent." In other words, Medicaid was going to fulfill a somewhat parental role. If your parents died or could no longer look after you, and you couldn't take care of your own needs, you could effectively become a ward of the state. Typically, this meant you would end up institutionalized.

Institutional care was still considered charitable by many people then, though whether it was better for its inmate-recipients or for those who didn't want to deal with others' disabilities and concomitant needs is debatable. Odd as it may sound, though, Medicaid has always excluded those in psychiatric facilities—or, as it calls them, "institutions for mental disease"—including certain residential treatment centers for substance abuse (those with more than sixteen beds). While that exclusion may sound like a way to maneuver people out of institutions, it does nothing to provide these people with better treatment options. Its effect is to leave out a whole swath of the disability community. It shows how the federal government didn't put mental health in the same category as physical, sensory, or intellectual disabilities; it was as if it were a different caste altogether. Though tweaked over the years, the exclusion remains in force, "an outdated, discriminatory federal rule that creates significant barriers to treatment for adults with severe mental illness," says the Treatment Advocacy Center, an Arlington, Virginia–based nonprofit dedicated to improving access to mental health therapies.[24]

In 1972, facing a growing number of disabled Vietnam vets, President Richard Nixon created Supplemental Security Income (SSI), which provides cash for the basic needs of low-income disabled people and senior citizens. At the same time, Nixon extended Medicaid benefits to all who were eligible for SSI. You no longer had to have your disability for at least seven months or surmount any of the other early restrictions. There are still restrictions aplenty, though, such as unreasonable income and asset limitations, and a marriage "penalty" that tightens those limits further for wedded recipients. And while these changes greatly increased funding for disabled Americans, they did not address institutionalization.

A slew of lawsuits over the past half century has endeavored to free institutionalized people. In 1971, a fifteen-year-old Alabaman named Ricky Wyatt sued to get out of a state mental hospital where he was incarcerated. He'd been a rambunctious youth, in and out of reform schools, raised by an aunt because his mother was in jail and his father was absent. Though never shown to have a disability, he was forcibly committed at fourteen to the Bryce State Hospital in Tuscaloosa, where he was by far the youngest of some five thousand residents, most of whom had been involuntarily committed for mental illness. A year later, he became the lead plaintiff in a class-action lawsuit, *Wyatt v. Stickney* (Stickney was Dr. Stonewall Stickney, the state commissioner of mental health). Wyatt testified that he'd been made to sleep on wet floors, awakened by being poked with a broom, tortured with scalding water that was thrown at him, and made to fight other residents so supervisors could place bets on who would win. The case led to a ruling that Wyatt and others could not be locked up like criminals, and they had a constitutional right to humane treatment that "will give each of them a realistic opportunity to be cured or to improve his or her mental condition."[25] Wyatt and his co-litigants were released, and statewide standards of care were established—the "Wyatt Standards," which would become a model for the nation, albeit one not always followed.

Then, in 1975, a Florida man named Kenneth Donaldson sued to be released from the state institution where he'd been confined for nearly fifteen years. The primary defendant was Dr. J. B. O'Connor, superintendent of the state hospital at Chattahoochee. The case of *O'Connor v. Donaldson* went all the way to the US Supreme Court, which found that people cannot be committed to a facility against their will unless they pose a danger to themselves or others.[26] But even that didn't put an end to the practice.

Also in 1975, in response to another class-action lawsuit, the state of New York passed a consent decree forcing New York City to shut down its notorious Willowbrook State School on Staten Island and find alternatives for its more than five thousand intellectually disabled residents. Created in 1947, ostensibly as a compassionate response to the thousands of children who were "mentally and physically defective and feeble minded, who never can become members of society," as then New York governor Thomas Dewey put it, its population quickly exceeded its capacity.[27] Within ten years of opening, it had more than four thousand inhabitants; a decade later the number had swelled to more than six thousand. Neglect and filth were rampant. Communicable diseases such as hepatitis and measles became epidemic. Beatings and even medical experimentation were common, as was sexual abuse. Even after the consent decree, it took another twelve years—till 1987, forty years after it began—to shut the place down.[28]

The publicity generated by Willowbrook—Geraldo Rivera did an award-winning TV special about it—contributed to passage of two potentially important pieces of legislation. In May 1980, President Jimmy Carter signed the Civil Rights of Institutionalized Persons Act (CRIPA), which authorizes the US attorney general to file civil rights suits on behalf of residents of prisons, nursing homes, and other facilities for folks with intellectual disabilities.[29] CRIPA does not, however, address system-wide deinstitutionalization nor create any new rights; instead, it empowers the Justice Department to enforce existing rights from prior case law. It's still in effect today.

Five months later, in October 1980, Carter signed the Mental Health Systems Act, which sought to improve government-funded psychiatric services, in part by providing grants to community mental health centers. That might have been a big boon for deinstitutionalization, but less than a year later, in August 1981, President Ronald Reagan repealed it as part of his Omnibus Budget Reconciliation Act, arguing that the Mental Health Systems Act cost too much. As a result, federal spending for mental health was slashed by some 30 percent, effectively ending the federal government's commitment to people with chronic psychiatric disabilities.

The results seem pretty clear: According to Harvard social scientist Christopher Jencks, the number of unhoused Americans in 1980, before Reagan entered the White House, was just over one hundred thousand.[30] As of 2020, the unhoused population as measured by the US Department of Housing and Urban Development is nearly six hundred thousand.[31]

Until a solution is found for providing housing and helping with the other daily needs of disabled folks, many will rely on a less formalized, less regimented system of mutual aid to get by. "Disabled people don't do mutual aid like abled people do," says the writer Leah Lakshmi Piepzna-Samarasinha.[32] Disabled peer-to-peer support tends to be low-key, they explain, built on "crip webs of trust." Sometimes it's as simple as "people checking on each other"—connections that are "about disabled [people] noticing and caring." This is in contrast to top-down government agencies or large-scale charities that tend to view disabled people as "faceless recipients of care," says Piepzna-Samarasinha. Disabled people have always received help from other disabled people, and maybe they always will. Sometimes these gestures may seem small and unimportant, but they can be vital. Piepzna-Samarasinha tells of a "queer disabled friend" who said, "We were maybe not going to save the world, but we were going to save each other."

For Piepzna-Samarasinha, that hit home. "The small, low-key things we do, in the crip genius ways we do them—with ease, without abled panic—are the opposite of nothing," they observe. "They are everything."

CHAPTER 14

SPARKS OF ACTIVISM EVERYWHERE

As disabled people make inroads into more and more aspects of American life, there are hints they may actually be gaining some power. In October 2019, Rutgers University calculated that more than 10 percent of elected officials in federal, state, and local government—nearly four thousand politicos in all—have disabilities, an unprecedented number for as long as Rutgers has been counting.[1] They include two US senators, five congressional representatives (another was elected in November 2020), and a governor.

Though their numbers still pale in comparison to the percentage of disabled people in the overall populace, these leaders hail from both major parties and are anything but homogeneous in their positions. In fact, just because they're disabled doesn't mean they embrace disability issues. Texas governor Greg Abbott, for example, who has used a wheelchair since a tree fell on him in 1984, when he was twenty-six, has repeatedly opposed the ADA. In 2014, when he was state attorney general, he tried to block disabled Texans from filing access lawsuits. "Abbott's office has fought a blind pharmacy professor in Amarillo who wanted reflective tape on the stairs to her office; two deaf defendants in Laredo who asked for a qualified sign language interpreter in their courtroom; and a woman with an amputated leg, [arguing] she was not disabled because she had a prosthetic limb," reports the *Dallas Morning News*. The plaintiffs had valid ADA cases, yet the newspaper says Abbott believes Texas should be immune from ADA lawsuits because it's unconstitutional for federal laws to force states to comply.[2]

ADAPT's Bob Kafka, who has lived in Austin for more than thirty years, acknowledges pride in having someone so significantly disabled achieve such high office. "But that doesn't give [him] a pass just because he's a guy in a wheelchair," he told a reporter back in 2013.[3] "He's totally two-faced on this disability stuff," said Stephanie Thomas, the disabled attorney and activist.[4]

Whatever a politician's qualities and duplicities, none dare express embarrassment or negativity toward their disabilities. They might need to explain them—as President Joe Biden acknowledged his childhood battle with stuttering—but it would be impossible today to try to pull off the kind of deception FDR did. Not only are secrets harder to keep than they used to be, but having a disability can give a candidate something in common with a sizable portion of the electorate. In 2014, according to the Pew Research Center's American Trends Panel, 71 percent of disabled Americans were sufficiently engaged to feel that election results really mattered to them, compared with just 59 percent of nondisabled Americans. Unfortunately, only 58 percent of disabled Americans actually voted in that year's midterm election, slightly less than the 63 percent of nondisabled Americans, but that may have had to do with difficulties casting a ballot.[5] By law, polling places must be accessible, though some still aren't; even at accessible locations, it can be tough to manipulate a ballot within the confines of a voting booth. Many disabled voters prefer mail-in ballots. In 2020, when voting by mail was more widely available, 74 percent of disabled voters cast ballots by mail or in early in-person drop boxes, compared to 66 percent of nondisabled voters, according to a separate Rutgers poll.[6]

If voting continues to become more open and accessible, it may help bring out more disabled voters, which in turn could elevate disability concerns in the halls of government and maybe even put more disabled candidates in office.

Politicians with disabilities are not really new. In the decades after FDR, a number of disabled legislators held prominent positions in the Capitol. Most were veterans, which no doubt made their disabilities more politically acceptable. But people largely didn't talk about these leaders' disabilities. Decades ago, you just didn't mention impairments. It wasn't considered polite. There was an unspoken bargain between you and whoever happened to be with you to pretend not to notice. Disability pride scarcely existed, at least not in mainstream circles.

Then, in 2016, a different kind of disabled veteran was elected to the US Senate: a woman. And she did talk about it.

Tammy Duckworth, Democrat from Illinois, was among the first American women to fly military combat missions. One Friday in November 2004, while serving in the Army National Guard during Operation Iraqi Freedom, her Blackhawk helicopter was hit by a rocket-propelled grenade. She lost both legs and partial use of her right arm. "Any part of me that was sticking outside of the armor . . . was injured, or is no longer with me," she told the press. During her recovery, she says, she was inspired by the disabled veterans before her who had gone into politics, who kept trying to serve their country and change the world.[7]

In 2012, Duckworth was elected to Congress; she served two terms as the representative from Illinois's Eighth Congressional District before being elected US senator in 2016. In 2018, a little over a year into her Senate term, she became the first senator to give birth while in office. That April, she received much press coverage when she wheeled into the Capitol (she uses either a wheelchair or prosthetic legs and crutches) with her baby daughter, Maile—just ten days old—cradled on her lap. "The first infant ever brought onto the Senate floor," said the *New York Times*.[8]

Duckworth says she doesn't consider herself a disability activist.[9] But when it comes to disability pride, she's all in. She felt the first tingling of pride the moment she recovered at Walter Reed, the national military hospital. "I was proud to have earned my wounds," is how she puts it. As a legislator, she's been a champion of measures that disabled people care about. In October 2018, she backed an amendment to the Federal Aviation Administration Reauthorization Act requiring airlines to make public how many wheelchairs and motorized scooters they damage or lose each month. (It was a shockingly high number: In 2019, before the COVID pandemic decimated air travel, the major air carriers lost or damaged nearly a thousand wheelchairs and scooters every month; in 2021, it still averaged more than eight hundred a month.)[10] "Travelers should be able to find out if certain airlines have high rates of breaking wheelchairs and other equipment that people depend on, just like we can find out if certain airlines have high rates of flight delays or cancellations," Duckworth said in a statement.[11]

In 2019, she got behind the Social Security Caregiver Credit Act, which would support state training programs for caregivers and enable certain family caregivers to receive Social Security credits for their unpaid labor. She supports the Disabled Access Credit Expansion Act, which would increase tax credits for small businesses that renovate for disability access, and the Supplemental Security Income Restoration Act, which would expand SSI eligibility and allow people to save more money without losing benefits. She pushed for the Office of Disability Policy Act, which would establish a new bureau to advise Congress on how future legislation might affect disabled Americans, and she favored the Disability Integration Act, the deinstitutionalization bill that would enable more people who need long-term care to live in a community setting. In 2020, she endorsed the Accessible Voting Act, a plan to increase voting accessibility for disabled and/or older Americans.

Alas, none of these—except the aviation amendment—have been enacted. They remain under consideration.

Duckworth believes the top priority for the disability community is bolstering the ADA. "We need to strengthen it [and] oppose efforts to chip away at it," she says. She keeps an eye on those who would attack it, the "greater effort by businesses to try to erode" its protections. The Senate offices themselves, she adds, have access barriers. She can't work out in the gym because it's not wheelchair accessible. "They have made accommodations for me in terms of making my office more accessible, but overall it is still lacking," she continues. "When I see accessibility issues around the Capitol, I certainly bring them up and we work to fix them."[12]

Then Senator Duckworth acknowledges a frustration that every disabled American knows too well. "The law was passed thirty years ago," she says, "and yet we still don't have full implementation."

Employment inequities remain one of the most galling disappointments. This persistent problem was on the mind of a young disabled man named Diego Mariscal when, in 2015, he launched a nonprofit business called 2Gether-International. Based in Washington, DC, the organization advises and trains aspiring disabled entrepreneurs and connects them with possible investors and clients. Mariscal, who was born in New Orleans with cerebral palsy but grew up in Monterrey, Mexico, says 2Gether-International operates entirely from grants, such as a recent $75,000 award from the DC Deputy Mayor's Office for Planning and Economic Development. Participants pay no fees; in fact, they receive $650 a month to seed their businesses.[13]

Mariscal's premise is that disabilities can be valuable assets to business performance, not hindrances. The skills disabled people use in managing their lives—hiring attendants, handling bureaucracies, constantly adapting—are perfectly aligned with what business professionals need. "From the moment disabled people wake up, they have to figure out how to get dressed, how to drive, how to communicate, how to live in a world that is not built to fit their needs," says his website.[14] "The mindset of disabled people is innately collaborative and communicative, oriented towards problem solving, good at working with limited resources, and used to overcoming daily challenges."

Mariscal admits he wasn't always so "disability positive." When he was growing up, his parents insisted he wasn't really disabled; he just "moved differently." It wasn't until he went to DC to attend American University that he learned about the ADA. As a Paralympic swimmer, he had known other disabled folks before, but never from a social justice or empowerment perspective. "That's when I began to gain a sense of pride and power," he says.

Mariscal's program is open to anyone who "identifies as disabled and has a viable business goal." He can't yet accommodate more than six participants at a time per twelve-week session, but he plans to expand. He would like to open more locations across the country, noting that he prefers "coworking spaces" that are shared with nondisabled colleagues. Disabled people, says Mariscal, should not be ghettoized.

Employment ghettoization is not an exaggeration. It exists most egregiously in what are called sheltered workshops—segregated working environments where disabled employees are paid less than minimum wage for doing menial tasks. According to the latest report from the US General Accounting Office, there could be as many as a half million disabled people who are paid less than one dollar an hour to stuff envelopes, put labels on jars, or perform janitorial duties. Among the alleged employers who exploit disabled labor in this way are franchise chains such as Super 8 motels and big-box stores such as Walmart and Home Depot. And it's perfectly legal.

Sheltered workshops have been around for nearly two hundred years. In 1840, the Perkins School for the Blind, near Boston, then called the New England Asylum for the Blind, began hiring blind people in a somewhat paternalistic environment, giving menial jobs to those who might not have found work elsewhere, but also not offering competitive wages. "Jobs for people who were blind were protected, or sheltered, from competition in order to create permanent job opportunities for them," says a 2011 report from the National Disability Rights Network, a multistate advocacy organization established by Congress in 1975 to protect disabled Americans from this kind of abuse.[15]

It might have seemed perfectly logical at the time for the first school for blind children to be "the first to confront the problem of what to do about graduates, equipped with wage-earning skills, who found every [other] employment door closed to them," writes Frances A. Koestler in her book *The Unseen Minority: A Social History of Blindness in the United States*.[16] The Perkins workshop was considered a kind of progressive model in its day; it was soon replicated at other schools for blind students. A 1908 survey of sixteen sheltered workshops found that most produced brooms, caning for chairs, and other handwoven products—"simple, handmade objects that . . . could be manufactured out of easily obtained materials, and could be sold in local markets," Koestler writes. The workers were paid about three dollars per week, not a living wage even then.

So it went, with scarce objection, for decade after decade, until the Great Depression. In 1933, Congress passed the National Industrial Recovery Act; its primary objective was economic stimulus, but it contained a provision to give disabled workers "a productivity-based sub-minimum wage" of 75 percent of the standard minimum wage in "competitive industries" and absolutely no wage floor in sheltered workshops, according to historian William G. Whittaker.[17] Other aspects of the act, however, such as requiring safe working conditions (at least for nondisabled workers) and maximum hours of labor, infuriated the business community as anticompetitive. The Supreme Court soon declared the 1933 act unconstitutional, but not before President Franklin Roosevelt issued an executive order explicitly allowing subminimum wages for disabled workers.[18] The potential abuse was now the law of the land.

In 1937, a group of blind employees at a sheltered workshop in Pittsburgh went on strike to protest their substandard pay. "The local press seemed more impressed with the 'oddity' of the event than with the fact that a group of disabled workers were angry enough to organize a militant rank-and-file job action in their place of employment," says the website of the Disability Social History Project.[19] The results of the strike are unknown. But, as if to settle any question as to whether subminimum wages were fair, Congress soon passed the Fair Labor Standards Act of 1938, Section 14(c) of which reopened the door to sheltered workshops that could pay as little as they wanted. Though Roosevelt's executive order allowing the subminimum wage expired, this act of Congress remains on the books today.

Sheltered workshops took off after that. "Between 1948 and 1976, the number of sheltered workshops in the USA increased from 85 to about 3000," writes Alberto Migliore, a senior research associate at the University of Massachusetts' Institute for Community Inclusion, which looks at policies and practices related to the hiring of intellectually disabled people.[20] During that time, he says, the workshops began focusing on intellectually or developmentally disabled people, since blind folks were finding better-paid positions elsewhere. In 1952, the sheltered workshop for blind people at the Perkins school closed for good, after 112 years.

Today, many sheltered workshops receive government grants on the pretext of being social service organizations. Most are small nonprofit agencies that hire a handful of people, but big ones such as Goodwill Industries may employ more than two thousand Section 14(c) workers across the US. They say they're providing valuable opportunities, but disability activists insist it's legalized discrimination—or even legalized slavery.[21]

In October 2018, the National Council on Disability published a report urging the federal government to ban sheltered workshops.[22] The harm they do goes deeper than inadequate compensation. They dictate all terms of employment, with little consideration for fair labor standards or workers' access needs. Disabled folks, often fresh out of school or training programs, are "fast tracked into segregated employment and do not have the benefit of individualized work assessments," says the National Disability Rights Network, a provider of protection and advocacy services in Washington, DC. "Loud and dusty industrial settings are often the only option for people with sensory sensitivities, or crowded and busy rooms are the settings for people with autism." Some of these workers would undoubtedly be able to do more complex, higher-level tasks if their needs were met. "Ironically, a person with a disability would receive more individualized accommodations in a competitive work environment," says the advocacy group, "because of the protections set forth in the ADA."[23]

If you think this sounds illegal, you're not alone. In 2001, Congress established the Office of Disability Employment Policy within the Department of Labor, a non-regulatory federal agency to eliminate "barriers to the training and employment" of disabled workers. It promotes "employment first" policies, which means that, through training programs and grants, it encourages publicly financed employment systems and job-placement services to integrate disabled workers in regular positions as opposed to sheltered workshops.[24] Five years later, Washington State became the first to implement this practice; since then, thirteen more states have followed suit: Alaska, California, Delaware, Illinois, Kansas, Maine, Mississippi, Ohio, Oklahoma, Oregon, Texas, Utah, and Wyoming.

These programs merely encourage fair employment for disabled workers; they don't outlaw the subminimum wage. Then, in 2012, a class-action lawsuit in Oregon became the first legal challenge against sheltered workshops. It accused the state's employment services of violating the ADA when they excluded thousands of intellectually or developmentally disabled people from normal job-placement efforts by failing to provide supports they needed to maintain regular jobs. As a result, the plaintiffs were "left with little choice but to toil away in sheltered workshop environments," writes Michelle Diament in *Disability Scoop*.[25] One witness testified that she was stuck working on an assembly line for sixty-six cents an hour. It took till December 2015 to reach a settlement. Oregon agreed to move more than a thousand disabled workers from sheltered workshops to jobs in the community at competitive wages. Some seven thousand others would receive employment support services to help them find work in the community, including nearly five thousand young folks under age twenty-four.[26]

It was a start. Thus encouraged, advocates urged more state interventions. A few states began actually outlawing the subminimum wage. Between 2017 and 2018, the Department of Labor completed nearly two hundred investigations into sheltered workshops and ordered repayment of nearly $2 million in back wages to disabled workers. Most of the time, though, officials look the other way. Only the most abusive situations get noticed.

One such abusive situation involved immigrant garment workers in California. Not disabled people per se, but the case got attention. In September 2021, the Golden State became the tenth state to officially outlaw the subminimum wage.

As promising as that might sound, it won't go into full effect until 2025.[27]

~

Political activism and employment reform are both vital to the future of the disability community. Yet the underlying malignancy of ableist bigotry can seep far and wide. If minds are closed, no amount of legislative or court victories will end the attitudinal barriers that suffuse our society. Could media be a more potent solution, as many seem to think? In 2009, Ohio University communications professors Margaret M. Quinlan and Benjamin R. Bates asserted that mass media has a definite effect on perceptions of people with disabilities.[28] The theme was amplified in 2013, when Towson University's Beth Haller and her colleague Lingling Zhang studied how media images of disabled people impact the disability community's own sense of identity. Positive representation, they found, led to an affirmation of disability identity "even when the media messages were perceived as unrealistic"; negative portrayals were associated with denial of a disability identity. Their use of "disability identity" is related to the idea of disability pride: proudly recognizing yourself as a member of that community. The research concludes unequivocally that representation plays a significant role in forming people's opinions. "Mass media are not only important agents for individuals to learn and formulate their attitudes, values, and beliefs," the researchers write, "but [they] also affect their self-esteem and self-perception."[29]

The connection between media representation and people's hearts and minds is so widely and firmly held across cultures that even the United Nations has gotten behind trying to improve disability depictions. In the UN's Convention on the Rights of Persons with Disabilities—the 2006 international human rights treaty modeled after the ADA but not yet endorsed by the US—the UN said the media "can be a powerful force to change societal misconceptions and present persons with disabilities as individuals that are a part of human diversity."[30]

Yet how exactly to put those principles into practice remains a challenge for a global entertainment industry that's often more concerned with reaping outsize profits than bending attitudes. Storm Smith, a producer at BBDO LA, the West Coast branch of the New York–based BBDO Worldwide ad agency, is a strong believer in the power of media to alter people's views. "One of the better ways to shake up perceptions is to get people from different perspectives in positions of influence, behind the scenes, to contribute to the stories we see," she says (as translated by Mandy David, her sign language interpreter).[31] "For example, I'm D/deaf. I'm a woman of Color. I'm queer. So I have an intersectional identity and can provide several unique perspectives. I can deliver content that's reflective of and relevant to these nontraditional demographics." Smith is adamant that she doesn't intend to speak for all people like herself. Which is why she feels it's so important to "invite more people to the table to provide the input that will help change attitudes, behaviors, and perspectives."

Smith's first official job title at BBDO was art director, but now she's a producer. That means she coordinates and contributes to a team of professionals, making sure they and their clients don't forget about diversity, inclusion, and accessibility. Tech giant Apple, for instance, invited her to contribute to its Everyone Can Code campaign, an ongoing educational initiative. She led the creation of video clips that showed—in sign language and with closed captioning—how young hard-of-hearing people can learn to write computer code as easily as they learn to sign. She worked with AT&T to fashion digital ads in celebration of the thirtieth anniversary of the ADA. She's addressed Facebook execs, the National Association of Broadcasters, the business schools of Harvard and UCLA, and a diverse group of entertainment "thought leaders" at a Ford Foundation media event. Smith tells audiences about herself and quotes statistics about disability in America, disabled people's buying power, and how supporting this growing market can improve a company's brand identity. Her message: *We are not a burden. Your brand can be locked in the past and remain part of the problem, or it can seize the future, take responsibility, and become part of the solution. Not changing, not keeping up, means missing out on a huge opportunity.*

She shares a depressing statistic: Some 55 percent of people still feel uncomfortable when they see disabled people on the screen or in ads.

Perhaps that's not surprising, considering the onslaught of regressive and reductive messaging that pops up randomly, unexpectedly. While watching TV, say, you may suddenly be bushwhacked by an anti-smoking public service announcement that shows a sad-looking person with a tracheostomy or artificial voice box, a reminder of the horrors of tobacco. Similar PSAs warn about the dangers of guns, firecrackers, riding a motorcycle without a helmet, and driving while drunk, while texting, or without a seatbelt. All good causes, without a doubt, but by sensationalizing the shock value of scars, broken bones, nerve damage, brain injuries, or throat conditions—exploiting them as fear grenades—these well-intentioned ads thoughtlessly demonize disabilities.

Smith has no illusions about what she's up against. Presenting better, more fair-minded narratives sometimes seems a hopelessly preposterous, soul-draining quest. Besides trying to convince image makers to include balanced, accurate portrayals of disabled people, she'd like corporations to earmark an accessibility budget so needed accommodations can be provided quickly and easily. No one, as far as she knows, has anything of the kind. "I'm so tired of confronting places about accessibility, tired of fighting," she says. "I don't want to hear, 'We can't. We don't have the funds.'"

Smith says she will keep hammering away at the insiders who are responsible for the stories we see. If all else fails, she says with a smile and a shrug, she'll simply confront them with the sheer force of her personality and righteous pride.

Part of Smith's message concerns what Professor Jasmine E. Harris calls the "aesthetics of disability"—what the average person thinks "disability" looks like, and what that connotes. In a January 2020 essay in the *New York Times*, Harris—then at the University of California, Davis, School of Law—wrote about this and its effect on our culture. This was during the first Harvey Weinstein trial; Weinstein, the sixty-seven-year-old former movie mogul accused of multiple counts of rape, criminal sexual assault, and predatory sexual assault, had entered a New York City courtroom hobbling, with a walker, and assisted by aides. He looked sad and defeated—more like a grumpy grandpa you might offer to help cross the street on his way to feeding pigeons in the park than the puffed-up executive producer of such critically acclaimed blockbusters as *The English Patient*, *Shakespeare in Love*, the *Lord of the Rings* trilogy, and *The King's Speech*. The image was so stark a contrast from the bombastic, swaggering, smiling tuxedoed he-man we'd seen sauntering through the glamorous red-carpet crowds at the Oscars year after year that it almost looked staged.

In that moment, Harris stressed, Weinstein looked like nobody's idea of a dangerous monster. Rather, he looked vulnerable. A defendant who appears physically disabled is more likely to be judged innocent, she wrote, just as a victim who appears disabled is more likely to be believed. "The aesthetics of disability can be used to manipulate the legal system while also reinforcing stereotypes of what people with disabilities look and sound like, and what they are capable of doing," wrote Harris.[32]

If it was a cynical ploy, it didn't do Weinstein much good. The evidence against him was too great. In the end, he was found guilty of rape and criminal sexual felony, acquitted only on charges of being a sexual predator. He was sentenced to twenty-three years in prison.

At any rate, Harris attributes presumptions based on impressions of disability to "the spread effect"—how one aspect of a person gets expanded and transferred to other aspects. Someone who smiles, for instance, is assumed to be friendly and kind; someone who appears disheveled and unkempt is assumed to be unreliable. The average American, she says, may not be attuned to common disability inferences and their repercussions, but these expectations and stereotypes are nonetheless influential. "Assumptions about what disability signifies, and what signifies disability, are woven into our culture," says Harris.

As a case in point, Harris says she's dyslexic, a fact that surprises many people. It shakes up their preconceived notions of what a disability looks like and, she hopes, broadens people's perspectives of the Other. She also has a sister who has spina bifida and uses a wheelchair, which Harris says shows that disability issues can directly impact the lives of people who don't seem like they would be affected by them. Similarly, she enjoys telling people that she's Latinx, which isn't apparent.

For Harris, this is more than a matter of not judging people by their looks; it's about expanding people's perceptions.[33] Most nondisabled people view disabilities through a flawed lens, she says. To them, a wheelchair signifies neediness, whereas for most wheelchair users it's a liberating tool, a mode of autonomy. In fact, the public may focus on a few visible markers of disability, such as wheelchairs or canes, or markers of accessibility, such as bigger bathroom stalls, ramps, sign language, and guide dogs—because they're easy to comprehend. This limited, simplistic view of what disabled people need and want relieves nondisabled folks of responsibility; it gets them off the hook. If there's accessible parking at a shopping mall, say, the developer/owner may figure their job is done: they don't have to provide any other accommodations.

Most nondisabled people fail to understand the marginalization and stigma of disability. They favor fairness, says Harris, and they tend to feel kindly toward disabled people because they think that's right and honorable. But that's about all. What's more, nondisabled people fail to grasp that disability isn't something alien, that it's a normal, common phenomenon; they are clueless to the fact that they themselves are potential members of the disability community. They don't twig to the differences between generosity, compassion, and charity on the one hand, and parity, respect, and the *right* to accessibility on the other.

The disability rights movement has so far failed to alter nondisabled people's views sufficiently, says Harris. Unlike the civil rights crusades of the 1960s, disability rights hasn't generated a groundswell of exposure and public interest. Even demonstrations such as the 504 sit-ins, the Denver bus protests, and the crawl up the Capitol steps "didn't arouse the kind of attention that the push to end racial discrimination did and still does," she says.

For the disability community, the next phase—the phase Harris says we're starting now—must involve shifting the social norms, tweaking the understanding of what disability means and looks like. She compares this to the LGBTQIA+ cause; it became harder for the majority culture to label LGBTQIA+ people as different and separate when, over the past few decades, more people who didn't *seem* to be queer began coming out. It became harder to talk in terms of *us* and *them*. It became harder to stereotype. Disabled people, on the contrary, are still too easy for nondisabled people to stereotype.

The disability community, Harris says, "needs to be strategic about who are going to be the public faces of the movement, its spokespeople, going forward." It's vital to present the whole spectrum of disability experiences. Otherwise, she says, the community risks coming off as one-dimensional, which would not only be inaccurate but foster internal divisions and resentments. "As a movement, disabled people can learn from movements that have come before," says Harris. After a thoughtful pause, she adds, "Segmentation and infighting plague every movement." In the struggles for racial justice, men have been more visible than women; in the women's rights movement, white women were the predominant activists, at least in the early campaigns; and in the LGBTQIA+ movement, white, gay male activists such as Harvey Milk were initially the most visible. "These so-called leaders really didn't represent their entire communities," she says.

Harris would like to see a required course in colleges and maybe high schools or middle schools about the aesthetics of disability. So far, only California, New Jersey, and Massachusetts include any disability history in their high school curricula. Her hope is that this education would give people a better sense of what prejudice and inequality really look like. "To the extent that we can meaningfully teach people to grapple with their biases, we can make change happen," she says.

TRENDING OR TRULY EMPOWERING?

I n the summer of 2020, the documentary film *Crip Camp: A Disability Revolution* was on nearly every disabled person's mind. Directed by Jim LeBrecht and Nicole Newnham, it had received backing from the Obamas' production company, Higher Ground. The film premiered at the Sundance Film Festival; quickly landed on Netflix, where everyone could see it, even during COVID; was translated into twenty-nine languages, with subtitles for D/deaf viewers; had audio description for blind viewers available in fifteen languages; and was nominated for an Oscar. (It lost.) The film showed the true story of a group of young disabled people who met in 1970 at a summer camp that was exclusively for disabled kids. Unlike others of its type, this camp didn't patronize; it empowered. Many of the campers found affirmation and a sense of community; they helped each other, accepted each other's limitations, drank together, sang together, flirted, and made out with each other. Most had been segregated to special ed classes in school and felt ostracized or ignored at home, but at this camp they felt free and valued. A number of them went on to become instrumental in the movement to pass Section 504 and, later, the ADA.

The message of the movie seems to be that from this sense of belonging came a capacity for righteous self-assertiveness. Many disabled viewers felt a connection—some remembered those days; others were too young or otherwise had no idea about this history. They watched together virtually, in online viewing parties. Social media discussions morphed into weekly webinars with guest presenters who delved into a variety of disability topics. "Crip Camp webinars every Sunday are like going to a church where I actually belong!" one disabled enthusiast posted on Facebook.

That summer, too, came the thirtieth anniversary of that sunny, humid day on the White House South Lawn when the ADA was signed into law. There could be no disability pride marches because of the pandemic. A celebration of "ADA30" at the Kennedy Center in Washington, DC, was canceled for the same reason. There was no commemoration scheduled at the White House—the occasion was scarcely noticed by then president Trump, not even in a tweet—unlike when President Obama held an official celebration of the ADA's twenty-fifth anniversary. Nevertheless, the day was celebrated with Zoom get-togethers promoted over social media. Major news outlets put out tributes and retrospectives: NPR,[1] CNN, Today.com, *USA Today*, and a variety of local papers. If it's not too reductive, the message they all shared was that the act was great but we have further to go. The *New York Times* took a different tack, running a whole series of pieces starting with essays two weeks before the anniversary and ending with an overview of disability history and reports on various aspects and leaders of the movement. Some elements were jarring, judged by a number of disabled critics as off-tune or patronizing, even pathologizing—such as a science article about gene editing that could effectively erase certain disabilities.[2] But in all, it was an attention getter, a major section dedicated to exploring "how the Americans with Disabilities Act has shaped modern life," and it invited readers to send in questions and tips so reporters could pursue more stories about disability and accessibility. This was hugely different from just five years earlier, when the paper carried only one op-ed (by me) marking that ADA anniversary.

Over the past decades, the idea of disability has shifted from a medical signifier to an emblem of cultural identity. Being disabled no longer means just being limited or functioning differently from the majority in some fundamental way; it links you to a diverse group of others who share a history, a set of similar experiences, and often a sociopolitical axe to grind, or at least a message—an agenda—for the rest of the world to heed.

At the end of *No Pity*, Joe Shapiro's seminal book about the early days of disability rights, he describes a May 1994 meeting in the East Room of the White House where President Bill Clinton told some 150 disability activists that they were carrying on their shoulders "not only your cause, but ours as well." Clinton was referring primarily to the progressive agenda to end health-care discrimination and extend universal medical coverage, but Shapiro laments that the disability movement remained "rarely recognized and little celebrated, [though] it gives America a model for a more fair society that values the talents of all."[3]

But now, can anyone say the disability community remains rarely recognized or little celebrated? Many nondisabled people may not like the ADA, but everyone has heard of it. You make a reservation at a hotel or restaurant, say, and you can't help hearing about "ADA accommodations." You might not be up on the details of what they entail, or the movement and the spirit behind them, but you know it's not referring to special arrangements for the American Dental Association or Americans for Democratic Action. Some people go so far as to try to overturn these rules, but they can no longer ignore them. And woe to the politician who speaks eloquently about an inclusive society and leaves out people with disabilities. It still happens, but they can be called on it. At a June 2020 Black Lives Matter protest in front of the White House following the murder of George Floyd by Minneapolis police, twenty or more disabled people held up signs emblazoned with "Black Disabled Lives Matter." Many of them had been organized by Keri Gray, the cancer survivor and diversity and inclusion consultant devoted to exploring the impact of race, gender, and disability.

Clearly, the disability community has come to enjoy an unprecedented degree of visibility—a presence that's evident in social media, fashion, TV, movies, Broadway, and politics. In her introduction to the brilliant collection *Disability Visibility: First-Person Stories from the Twenty-First Century*, published in 2020, the disability activist Alice Wong remarks on the difference: "In 2014, disabled people throughout the United States were preparing for the following year's twenty-fifth anniversary of the ADA. I wanted to mark the upcoming milestone, but wasn't affiliated with any major advocacy or media organization and wasn't certain how I could contribute as an individual." Wong says she wanted to see more stories about "the disabled experience in the present while honoring the past." She felt there should be more attention paid to the lives of everyday disabled people, not just the few "supercrips" who always got attention and praise. She wanted to increase the diversity of disability representation. "I believe I am living in a time where disabled people are more visible than ever before," Wong continues. "And yet while representation is exciting and important, it is not enough. I want and expect more. *We all should expect more. We all deserve more.*"[4]

The demand for *more* is hard to argue with. We may have become more conspicuous, but we still don't have enough accurate or diverse representation. We may have laws against discrimination, but we still have discrimination. We may have legal protections, yet a third to a half of those killed by police are disabled.[5] Disabled, sick, and elderly people were targeted to be deprived of needed care during a pandemic simply because they were considered the most expendable, or at least the least likely to benefit. We may have rights, but we don't yet have justice.

Before I started research for this book, I thought I understood what the disability movement was all about. I understood about not medicalizing us, about embracing our identity as a marginalized minority, about not just tolerating but valuing disabled people's perspectives and contributions, about respecting us as full human beings. I didn't cotton to the fact that these basic principles leave so many people out. I knew that folks with mobility, sensory, and cognitive impairments were members of the disability community, of course, but I didn't understand autistic self-advocacy, neurodiversity, or psychiatric disabilities. I didn't know about intersectionality or heed the wisdom of the Disability Justice framework. As a white cisgender heterosexual man, a person of privilege, I hadn't contemplated the extent of the racism, sexism, homophobia, transphobia, or other exclusionary, dismissive, hateful practices *within* the disability community. The disability tent is much bigger than I'd realized. We are not monolithic.

I've come to know a new generation that's pointing out the many disabled folks who've been erased from the mainstream disability identity. That's vital. After all, being left out is sort of what started the disability rights movement in the first place: who is included and who is excluded from society?

Today, we the disabled may not always be united, we may have factions, but we're not fractured. We are dynamic, whether opposing cuts in Medicaid, education, health care, and affordable housing or objecting when the Trump administration floated the idea of using "neurobehavioral" tech to combat shootings—collecting data from smart devices and elsewhere to predict violent behavior, in effect blaming mental illness for mass brutality. "This is scary and dangerous," autistic activist Lydia X. Z. Brown told Vanity Fair. "Negatively racialized disabled people WILL be the most likely to be victimized/targeted by increased psychiatric and police surveillance."[6]

People are tired of having to explain themselves, their issues, and why those issues matter. They want to see more disabled people in leadership positions, more disabled people aiding and empowering other disabled people. They're fed up with of politicians and social service do-gooders who talk to them like they're children. They feel "heard" when disabled people are the ones staffing agencies and providing guidance.

At the same time, disabled people are sick of feeling isolated. Many of them are lonely. They want the world to know that they are sexual beings. They are fed up with feeling left out, locked out.

In its diversity and complexity, the disability community is ceaselessly engaged in heartfelt endeavors to challenge the status quo—not because they want to but because they have to. Too many disabled people are still institutionalized. Too many feel threatened by the ongoing encroachment of so-called right-to-die laws. Too many disabled folks are policed.

Yet I have hope. Even if they come haphazardly, drip by drip, the efforts to upend ableism in all its manifestations may cause a ripple effect. In small towns and big cities, from coast to coast, disabled people of all colors, genders, ages, orientations, backgrounds, political leanings, ability levels, sizes, religions, and socioeconomic circumstances are doing their part. Their crusades may be varied, their targets wide-ranging and diverse, but their dream is largely the same: to improve the lot of the disability community, and therefore all of society.

There's Tyrone Starkie, a man in his thirties with a form of muscular dystrophy, who helped start a nonprofit called Community Heroes. Through its website and social media, the Goldsboro, North Carolina–based group highlights disabled people who are giving back to at-risk populations.[7] Starkie knows what it's like to be stared at, both as a disabled person and as a Black man married to a white woman in the South. Strangers, he says, often make rude comments; they assume his wife is his nurse. It makes him angry. "You have to laugh," he says, not laughing. He decided to channel his frustration into giving back. Through

Community Heroes, he aims to spotlight and inspire, to promote the dream of an all-inclusive society.[8]

In Parker, Colorado, Wayne Connell became frustrated by people's reactions after his wife, Sherri, was diagnosed with multiple sclerosis and Lyme disease. Many outsiders didn't believe she needed certain modifications because her disabilities weren't visible. So, in 1996, Connell started the Invisible Disabilities Association, a nonprofit all-volunteer group to help raise awareness and offer support for others like Sherri. It gives annual awards to organizations and individuals making a positive difference. The association started the Invisible Disabilities Community, an online peer-support group. It also received government approval to designate the third week in October as Invisible Disabilities Week. No matter the diagnosis, the group maintains, invisible disabilities and needs are real.[9]

In Frisco, Texas, Michele Campanelli-Erwin is waging a quiet war to get air carriers to allow passengers to stay in their wheelchairs, just like buses and trains do. In the early 2000s, she became incensed at how difficult it was to fly to Disney World with her son, Grayson, who uses a wheelchair because of spinal muscular atrophy. Soon after, she launched All Wheels Up, a research and advocacy initiative that makes a point of arguing its case for better airplane access in technical, engineering-savvy language that business executives can't ignore.[10]

If I listed all the examples of grassroots advocacy, this book would weigh a ton.

~

"What's wrong with that kid?" I heard a lot growing up.

Other kids were always pointing, staring, questioning. They weren't bullying, not exactly, and I guess I now understand their curiosity. But that kind of attention is something you don't forget. I tried my best to ignore these interruptions, these incursions. If I'm honest, I wanted to minimize my disability the way every successful disabled role model I knew of at the time did. To get on with my life and hope nobody noticed my wheelchair, curved spine, or soggy-hotdog arms. But that was impossible.

"Tell them you have amyotonia," my mother advised.

Amyotonia was my diagnosis before doctors had settled on spinal muscular atrophy; it's a fancy, nonspecific term for muscle weakness. She might as well have asked me to recite a *Hamlet* soliloquy.

"If it's easier, just tell them you can't walk," said Mom.

I tried. I didn't like saying it. It sounded defeatist. I tried making it come out neutral, almost clinical, never pitiful. Sometimes this admission just brought more queries. "*Why* can't you walk? Did you get hurt? I'll bet you fell down. Will you get better soon?"

The endless questioning made me feel like an exhibit in the museum. Mom kept insisting I be truthful and brave, not confrontational, but I didn't like having the job of explaining my existence to strangers.

"Tell them you were born this way," she suggested next.

Those words weren't hard to say. They were truthful, simple, straightforward, easy to pronounce. And somehow they worked! No more follow-up inquiries or remarks.

In the years since, I've come to understand why that simple declaration of "I was born this way" proved so effective, why it satisfied the curious onlookers. Even if my disability had come later—if I hadn't been *born* this way—the straightforward statement communicated that nothing was wrong. I could as easily have said, *I just am this way* or *This is the way I am.* I think that was my mother's point. My disability was nothing to shy away from or be embarrassed about.

Later, as a young adult, I'd try to remember another sentence she taught me a line from a seventeenth-century sonnet by John Milton: "They also serve who only stand and wait." Milton was going blind, and I believe he was affirming that his existence still mattered, his life still had purpose. It told me that my life mattered. I had purpose. It was, I think now, an early expression of disability pride.

We the disabled serve a purpose. We count. We matter, just as we are.

Over time, I've come to see that my disability is about more than myself. It's a connection to a rich, multifaceted history and culture. I am inextricably linked to a community that endures. The more I know about my disabled siblings—past and present—the better I feel about being a member of the club. Recognizing and celebrating disability as an identity helps me know there's nothing wrong with the way I am. It also tells me I'm not alone.

Today when kids stare, point, or question, I always try to stop and explain. "I can't walk. I don't have muscles like you do. I drive my chair with this little joystick, you see?" I say, demonstrating. "Pretty cool, huh?" Sometimes the adult with them pulls them away, discourages their inquisitiveness. But I try to encourage it.

It's different when the interrogations come from adults. Especially medical professionals. "How do you live? You're really an inspiration!" I hear too often. I smile, take the compliment if I can stomach it, but I can't help feeling I'm a puzzle to them, an anomaly that disrupts their considered expertise. It feels like they're saying, *Why aren't you more pitiful—or dead?* As though I'm living on borrowed time. Even now, at my age, it can make me wonder, *Do I belong here?*

I understand the struggle to feel okay in one's own skin, the epiphany that comes from learning to love a body or mind that society seems to call shameful. Almost everyone I interviewed for this book acknowledged they, too, had gone through a similar transition; they'd had to wrestle with bitter self-loathing before coming out into the sunlight. The more we make friends with our disabilities and come to value, even cherish, our existence, the easier that path may become for other disabled people. Maybe one day disability pride will be universally acknowledged, and those who would question and doubt our place in society will be the oddballs, the out-of-touch, the ignorant.

The ADA empowered many of us to dream of such a reality. To imagine a fully inclusive society where unramped stairs and stares of pity are reminders of a vile past, known only in history books. Thirty-plus years on, perhaps some of that change has already started happening. Little hints of progress keep popping up. But, without a doubt, the pace of improvement is discouragingly slow. Sometimes, evolution is so tiny and gradual you miss it entirely. Yet new ideas, new views, new spokespeople, new websites, new performers, new books and articles and surveys, new legislative wins, new advocates and activists keep arriving on the scene. You couldn't get disabled people to hide their opinions and talents (or their disabilities) if you tried.

ACKNOWLEDGMENTS

Thanks, first, to you: the readers. Without you, there would be nothing here.

Writing the end of a book is a fearsome task; I want to be sure I haven't left out anything important, though odds are I've inadvertently overlooked some crucial detail, meaningful event, and people who matter. I'm grateful for all the great disabled people and their allies—past, present, and future—without whom my life and my book wouldn't have been possible. I only wish I could've included more of you herein.

That said, here's a partial list of the folks who helped shape the words and ideas on these pages. I'm beholden to my loyal, enthusiastic editors, Joanna Green and Catherine Tung, who took my raw concept and molded it into a narrative arc. Susan Lumenello and Rebekah Cotton made sure I didn't repeat myself too much, too much. I'm indebted to my devoted, passionate agent, Jennifer Lyons, to whom I owe nothing less than my entire authorial career—you've always believed in me, Jennifer, even back in high school! I owe much of this project to the many folks who aided and abetted its completion, including my family of origin, for unflagging encouragement and financial support; Kim, the transcriber (and sometimes researcher); Janine, my late publicist; my many friends and colleagues who read early drafts; Judy and Joe, for their many referrals; and myriad others.

Finally, a great big heartfelt hug to M.L., Paula, and Miranda, for just being you.

NOTES

INTRODUCTION: TOO DEFIANT?

1. Email interview with Jillian Mercado, Dec. 2019.

2. Diana Pearl, "Aerie Continues Its 'Real' Streak, Casting Models with Illnesses and Disabilities," *Adweek*, July 12, 2018.

3. Mary Hanbury, "These Photos Reveal Why Women Are Abandoning Victoria's Secret for American Eagle's Aerie Underwear Brand," *Business Insider*, July 20, 2018.

4. Interview with Aaron Rose Philip, Feb. 2020.

5. Michael Paulson, "Ali Stroker on Winning the Tony: 'I Was Meant to Be in This Seat,'" *New York Times*, June 12, 2019.

6. Jessica Moulite, "Exclusive: Rep. Ayanna Pressley Reveals Beautiful Bald Head and Discusses Alopecia for the First Time," *The Root*, Jan. 16, 2020, https://www.the root.com/exclusive-rep-ayanna-pressley-reveals-beautiful-bald-1841039847.

7. Rep. Ayanna Pressley and Rebecca Cokley, "There Is No Justice That Neglects Disability," *Stanford Social Innovation Review* (Winter 2022), https://ssir.org/articles /entry/there_is_no_justice_that_neglects_disability#.

8. "Official Trailer: Rollin' with Zach," http://www.oprah.com/ own-rollin-with-zach/official-trailer-rollin-with-zach, accessed Nov. 19, 2021.

9. Bridget LeRoy, "Serge Kovaleski: A Reporter Reflects," *Independent*, Aug. 29, 2018, https://indyeastend.com/news-opinion/features/serge-kovaleski-a-reporter -reflects.

10. Christina Samuels, "Special Education Bias Rule Put on Hold for Two Years by DeVos Team," *On Special Education*, June 29, 2018, https://blogs.edweek.org /edweek/speced/2018/06/special_education_bias_rule_postponed.html.

11. Tom Ridge, "Trump's Budget Is Full of Cuts Aimed at People With Disabilities," *New York Times*, Apr. 17, 2019, https://www.nytimes.com/2019/04/17/opinion /disability-budget-cuts-trump.html.

12. For information on SMA, see the "Spinal Muscular Atrophy Fact Sheet," National Institutes of Health, last modified Nov. 15, 2021, https://www.ninds.nih.gov /Disorders/Patient-Caregiver-Education/Fact-Sheets/Spinal-Muscular-Atrophy -Fact-Sheet.

13. Hanne Marie Bøe Lunde et al., "Survival and Cause of Death in Multiple Sclerosis," *Journal of Neurology, Neurosurgery & Psychiatry* 88, no. 8 (June 2017): 621–25, https://jnnp.bmj.com/content/88/8/621.

14. "'World's Smallest' Surviving Premature Baby Released from US Hospital," BBC News, May 30, 2019, https://www.bbc.com/news/world-us-canada-48458780.

15. "United Nations and Disability," United Nations, https://www.un.org /disabilities/documents/historyinfographic.pdf, accessed Nov. 19, 2021.

16. Joseph P. Shapiro, *No Pity: People with Disabilities Forging a New Civil Rights Movement* (New York: Three Rivers Press, 1993), 4.

17. Interview with Judith Heumann, Feb. 2020.

CHAPTER I: CREATING RIGHTS

1. Rebecca Cokley, "Reflections from an ADA Generation," TEDx Talks, July 25, 2018, https://www.youtube.com/watch?v=nmDk6ZE3npY.

2. Cokley, "Reflections from an ADA Generation."

3. Some D/deaf people make a distinction between "deaf" in lower case, which describes an audiological condition, and "Deaf" in upper case, which describes those who share a cultural identity and for whom sign language is a first language. To avoid offense, this book uses both.

4. Interview with Joe Shapiro, Jan. 2020.

5. Kim E. Nielsen, *A Disability History of the United States* (Boston: Beacon Press, 2012).

6. Natasha Frost, "Quarantined for Life: The Tragic History of US Leprosy Colonies," History.com, Mar. 31, 2020, https://www.history.com/news/leprosy-colonies -us-quarantine.

7. Jose P. Ramirez Jr., *Squint: My Journey with Leprosy* (Jackson: University Press of Mississippi, 2009).

8. Rigoberto Hernandez, "Bonus Episode: Interview with Kim Nielsen," *Distillations*, Aug. 13, 2020, https://www.sciencehistory.org/distillations/podcast/bonus -episode-interview-with-kim-nielsen.

9. See "30 Facts About Harriet 'Moses' Tubman," Black History Studies, https:// blackhistorystudies.com/resources/resources/facts-about-harriet-tubman, accessed Jan. 6, 2022.

10. See "Sojourner Truth Was a Disabled Social Justice Activist," *Intersected Disability* (blog), Feb. 1, 2019, http://intersecteddisability.blogspot.com/2019/02 /sojourner-truth-was-disabled-disability.html.

11. Eliza Suggs, *Shadow and Sunshine* (Chapel Hill: University of North Carolina Press, 1906), https://docsouth.unc.edu/neh/suggs/suggs.html.

12. Vann R. Newkirk II, "A Generation of Bad Blood," *Atlantic*, June 17, 2016, https://www.theatlantic.com/politics/archive/2016/06/tuskegee-study-medical -distrust-research/487439.

13. Terence McArdle, "The Veterans Were Desperate. Gen. MacArthur Ordered U.S. Troops to Attack Them," *Washington Post*, July 28, 2017.

14. McArdle, "The Veterans Were Desperate."

15. See "ADA 30," NYC Mayor's Office for People with Disabilities, https:// www1.nyc.gov/site/mopd/events/our-history.page?slide=4, accessed Nov. 19, 2021.

16. Paul K. Longmore and David Goldberger, "The League of the Physically Handicapped and the Great Depression: A Case Study in the New Disability History," *Journal of American History* 87, no. 3 (Dec. 2000): 888–922, https://doi.org /10.2307/2675276.

17. Mary Bellis, "History of the Wheelchair," ThoughtCo., July 2, 2019, https://www.thoughtco.com/history-of-the-wheelchair-1992670.

18. "What Was the First Electric Wheelchair?," Karman, Oct. 22, 2018, https://www.karmanhealthcare.com/what-was-the-first-electric-wheelchair.

19. Young Minds Advocacy, https://www.ymadvocacy.org/the-community-mental-health-act-of-1963, accessed Nov. 19, 2021.

20. *Public Papers of the Presidents of the United States: John F. Kennedy*, 1963, p. 137, available at https://www.govinfo.gov/app/details/PPP-1963-book1, accessed Mar. 6, 2022.

21. Talila "T.L." Lewis, "Ableism 2020: An Updated Definition" (a blog post), dated Jan. 25, 2020, https://www.talilalewis.com/blog, accessed Nov. 19, 2021.

22. Eileen AJ Connelly, "Overlooked No More: Brad Lomax, a Bridge between Civil Rights Movements," *New York Times*, July 8, 2020, https://www.nytimes.com/2020/07/08/obituaries/brad-lomax-overlooked.html.

23. "Director, Community Resources for Independent Living: Oral History Transcript: An African-American Woman's Perspective on the Independent Living Movement in the Bay Area, 1960s–1980s / Johnnie Lacy," Online Archive of California, https://oac.cdlib.org/view?docId=hb8x0nb6d8&brand=oac4&chunk.id=meta, accessed February 26, 2022.

24. Vilissa Thompson, "Johnnie Lacy, Defiantly Black & Disabled," *Ramp Your Voice!*, Feb. 10, 2017, http://www.rampyourvoice.com/black-history-month-2017-johnnie-lacy-defiantly-black-disabled.

25. Robert L. Burgdorf Jr., "Why I Wrote the Americans with Disabilities Act," *Washington Post*, July 24, 2015, https://www.washingtonpost.com/posteverything/wp/2015/07/24/why-the-americans-with-disabilities-act-mattered.

26. Mills v. Board of Education of District of Columbia. See Justia US Law, https://law.justia.com/cases/federal/district-courts/FSupp/348/866/2010674/, accessed Nov. 19, 2021.

27. Pennsylvania Association for Retarded Citizens (PARC) v. Commonwealth of Pennsylvania. See the Public Interest Law Center, https://www.pubintlaw.org/cases-and-projects/pennsylvania-association-for-retarded-citizens-parc-v-commonwealth-of-pennsylvania, accessed Nov. 19, 2021.

28. Public Law 94-142, Nov. 29, 1975, https://www.govinfo.gov/content/pkg/STATUTE-89/pdf/STATUTE-89-Pg773.pdf, accessed Nov. 19, 2021.

29. Andrew Grim, "Sitting-in for Disability Rights: The Section 504 Protests of the 1970s," National Museum of American History, July 8, 2015, https://americanhistory.si.edu/blog/sitting-disability-rights-section-504-protests-1970s.

30. "Dennis Billups," Disability Changemakers, https://disabilitychangemakers.org/dennis-billups, accessed Nov. 19, 2021.

31. "Lynette Taylor on Her Experience as an Interpreter at the Section 504 Protests," Paul K. Longmore Institute on Disability, https://diva.sfsu.edu/collections/longmoreinstitute/bundles/231044, accessed Nov. 19, 2021.

32. "Joe Quinn on his Experience at the 504 Sit-In as a Deaf Interpreter and Protester," Paul K. Longmore Institute on Disability, https://diva.sfsu.edu/collections/longmoreinstitute/bundles/230603, accessed Nov. 19, 2021.

33. *Drunk History*, season 5, episode 5, "Civil Rights," aired Feb. 20, 2018, on Comedy Central; Kitty Cone, "Short History of the 504 Sit-In," Disability Rights

Education & Defense Fund, https://dredf.org/504-sit-in-20th-anniversary/short -history-of-the-504-sit-in, accessed Nov. 19, 2021.

34. "The History of the Independent Living Movement," Northeast Independent Living Program, https://www.nilp.org/history-of-independent-living-movement, accessed Nov. 19, 2021.

35. National Council on Disability, https://ncd.gov/about, accessed Nov. 19, 2021.

36. Brenda Jo Brueggemann, "The Coming out of Deaf Culture and American Sign Language: An Exploration into Visual Rhetoric and Literacy," *Rhetoric Review* 13, no. 2 (Spring 1995): 409–20.

37. Myrtle R. Walgreen and Margueritte Harmon Bro, *Never a Dull Day: An Autobiography* (Chicago: Henry Regnery, 1963), 313–14.

38. Richard W. Stevenson, "Justin Dart Jr., 71, Advocate for Rights of Disabled People," *New York Times*, June 24, 2002, https://www.nytimes.com/2002/06/24/us /justin-dart-jr-71-advocate-for-rights-of-disabled-people.html.

39. Arlene Mayerson, "The History of the Americans with Disabilities Act: A Movement Perspective," Disability Rights Education & Defense Fund, 1992, https:// dredf.org/about-us/publications/the-history-of-the-ada.

40. William J. Eaton, "Disabled Persons Rally, Crawl Up Capitol Steps," *Los Angeles Times*, Mar. 13, 1990, https://www.latimes.com/archives/la-xpm-1990 -03-13-mn-211-story.html.

41. Becky Little, "When the 'Capitol Crawl' Dramatized the Need for Americans with Disabilities Act," History Channel, July 24, 2020, https://www.history .com/news/americans-with-disabilities-act-1990-capitol-crawl.

42. Lennard Davis, *Enabling Acts: The Hidden Story of How the Americans with Disabilities Act Gave the Largest US Minority Its Rights* (Boston: Beacon Press, 2015), 192.

CHAPTER 2: SUCCESSES, DISAPPOINTMENTS, AND SHORTCOMINGS

1. "A Law for Every American," *New York Times*, July 27, 1990, https://www.ny times.com/1990/07/27/opinion/a-law-for-every-american.html.

2. Doris Zames Fleischer and Frieda Zames, "Disability Rights: The Overlooked Civil Rights Issue," *Disability Studies Quarterly* 25, no. 4 (Fall 2005), https://dsq-sds .org/article/view/629/806.

3. Introduction to the ADA, ADA.gov, https://www.ada.gov/ada_intro.htm, accessed Nov. 19, 2021.

4. "What Is Considered an 'Undue Hardship' for a Reasonable Accommodation?," ADA National Network, updated Feb. 2022, https://ADAta.org/faq/what -considered-undue-hardship-reasonable-accommodation.

5. See "The ADA and the End to Sheltered Workshops," Disability Employment TA Center, https://aoddisabilityemploymenttacenter.com/the-ada-and-the-end-to -sheltered-workshops, accessed Jan. 6, 2022.

6. "Charge Statistics (Charges Filed with EEOC) FY 1997 through FY 2020," US Equal Employment Opportunity Commission, https://www.eeoc.gov/statistics/charge -statistics-charges-filed-eeoc-fy-1997-through-fy-2019, accessed Nov. 19, 2021.

7. Heather Cobun, "EEOC Alleges Woman Was Fired Due to High-Risk Pregnancy," *Daily Record*, Sept. 19, 2019, https://thedailyrecord.com/2019/09/19/eeoc -doodycalls-pregnancy-discrimination.

8. "DoodyCalls Will Pay $40,000 to Settle EEOC Pregnancy and Disability Discrimination Suit," press release, US Equal Employment Opportunity Commission, Dec. 14, 2020, https://www.eeoc.gov/newsroom/doodycalls-will-pay-40000-settle-eeoc-pregnancy-and-disability-discrimination-suit.

9. Jeanmarie Evelly, "In Settlement Win for Disabled NYers, City Agrees to Fix Inaccessible Sidewalks," *City Limits*, July 24, 2019, https://citylimits.org/2019/07/24/nyc-sidewalks-accessibilty-disabled-settlement.

10. Dana Rubinstein, "New York City Makes a $1.55B, 500-person Commitment to Accessible Street Corners," *Politico*, July 23, 2019, https://www.politico.com/states/new-york/city-hall/story/2019/07/23/new-york-city-makes-a-155b-500-person-commitment-to-accessible-street-corners-1117253.

11. Mark Hallum, "'Burdens of Discovery' Bog Down NYC Subway Accessibility Lawsuit," *AM New York*, Jan. 28, 2020, https://www.amny.com/transit/burdens-of-discovery-bog-down-nyc-subway-accessibility-lawsuit.

12. Clayton Guse, "MTA Bypasses Americans with Disabilities Act in Planned Renovations to Queens Subway Stops," *New York Daily News*, Jan. 15, 2020, https://www.nydailynews.com/new-york/ny-mta-construction-no-7-line-subway-accessibility-elevators-20200115-7ykacmj4indedeyk2moncou5je-story.html.

13. Hallum, "'Burdens of Discovery' Bog Down NYC Subway Accessibility Lawsuit."

14. "Americans with Disabilities Act: Accessibility Standards," US Access Board, https://www.access-board.gov/ada, accessed Nov. 19, 2021.

15. "2010 ADA Standards for Accessible Design," US Department of Justice, Sept. 15, 2010, https://www.ada.gov/regs2010/2010ADAStandards/2010ADAstandards.htm.

16. "Americans with Disabilities Act: Insurance Coverage Considerations," Marsh & McClennan Cos., Aug. 2017, https://www.marsh.com/us/insights/research/americans-with-disabilities-act-insurance-coverage-considerations.html.

17. "Summary of the Air Carrier Access Act," WheelchairTravel.org, https://wheelchairtravel.org/air-travel/air-carrier-access-act-summary, accessed Nov. 19, 2021.

18. "Air Travel Consumer Reports," Office of Aviation Enforcement and Proceedings, US Department of Transportation, July 2019, https://www.transportation.gov/sites/dot.gov/files/docs/resources/individuals/aviation-consumer-protection/344411/july-2019-atcr.pdf, accessed Nov. 19, 2021.

19. John Morris, "Heartbreaking: Airline's Negligence Led to Wheelchair User's Death," WheelchairTravel.org, Nov. 5, 2021, https://wheelchairtravel.org/heartbreaking-airlines-negligence-led-to-wheelchair-users-death.

20. Lynn McDonough, "Service Animals at 30,000 Feet," *Regulatory Review*, Feb 9, 2021, https://www.theregreview.org/2021/02/09/mcdonough-service-animals-30000-feet.

21. Minh N. Vu, Kristina M. Launey, and Susan Ryan, "Number of ADA Title III Lawsuits Filed in 2018 Tops 10,000," *Seyfarth Shaw*, Jan. 22, 2019, https://www.ADAtitleiii.com/2019/01/number-of-ADA-title-iii-lawsuits-filed-in-2018-tops-10000.

22. Jack McElaney, "Domino's Pizza v. Guillermo Robles, No. 18-1539," *Digital Accessibility Digest*, June 28, 2021, https://www.microassist.com/digital-accessibility/dominos-pizza-guillermo-robles.

23. Tucker Higgins, "Supreme Court Hands Victory to Blind Man Who Sued Domino's Over Site Accessibility," MSNBC, updated Oct. 8, 2019, https://www.cnbc.com/2019/10/07/dominos-supreme-court.html.

24. Christopher Zara, "Disney Store Is the Latest Retailer Hit with an ADA Lawsuit over Braille Gift Cards," Fast Company, Nov. 1, 2019, https://www.fastcompany.com/90425629/disney-store-is-the-latest-retailer-hit-with-an-ADA-lawsuit-over-braille-gift-cards.

25. See "H.R. 620—ADA Education and Reform Act of 2017," Congress.gov, https://www.congress.gov/bill/115th-congress/house-bill/620, accessed Nov. 19, 2021.

26. See "CS/CS/CS/HB 727: Accessibility of Places of Public Accommodation," Florida Senate, https://www.flsenate.gov/Session/Bill/2017/00727/?Tab=BillHistory, accessed Nov. 19, 2021.

27. "Attorney General Laxalt Successfully Intervenes in Effort to Curb Abusive Litigation Practices That Take Advantage of Nevada's Small Businesses," State of Nevada, Oct. 13, 2017, https://ag.nv.gov/News/PR/2017/Attorney_General_Laxalt_Successfully_Intervenes_in_Effort_to_Curb_Abusive_Litigation_Practices_that_Take_Advantage_of_Nevada%E2%80%99s_Small_Businesses.

28. Jane Ann Morrison, "AG Intervenes in ADA Litigation 'To Protect the Public's Interest,'" *Las Vegas Review-Journal*, Nov. 8, 2017, https://www.reviewjournal.com/news/news-columns/jane-ann-morrison/ag-intervenes-in-ada-litigation-to-protect-the-publics-interest; *Zimmerman v. Home Depot USA*, CaseText.com, Nov. 13, 2017, https://casetext.com/case/zimmerman-v-home-depot-united-statesa-inc-1.

29. Sutton v. United Air Lines, Inc. (97-1943) 527 U.S. 471 (1999) 130 F.3d 893, affirmed, Legal Information Institute, https://www.law.cornell.edu/supct/html/97-1943.ZO.html, accessed Nov. 19, 2021.

30. Toyota Motor Mfg., Ky., Inc. v. Williams, 534 U.S. 184 (2002), US Supreme Court, https://supreme.justia.com/cases/federal/us/534/184, accessed Nov. 19, 2021.

31. See "ADA Amendments Act of 2008, PL 110-325 (S 3406)," US Equal Employment Opportunity Commission, Sept. 25, 2008, https://www.eeoc.gov/statutes/ada-amendments-act-2008.

32. "Remarks by the President on 20th Anniversary of the Americans with Disabilities Act," White House press release, July 26, 2010, https://obamawhitehouse.archives.gov/the-press-office/remarks-president-20th-anniversary-americans-with-disabilities-act.

33. "The Olmstead Supreme Court Decision in a Nutshell," OlmsteadRights.org, https://bit.ly/3oOfit2, accessed Nov. 19, 2021.

34. "About *Olmstead*," US Department of Justice, Civil Rights Division, https://www.ada.gov/olmstead/olmstead_about.htm, accessed Nov. 19, 2021.

35. Executive Order: Community-Based Alternatives for Individuals With Disabilities, George W. Bush, White House, June 18, 2001, http://www.accessiblesociety.org/topics/programs-policy/olmsteadexecordertext.htm.

36. "What Is the Disability Integration Act?," http://www.disabilityintegrationact.org, accessed Nov. 19, 2021.

37. S.117—Disability Integration Act of 2019, Congress.gov, https://bit.ly/3x50fil, accessed Nov. 19, 2021.

38. Persons with a Disability: Labor Force Characteristics Summary, US Bureau of Labor Statistics, Feb. 24, 2021, https://www.bls.gov/news.release/disabl.nr0.htm.

39. Karina Hernandez, "People with Disabilities Are Still Struggling to Find Employment—Here Are the Obstacles They Face," CNBC, Mar. 3, 2020, https:// www.cnbc.com/2020/03/02/unemployment-rate-among-people-with-disabilities -is-still-high.html.

40. Molly Taft, "Why Can't Uber and Lyft Be More Wheelchair-Friendly?" *Bloomberg CityLab*, Dec. 11, 2018, https://www.bloomberg.com/news/articles /2018-12-11/uber-promises-to-ramp-up-access-for-wheelchair-users.

41. Taft, "Why Can't Uber and Lyft Be More Wheelchair-Friendly?"

42. See Drake v. Salt River Pima-Maricopa Indian Cmty., https://casetext.com /case/drake-v-salt-river-pima-maricopa-indian-cmty, accessed Nov. 19, 2021.

43. "Understanding Supplemental Security Income SSI Income—2021 Edition," Social Security Administration (hereafter SSA), https://www.ssa.gov/ssi/text -income-ussi.htm, accessed Mar. 7, 2022.

44. "A Guide to Supplemental Security Income (SSI) for Groups and Organizations," SSA, Jan. 2022, p. 9, https://www.ssa.gov/pubs/EN-05-11015.pdf.

45. "Why Are Resources Important in the SSI Program?" Social Security: Spotlight on Resources—2021 Edition, SSA, https://www.ssa.gov/ssi/spotlights/spot -resources.htm, accessed Mar. 7, 2022.

46. *Working While Disabled: How We Can Help*, SSA, Jan. 2022, p. 5, https:// www.ssa.gov/pubs/EN-05-10095.pdf.

47. "Adults with a Disability that Began Before Age 22," Disability Benefits: How You Qualify, SSA, https://www.ssa.gov/benefits/disability/qualify.html, accessed Mar. 7, 2022.

48. Marti Hause and Ari Melber, "Half of People Killed by Police Have a Disability: Report," NBCNews.com, Mar. 14, 2016, https://www.nbcnews.com/news /us-news/half-people-killed-police-suffer-mental-disability-report-n538371.

CHAPTER 3: WHAT IS PRIDE—AND WHY DOES IT MATTER?

1. Deborah Marks, *Disability: Controversial Debates and Psychosocial Perspectives* (London: Routledge, 1999), 25.

2. "Ableism and Internalized Ableism," *Disability Rights Bastard* (blog), Apr. 23, 2013, https://disabilityrightsbastard.wordpress.com/2013/04/23/ableism-and -internalized-ableism.

3. Imani Barbarin, "7 Lying Thoughts That Prove Internalized Ableism Is Real," *Crutches and Spice* (blog), Oct. 6, 2017, https://crutchesandspice.com/2017/10/06 /7-lying-thoughts-that-prove-internalized-ableism-is-real.

4. Shane Burcaw, "I Was Ashamed of My Body," *Squirmy & Grubs* (vlog), Jan. 23, 2021, https://www.youtube.com/watch?v=SNO8v-Gt4HQ.

5. Nadina LaSpina, *Such a Pretty Girl: A Story of Struggle, Empowerment, and Disability Pride* (New York: New Village Press, July 2019), 207.

6. "1993 Disability Pride March in NYC," https://www.youtube.com/watch?v =M7OcgdnZejs, accessed Feb. 26, 2022.

7. "NYC's Inaugural Disability Pride Parade Draws Thousands," *New York Post*, July 12, 2015, https://nypost.com/2015/07/12/inaugural-disability-pride-parade -draws-thousands.

8. Disability Pride NYC, http://disabilitypridenyc.org/our-sponsors, accessed Nov. 19, 2021.

9. "July Is 'Disability Pride Month' in New York," Services for the Underserved, https://sus.org/july-is-disability-pride-month-in-new-york, accessed Nov. 19, 2021.

10. Mary Johnson, "Pride & Identity," *Electric Edge*, Mar./Apr. 1998, http://www.raggededgemagazine.com/mar98/pride.htm.

11. "Ed Roberts: Free Wheeling," documentary, Jan. 20, 2012, https://www.youtube.com/watch?v=ci3ek-tqiGQ.

12. Laura Hershey, "You Get Proud by Practicing," The Nth Degree, http://www.thenthdegree.com/proudpoem.asp, accessed Jan. 6, 2022.

13. Eli Clare, "Shame and Pride," in *Brilliant Imperfection: Grappling with Cure* (Durham, NC: Duke University Press, 2017), 103.

14. Interview with Emily Ladau, Jan. 2020.

15. Jennifer Natalya Fink, *All Our Families: Disability Lineage and the Future of Kinship* (Boston: Beacon Press, 2022), 6.

16. Email interview with Beth Haller, Jan. 2020.

17. Joseph Shapiro, "Disability Pride: The High Expectations of a New Generation," *New York Times*, July 17, 2020, https://www.nytimes.com/2020/07/17/style/americans-with-disabilities-act.html.

18. "Data and Statistics about ADHD," US Centers for Disease Control and Prevention, last reviewed Sept. 23, 2021, https://www.cdc.gov/ncbddd/adhd/data.html.

19. Benjamin Zablotsky and Josephine M. Alford, NCHS Data Brief, no. 358, Mar. 2020, https://www.cdc.gov/nchs/data/databriefs/db358-h.pdf.

20. See Attention-Deficit/Hyperactivity Disorder (ADHD), National Institute of Mental Health, https://www.nimh.nih.gov/health/statistics/attention-deficit-hyperactivity-disorder-adhd.shtml, accessed Nov. 20, 2021.

21. Ericka Polanco-Webb, "Should You Use Special Needs or Disabilities?" *Chicago Parent*, Nov. 2, 2020, https://www.chicagoparent.com/parenting/special-needs/special-needs-vs-disability.

22. Jamie Davis Smith, "My Daughter Doesn't Have 'Special' Needs. She's Disabled," *Washington Post*, Sept. 28, 2017, https://www.washingtonpost.com/news/parenting/wp/2017/09/28/my-daughter-doesnt-have-special-needs-shes-disabled.

23. Lisa Lightner, "Special Needs vs Disabled? The 'New' Term to Say Instead of Special Needs," *A Day in Our Shoes* (blog), June 19, 2020, https://adayinourshoes.com/disabled-instead-of-special-needs.

24. Andrew Pulrang, "Words Matter, and It's Time to Explore the Meaning of 'Ableism,'" *Forbes*, Oct. 25, 2020. https://www.forbes.com/sites/andrewpulrang/2020/10/25/words-matter-and-its-time-to-explore-the-meaning-of-ableism.

25. Talila A. Lewis, "January 2021: Working Definition of Ableism," Jan. 1, 2021, www.TalilaLewis.com/blog.

26. Eli Clare, *Brilliant Imperfection*, xvi.

27. Fink, *All Our Families*, xi.

28. Meghan Mutchler, "Roosevelt's Disability an Issue at Memorial," *New York Times*, Apr. 10, 1995.

29. See Hugh Gregory Gallagher, *FDR's Splendid Deception: The Moving Story of Roosevelt's Massive Disability—and the Intense Efforts to Conceal It from the Public* (New York: Dodd, Mead, 1985).

30. C. Todd Stephenson, "Depicting Disability: The Franklin Delano Roosevelt Memorial in Washington, D.C.," National Council for the Social Studies, http:// www.socialstudies.org/sites/default/files/publications/se/6005/600512.html, accessed Nov. 20, 2021.

31. Charles Krauthammer, "FDR in a Wheelchair? No," *Washington Post*, June 14, 1996, https://www.washingtonpost.com/archive/opinions/1996/06/14/fdr-in -a-wheelchair-no/dc7aa3a9-2c20-43ad-89cd-da59b0016f09.

32. Carl Weiser, "Activists for Disabled Upset by FDR Memorial," *Tulsa World*, May 26, 1996, https://www.tulsaworld.com/archive/activists-for-disabled-upset-by -fdr-memorial/article_be792b3b-2d09-5cb8-a2b9-1623efd05d77.html.

33. Hugh Sidey, "Truth in Memory: Omission of F.D.R.'s Handicap Is a Crime against His Spirit," *Time*, May 20, 1996, http://content.time.com/time/subscriber /article/0,33009,984585-2,00.html.

34. Destination DC, https://washington.org/research/washington-dc-visitor -research, accessed Mar. 8, 2022.

35. Theresa Vargas, "A Disabled President's Memorial Still Isn't Fully Accessible to Disabled Visitors, a New Report Finds," *Washington Post*, May 19, 2021, https:// www.washingtonpost.com/local/fdr-memorial-braille-unreadable/2021/05/19 /530030fe-b8d7-11eb-a5fe-bb49dc89a248_story.html.

36. Gerard Goggin and Christopher Newell, "Fame and Disability: Christopher Reeve, Super Crips, and Infamous Celebrity," *M/C Journal* 7, no. 5 (Nov. 2004), https://doi.org/10.5204/mcj.2404.

CHAPTER 4: DISABILITY STUDIES AND THE AFTERLIFE OF CULTURAL ICONS

1. Pamela Cushing and Tyler Smith, "A Multinational Review of English-Language Disability Studies Degrees and Courses," *Disability Studies Quarterly* 29, no. 3 (2009), https://dsq-sds.org/article/view/940.

2. "The Best Disability Studies Colleges of 2019," Universities.com, https://www .universities.com/programs/disability-studies-degrees, accessed Nov. 19, 2021.

3. Tammy Berberi and Pascale Antolin, "Tammy Berberi on Disability Studies," *Angles* 3 (2016), https://doi.org/10.4000/angles.1706.

4. "Mission and History," Society for Disability Studies, https://disstudies.org /index.php/about-sds/mission-and-history, accessed Nov. 26, 2021.

5. "Mission and History," Society for Disability Studies.

6. Michael Oliver, *The Politics of Disablement: A Sociological Approach* (London: Palgrave Macmillan, 1990).

7. Nancy E. Rice, *Encyclopedia Britannica*, s.v. "disability studies," Dec. 5, 2018, https://www.britannica.com/topic/disability-studies.

8. David Brindle, "Mike Oliver Obituary," *Guardian*, Mar. 19, 2019, https:// www.theguardian.com/society/2019/mar/19/mike-oliver-obituary.

9. Cecilia Capuzzi Simon, "Disability Studies: A New Normal," *New York Times*, Nov. 3, 2013.

10. Berberi and Antolin, "Tammy Berberi on Disability Studies."

11. Allegra Stout and Ariel Schwartz, "'It'll Grow Organically and Naturally': The Reciprocal Relationship Between Student Groups and Disability Studies on College Campuses," *Disability Studies Quarterly* 34, no. 2 (2014), https://dsq-sds .org/article/view/4253/3593.

12. Natasha A. Spassiani and Carli Friedman, "Stigma: Barriers to Culture and Identity for People with Intellectual Disability," *Inclusion* (Dec. 2014): 329–41, https://doi.org/10.1352/2326-6988-2.4.329.

13. Kathleen R. Bogart, Nicole M. Rosa, and Michael L. Slepian, "Born That Way or Became That Way: Stigma Toward Congenital Versus Acquired Disability," *Group Processes & Intergroup Relations*, Jan. 2018, http://www.columbia.edu /~ms4992/Pubs/2019_Bogart-Rosa-Slepian_GPIR.pdf.

14. J. Lorand Matory, *Stigma and Culture: Last-Place Anxiety in Black America* (Chicago: University of Chicago Press, 2015), 384.

15. Maria Lazarte, "Wheelchair Ride for Guerrilla Art," International Organization for Standardization, Nov. 29, 2013, https://www.iso.org/news/2013/11/Ref1803.html.

16. Brendan Murphy, "Symbol of Access for Mobility-Impaired People," 1994, http://static1.1.sqspcdn.com/static/f/149733/1836063/1219242077070/MA_ADA +Symbol.pdf?token=T2bINwwG50Mrim7jx2XPD67uDvw%3D.

17. Billy Baker, "Wheelchair Icon Revamped by Guerrilla Art Project," *Boston Globe*, Dec. 13, 2013, https://www.bostonglobe.com/metro/2013/12/13/disability -icon-revamped-guerilla-art-project/HZDJAIORZvL68dukN9L0TL/story.html.

18. Niraj Chokshi, "The Handicap Symbol Gets an Update—at Least in New York State," *Washington Post*, July 29, 2014, https://www.washingtonpost.com/blogs /govbeat/wp/2014/07/29/the-handicap-symbol-gets-an-update-at-least-in-new -york-state.

19. "Thoughts on the International Access Symbol," The Nth Degree, http:// www.thenthdegree.com/intacces.asp, accessed Mar. 20, 2022.

20. Harriet A. Washington, *Medical Apartheid: The Dark History of Medical Experimentation on Black Americans from Colonial Times to the Present* (New York: Doubleday, 2006), 86–92.

21. Mwatuangi, "Black Disability History, Vol. I: Reclaiming the Black Disabled Experience," *Medium*, Feb. 13, 2020, https://medium.com/afrosapiophile/black -disability-history-vol-i-reclaiming-the-history-of-the-black-disabled-experience -bd21f2a02656.

22. Clara Yang, "DWW: Thomas 'Blind Tom' Wiggins, Pianist," University of North Carolina, College of Arts and Sciences, Sept. 16, 2020, https://music.unc.edu /2020/09/16/dww-thomas-blind-tom-wiggins-pianist.

23. Jim Downs, "The Continuation of Slavery: The Experience of Disabled Slaves During Emancipation," *Disability Studies Quarterly* 28, no. 3 (Summer 2008), https://dsq-sds.org/article/view/112/112.

24. *Shaw University Bulletin*, 1962, https://archive.org/details/shawuniversity bualum1962/page/22/mode/2up.

25. Deborah Marks, *Disability: Controversial Debates and Psychosocial Perspectives* (London: Routledge, 1999), 35.

26. Haben Girma, "Opinion: Hey, Texas, Students Need to Learn about Helen Keller. Don't Remove Her," *Washington Post*, Sept. 19, 2018, https://wapo.st/30J4mEE.

27. Chris Boyette and Madeline Holcombe, "In Reversal, Texas Board Votes to Teach Students about Helen Keller, Hillary Clinton," CNN, Nov. 14, 2018, https:// www.cnn.com/2018/11/14/us/texas-curriculum-hillary-clinton-helen-keller-trnd /index.html.

28. Interview with Emily Ladau, January 2020.

CHAPTER 5: NEURODIVERSITY AND AUTISTIC SELF-ADVOCACY

1. Anita Cameron, "Why Are Black Disabled Activists Being Ignored or Forgotten?," Geek Club Books, Jan. 27, 2021, https://geekclubbooks.com/why-are-black-disabled-activists-being-ignored-or-forgotten.

2. Interview with Lydia X. Z. Brown, Mar. 2020.

3. See Marianthi Kourti, "All the Weight of)ur Dreams: On Living Racialised Autism," *Disability & Society* 33, no. 7 (May 20, 2018), https://www.tandfonline.com/doi/full/10.1080/09687599.2018.1471811.

4. Interview with Brown.

5. Interview with Brown.

6. See "Autistic People of Color Fund," Autism and Race, last updated Dec. 2020, https://autismandrace.com/autistic-people-of-color-fund.

7. Interview with Steve Silberman, Feb. 2020.

8. Harvey Blume, "Neurodiversity: On the Neurological Underpinnings of Geekdom," *Atlantic*, Sept. 1998, https://www.theatlantic.com/magazine/archive/1998/09/neurodiversity/305909.

9. See Kassiane Alexandra Sibley, "PSA from the Actual Coiner of 'Neurodivergent," *Sherlock's Flat Affect* (blog), accessed Jan. 7, 2022, https://sherlocksflataffect.tumblr.com/post/121295972384/psa-from-the-actual-coiner-of-neurodivergent.

10. Lina Zeldovich, "How History Forgot the Woman Who Defined Autism," *Scientific American*, Nov. 10, 2018, https://www.scientificamerican.com/article/how-history-forgot-the-woman-who-defined-autism.

11. Zeldovich, "How History Forgot the Woman."

12. See "'Autistic Disturbances of Affective Contact' (1943), by Leo Kanner," Embryo Project Encyclopedia, May 23, 2014, https://embryo.asu.edu/pages/autistic-disturbances-affective-contact-1943-leo-kanner.

13. Clara Claiborne Park, *The Siege: The First Eight Years of an Autistic Child* (New York: Little Brown, 1967).

14. Richard Pollak, *The Creation of Dr. B: A Biography of Bruno Bettelheim* (New York: Simon & Schuster, 1997).

15. Hans Asperger, "'Autistic Psychopathy' in Childhood," in *Autism and Asperger Syndrome*, ed. and trans. Uta Frith (Cambridge: Cambridge University Press, 1992), 37–92, https://cpb-us-e1.wpmucdn.com/blogs.uoregon.edu/dist/d/16656/files/2018/11/Asperger-Autistic-Psychopathy-in-Childhood-2h51vw4.pdf.

16. Edith Sheffer, *Asperger's Children: The Origins of Autism in Nazi Vienna* (New York: W. W. Norton, 2018).

17. See "Autism Spectrum Disorder (ASD)," Centers for Disease Control and Prevention, last reviewed Dec. 21, 2021, https://www.cdc.gov/ncbddd/autism/data.html.

18. Jim Sinclair, "Self-Introduction to the Intersex Society of North America," 1997, https://web.archive.org/web/20090207013228/http:/web.syr.edu:80/~jisincla/brief_bio.htm.

19. Charlotte Brownlow, "Representations of Autism: Implications for Community Healthcare Practice," *Community Practitioner*, July 1, 2009, https://web.archive.org/web/20160505152712/https://www.highbeam.com/doc/1P3-1777521561.html.

20. See Vanessa Blanchard, "10 Autistic Phrases Explained," *Spectroomz* (blog), July 22 (no year given), https://www.spectroomz.com/blog/allistic-definition, accessed Jan. 7, 2022.

21. Jim Sinclair, "Don't Mourn for Us," Autism Network International's newsletter, *Our Voice* 1, no. 3 (1993), http://www.autreat.com/dont_mourn.html.

22. Amy Sequenzia, "Intelligence Is an Ableist Concept," *Ollibean* (blog), Jan. 27, 2018, https://ollibean.com/intelligence-is-an-ableist-concept.

23. See "About Me: Hari as Possibility," *Uniquely Hari* (blog), https://uniquely hari.blogspot.com/p/about-me.html, accessed Jan. 7, 2022.

24. Interview with Ari Ne'eman, May 2020.

25. Norman Davies, *Heart of Europe: The Past in Poland's Present* (Oxford: Oxford University Press, 1984).

26. James I. Charlton, *Nothing About Us Without Us: Disability Oppression and Empowerment* (Berkeley: University of California Press, 2000), 8.

27. AJ Wakefield et al., "RETRACTED: Ileal-Lymphoid-Nodular Hyperplasia, Non-Specific Colitis, and Pervasive Developmental Disorder in Children," *The Lancet*, Feb. 28, 1998, https://www.thelancet.com/journals/lancet/article/PIIS0140 -6736(97)11096-0/fulltext.

28. Laura Eggertson, "Lancet Retracts 12-Year-Old Article Linking Autism to MMR Vaccines," *Canadian Medical Association Journal* (Feb. 4, 2010), https://www .ncbi.nlm.nih.gov/pmc/articles/PMC2831678.

29. *Start Here: A Guide for Parents of Autistic Kids* (Washington, DC: Autistic Press, 2021), https://autisticadvocacy.org/wp-content/uploads/2021/04/booklet -interior-4.1.pdf.

30. See "The Basics," Autastic.com, https://www.autastic.com/category/the -basics, accessed Jan. 7, 2022.

31. See Haley Moss website, https://haleymoss.com.

32. Haley Moss, *The Young Autistic Adult's Independence Handbook* (London: Jessica Kingsley Publishers, 2021).

33. "ASAN Welcomes Ban of Electric Shock Torture," Autistic Self Advocacy Network, press release, Mar. 4, 2020, https://autisticadvocacy.org/2020/03/asan -welcomes-ban-of-electric-shock-torture.

34. Brendan Pierson, "D.C. Circuit Overturns FDA Ban on Shock Device for Disabled Students," Reuters, July 7, 2021, https://www.reuters.com/legal/litigation /dc-circuit-overturns-fda-ban-shock-device-disabled-students-2021-07-06.

35. "AWN Condemns Court Ruling Upholding Use of Electric Shock Torture," Autistic Women & Nonbinary Network, press release, July 7, 2021, https://awn network.org/awn-condemns-court-ruling-upholding-use-of-electric-shock-torture, accessed Nov. 20, 2021.

36. See the website of Dr. T. C. Waisman, https://adaptcoach.com, accessed Jan. 7, 2022.

37. See Autistic Strategies Network website, https://autisticstrategies.net, accessed Jan. 7, 2022.

38. See the website of the Autism Intervention Research Network on Physical Health, https://airpnetwork.ucla.edu, accessed Jan. 8, 2022.

39. See Juan Carlos Chavez, "Program in Tampa Addresses Autism in Spanish for Hispanic Families," *Tampa Bay Times*, Apr. 12, 2021, https://www.tampabay.com /news/health/2021/04/12/program-in-tampa-addresses-autism-in-spanish-for -hispanic-families.

40. Meghan Holohan, "'More Visibility Is Needed': Pennsylvania State Rep One of Few with Autism," Today.com, Jan. 15, 2021, https://www.today.com/health/pa -state-rep-jessica-benham-one-1st-politicians-autism-t205917.

41. See "IACC Member Biographies," Interagency Autism Coordinating Committee, https://iacc.hhs.gov/about-iacc/members/bios, accessed Jan. 8, 2022.

42. See "Diversity and Inclusion at SAP," corporate website, https://www.sap.com /corporate/en/company/diversity.html, accessed Nov. 20, 2021.

43. Robert D. Austin and Gary P. Pisano, "Neurodiversity as a Competitive Advantage: Why You Should Embrace It in Your Workforce," *Harvard Business Review* (May–June 2017), https://hbr.org/2017/05/neurodiversity-as-a-competitive -advantage.

44. Magda Mostafa, "An Architecture for Autism," *International Journal of Architectural Research* 2, no. 1 (March 2008), https://www.researchgate.net/publication /26503573_An_An_Architecture_for_Autism_Concepts_of_Design_Intervention _for_the_Autistic_User.

45. Email interview with Thomas Armstrong, Jan. 2020.

46. *In My Language*, dir. Amanda Baggs, posted on Interacting with Autism, http:// www.interactingwithautism.com/section/understanding/media/representations /details/12#:~:text=This%20extraordinary%20short%20film%20by,out%20of%20 their%20comfort%20zone, accessed Feb. 22, 2022.

CHAPTER 6: DISABILITY JUSTICE

1. Mia Mingus, "Access Intimacy: The Missing Link," *Leaving Evidence* (blog), May 5, 2011, https://leavingevidence.wordpress.com/2011/05/05/access-intimacy -the-missing-link.

2. "Disability Justice: Theory & Practice," a talk by Mia Mingus at the Society for Disability Studies' *Getting It Right* conference in Atlanta, Georgia, Oct. 28, 2015.

3. Molly Phillips-Nugent, "Access Is More Than Just Inclusion," *Forbes*, Jan. 17, 2019, https://www.forbes.com/sites/civicnation/2019/01/17/access-is-more-than -just-inclusion.

4. Erin E. Andrews et al., "#SaytheWord: A Disability Culture Commentary on the Erasure of 'Disability,'" *Rehabilitation Psychology* (May 2019): 111–18, https:// pubmed.ncbi.nlm.nih.gov/30762412.

5. Neil Genzlinger, "Stacey Milbern, 33, a Warrior in the Disability Justice Movement, Dies," *New York Times*, June 6, 2020, https://www.nytimes.com/2020 /06/06/us/stacey-milbern-dead.html.

6. Devin Katayama, "What Disability Justice Activist Stacey Park Milbern Taught Us," KQED, May 29, 2020, https://www.kqed.org/news/11821598/what -stacey-park-milbern-taught-us.

7. Patricia Berne, *Skin, Tooth, and Bone: The Basis of Movement Is Our People; a Disability Justice Primer* (San Francisco: Sins Invalid, 2016).

8. "10 Principles of Disability Justice," *Sins Invalid* (blog), Sept. 17, 2015, https:// www.sinsinvalid.org/blog/10-principles-of-disability-justice.

9. Leah Lakshmi Piepzna-Samarasinha, *Care Work: Dreaming Disability Justice* (Vancouver: Arsenal Pulp Press, 2018), 21–22.

10. Piepzna-Samarasinha, *Care Work*, 23.

11. Zoe Guy, "Activist Lydia X. Z. Brown on Disability Justice, Mutual Aid, and How Race and Disability Intersect," *Marie Claire*, Mar. 17, 2021, https://www .marieclaire.com/politics/a35866693/lydia-x-z-brown-interview-2021.

12. Interview with Brown.

13. David M. Perry and Lawrence Carter-Long, "Media Coverage of Law Enforcement Use of Force and Disability," Ruderman Foundation, Mar. 2016, https:// rudermanfoundation.org/wp-content/uploads/2017/08/MediaStudy-Police Disability_final-final.pdf.

14. See #DeafInPrison Campaign Fact Sheet, HEARD, https://behearddc.org /wp-content/uploads/2018/11/DeafInPrison-Fact-Sheet-.pdf, accessed Nov. 20, 2021.

15. Abigail Abrams, "Black, Disabled and at Risk: The Overlooked Problem of Police Violence Against Americans with Disabilities," *Time*, July 6, 2020, https:// time.com/5857438/police-violence-black-disabled.

16. Lydia X. Z. Brown, "Rebel—Don't Be Palatable: Resisting Co-Optation and Fighting for the World We Want," in *Resistance and Hope: Essays by Disabled People*, ed. Alice Wong (San Francisco: Disability Visibility Project, 2018).

17. Interview with Brown.

18. Dan Merica, "Clinton Ignores Trump, Delivers Speech on Helping Disabled," CNN, Sept. 21, 2016, https://www.cnn.com/2016/09/21/politics/hillary -clinton-economy-disabled.

19. "RespectAbility Receives Ford Foundation Grant to Create Paid Fellowships," Open Minds Industry Bulletin, Dec. 28, 2016, https://openminds.com /market-intelligence/bulletins/respectability-ford-foundation-grant.

20. See "#ProtectHarriet: The Harriet Tubman Collective's Response to Respect- Ability's Racism & Ford Foundation Enabling the Same," Harriet Tubman Collective, Jan. 19, 2017, https://harriettubmancollective.tumblr.com/post/156079791938/protect harriet, accessed Nov. 20, 2021.

21. Perry and Carter-Long, "Media Coverage of Law Enforcement Use of Force and Disability."

22. Lydia X. Z. Brown, Leroy Moore, and Talila Lewis, "Accountable Reporting on Disability, Race, and Police Violence: Community Response to the 'Ruderman White Paper on the Media Coverage of Use of Force And Disability,'" Harriet Tubman Collective, https://harriettubmancollective-blog.tumblr.com /post/174479075753/accountable-reporting-on-disability-race-and/amp, accessed Nov. 20, 2021.

23. David Carter, *Stonewall: The Riots That Sparked the Gay Revolution* (New York: St. Martin's Griffin, 2004).

24. J. M. Ellison, "4 Activists Who Make Me Proud to Be Disabled and Transgender," *Rooted in Rights* (blog), June 14, 2018, https://rootedinrights.org/4-activists -who-make-me-proud-to-be-disabled-and-transgender.

25. Sewell Chan, "Overlooked: Marsha P. Johnson," *New York Times*, Mar. 8, 2018, https://www.nytimes.com/interactive/2018/obituaries/overlooked-marsha -p-johnson.html.

26. Wyatt Buchanan, "Jazzie Collins, S.F. Transgender Activist, Dies," SFGate.com, July 13, 2013, https://www.sfgate.com/bayarea/article/Jazzie-Collins-S-F-transgender-activist-dies-4663968.php.

27. Emily Green, "Groundbreaking Shelter for LGBT Homeless Opening in the Mission," *San Francisco Chronicle*, June 16, 2016, https://www.sfchronicle.com/bayarea/article/Groundbreaking-shelter-for-LGBT-homeless-opening-6331449.php.

28. Kimberlé Crenshaw, "Demarginalizing the Intersection of Race and Sex: A Black Feminist Critique of Antidiscrimination Doctrine, Feminist Theory and Antiracist Politics," *University of Chicago Legal Forum* 1989, no. 1, article 8, http://chicagounbound.uchicago.edu/uclf/vol1989/iss1/8, accessed Mar. 8, 2022.

29. See "The Heumann Perspective: Keri Gray," June 1, 2017, https://www.youtube.com/watch?v=gMKfRojET4c.

30. Keri Gray Group, "Melanin + Curves + Scars," accessed Jan. 31, 2022, https://withkeri.com/category/melanin-curves-scars.

31. Jaimee A. Swift, "Loving Your Black Disabled Womanhood as Radical Praxis," *Black Women Radicals* (blog), Dec. 2019, https://www.blackwomenradicals.com/blog-feed/loving-your-black-disabled-womanhood-as-radical-praxis-keri-gray-on-self-acceptance-visibility-and-the-politics-of-being-unapologetic.

32. See "Adults with Disabilities: Ethnicity and Race," US Centers for Disease Control and Prevention, last reviewed Sept. 16, 2020, https://www.cdc.gov/ncbddd/disabilityandhealth/materials/infographic-disabilities-ethnicity-race.html.

33. Rebecca Vallas and Shawn Fremstad, "Disability Is a Cause and Consequence of Poverty," Center for American Progress, Sept. 19, 2014, https://talkpoverty.org/2014/09/19/disability-cause-consequence-poverty.

34. Interview with Katherine (Kat) Pérez, Jan. 2020.

35. Interview with Sachin Pavithran, Jan. 2020.

36. Nomy Lamm, "This Is Disability Justice," *This Body Is Not an Apology* (blog), Sept. 2, 2015, https://thebodyisnotanapology.com/magazine/this-is-disability-justice.

CHAPTER 7: VISIBILITY, COMMUNITY, AND CONTEXT

1. Alice Wong, "My Medicaid, My Life" *New York Times*, May 3, 2017, https://www.nytimes.com/2017/05/03/opinion/my-medicaid-my-life.html.

2. Wong, "My Medicaid, My Life."

3. White House, "President Obama Greets Alice Wong via Robot," press release, July 20, 2015, https://obamawhitehouse.archives.gov/photos-and-video/photo/2015/07/president-obama-greets-alice-wong-robot.

4. Mahita Gajanan, "These 16 People and Groups Are Fighting for a More Equal America: Alice Wong," *Time*, Feb. 20, 2020, https://time.com/5783951/equality-activists.

5. Wong, "My Medicaid, My Life."

6. Andrew Perrin and Sara Atske, "Americans with Disabilities Less Likely Than Those Without to Own Some Digital Devices," Pew Research Center, Sept. 10, 2021, https://www.pewresearch.org/fact-tank/2021/09/10/americans-with-disabilities-less-likely-than-those-without-to-own-some-digital-devices.

7. Shawn Fremstad, "Half in Ten: Why Taking Disability into Account Is Essential to Reducing Income Poverty and Expanding Economic Inclusion," Center for

Economic and Policy Research, Sept. 2009, https://www.cepr.net/documents
/publications/poverty-disability-2009-09.pdf.

8. s. e. smith, "Why Aren't More Disabled People Online?," *Rooted in Rights*,
July 5, 2017, https://rootedinrights.org/why-arent-more-disabled-people-online.

9. smith, "Why Aren't More Disabled People Online?"

10. s. e. smith, "Websites Need to Be More Accessible for Disabled People," *Vox*,
Feb. 5, 2019, https://www.vox.com/the-goods/2019/2/5/18210912/websites-ada
-compliance-lawsuits.

11. Interview with Nell Koneczny, Feb. 2020.

12. Interview with Dominick Lawniczak Evans, Dec. 2019.

13. Dominick Evans and Ashtyn Law, "FilmDis White Paper on Disability Representation on Television: Examining 180 TV Shows from March 2018 to March
2019," FilmDis, http://www.filmdis.com/our-work/research-projects, accessed Nov.
20, 2021.

14. See "I'm Not Your Inspiration, Thank You Very Much: Stella Young," TED
Talk, June 9, 2014, https://www.youtube.com/watch?v=8K9Gg164Bsw.

15. Interview with Rosemarie Garland-Thomson, May 2019.

16. Rosemarie Garland-Thomson, "Becoming Disabled," *New York Times*, Aug.
19, 2016, https://www.nytimes.com/2016/08/21/opinion/sunday/becoming
-disabled.html.

17. Interview with Garland-Thomson.

18. "Invacare Storm Series 3G Torque SP and Torque 3 Power Wheelchairs,"
company brochure, http://www.invacare.com/doc_files/12-240%20rev0617%203G
%20Storm%20Torque%20Brochure%20FINAL%20no%20crops.pdf, accessed Nov.
20, 2021.

CHAPTER 8: THE POLITICS OF BEAUTY

1. Susan M. Schweik, *The Ugly Laws: Disability in Public* (New York: New York
University Press, 2009).

2. Paul K. Longmore, *Why I Burned My Book and Other Essays on Disability*
(Philadelphia: Temple University Press, 2003), 36.

3. Melissa Blake, "After an Internet Troll Told Me I Was 'Too Ugly,' I Spent a
Year Posting Selfies," *Refinery 29*, Sept. 30, 2020, https://www.refinery29.com/en-us
/2020/09/10031949/melissa-blake-writer-twitter-selfies-trollgate-interview.

4. Reggie Ugwu, "This Is Lupita Nyong'o. Hollywood, Please Keep Up," *New
York Times*, March 20, 2019, https://www.nytimes.com/2019/03/20/arts/lupita
-nyongo-us.html.

5. See ABC's *The View*, March 28, 2019, https://www.youtube.com/watch?v
=CZRwlmyMf7g.

6. Judith Cummings, "Disabled Model Defies Sexual Stereotypes," *New York
Times*, June 8, 1987, www.nytimes.com/1987/06/08/style/disabled-model-defies
-sexual-stereotypes.html.

7. Rachel Kassenbrock, "She Posed in Lingerie to Prove People with Disabilities
Are 'Capable, Sexual Beings,'" *The Mighty*, July 30, 2015, https://themighty.com
/2015/07/quadriplegic-woman-poses-in-lingerie-to-end-stereotypes.

8. Interview with Ellen Stohl, Apr. 2019.

9. Yvonne Villarreal, "Creative Minds: Gay Rosenthal of 'Push Girls,'" *Los Angeles Times*, June 8, 2012, https://www.latimes.com/entertainment/tv/la-xpm-2012 -jun-08-la-ca-creative-minds-20120610-story.html.

10. Maria Elena Fernandez, "Push Girls on Sundance: Summer's Most Surprising Show," *Daily Beast*, May 31, 2012, https://www.thedailybeast.com/push-girls -on-sundance-summers-most-surprising-show.

11. Linda Holmes, "'Push Girls': A Fresh Take on Women Riding on '26-Inch Rims,'" NPR's Pop Culture Happy Hour, June 4, 2012, https://www.npr.org/2012/06 /04/154277774/push-girls-a-fresh-take-on-women-riding-on-26-inch-rims.

12. "Disabled Models Make London Fashion Week Debut," *UK Fashion Network*, Feb. 17, 2017, https://uk.fashionnetwork.com/news/Disabled-models-make -london-fashion-week-debut,794704.html.

13. Adam Bailey, "Jack Eyers: From Catwalk to Canoe," Paralympics.org, May 17, 2018, https://www.paralympic.org/news/jack-eyers-catwalk-canoe.

14. Paul Wilson, "Men's Health Heroes: Jack Eyers," *Men's Health* (UK), Nov. 4, 2015, https://www.menshealth.com/uk/building-muscle/a755037/mens-health -heroes-jack-ayers.

15. See Jack Eyers website, https://www.jackeyers.com, accessed Nov. 21, 2021.

16. Lia Martirosyan, "Jack Eyers—Modeling *His* Way!" *Ability*, Jan. 2014, https://abilitymagazine.com/jack-eyers-modeling-way.

17. Erin Nyren, "Selma Blair Says She Has Multiple Sclerosis in Heartfelt Instagram Post," *Variety*, Oct. 20, 2018, https://variety.com/2018/biz/news/selma-blair -multiple-sclerosis-ms-1202987565.

18. Julie Miller, "'There's No Tragedy for Me': Selma Blair's Transformation," *Vanity Fair*, March 2019, https://www.vanityfair.com/hollywood/2019/02/selma -blairs-transformation.

19. Katie Tastrom, "What the Media Got Wrong About Selma Blair," *Rooted in Rights*, Mar. 19, 2019, https://rootedinrights.org/what-the-media-got-wrong-about -selma-blair.

20. Tastrom, "What the Media Got Wrong."

21. See Authored website, https://authoredapparel.com, accessed Nov. 21, 2021.

22. See IZ Adaptive website, https://izadaptive.com, accessed Nov. 21, 2021.

23. See Tommy Hilfiger Adaptive website, https://usa.tommy.com/en/tommy -adaptive, accessed Nov. 21, 2021.

24. See Zappos Adaptive website, https://www.zappos.com/e/adaptive, accessed Nov. 21, 2021.

25. Annie Groer, "For People with Disabilities, Finding Clothing That Is Stylish and Meets Their Needs Is Getting Easier," *Washington Post*, Aug. 3, 2019, https:// www.washingtonpost.com/health/for-people-with-disabilities-finding-clothing -that-is-stylish-and-meets-their-needs-is-getting-easier/2019/08/02/1889990a -87cf-11e9-98c1-e945ae5db8fb_story.html.

26. "About," Rebirth Garments, http://rebirthgarments.com/about, accessed Nov. 30, 2021.

27. Stephanie Thomas biography, Business of Fashion, https://www.business offashion.com/community/people/stephanie-thomas, accessed Nov. 2021.

28. Interview with Aaron Rose Philip, Feb. 2020.

CHAPTER 9: CASTING AND MISCASTING

1. Maya Salam, "Ali Stroker Makes History as First Wheelchair User to Win a Tony," *New York Times*, June 9, 2019, https://www.nytimes.com/2019/06/09/theater /ali-stroker-oklahoma-tony-awards.html.

2. Jessica Gelt, "Reactions to Ali Stroker's Historic Tony Awards Win Will Make Your Heart Soar," *Los Angeles Times*, June 9, 2019, https://www.latimes.com /entertainment/arts/la-et-cm-ali-stroker-disabled-tony-award-win-reactions -20190609-story.html.

3. "Ali Stroker, Tony Award Winning Actor," #AerieREAL Life, Jan. 23, 2020, https://www.ae.com/aerie-real-life/2020/01/23/ali-stroker-tony-award-winning -actor.

4. Emma Purcell, "Ali Stroker: We Speak to the Tony Award-Winning Disabled Actress and Singer," *Disability Horizons*, Apr. 22, 2020, https://disabilityhorizons .com/2020/04/ali-stroker-we-speak-to-the-tony-award-winning-disabled-actress -and-singer.

5. "Modern Icons: Ali Stroker," White+Warren, https://www.whiteandwarren .com/blogs/journal/modern-icons-ali-stroker, accessed Nov. 21, 2021.

6. "Modern Icons: Ali Stroker," White+Warren.

7. Longmore, *Why I Burned My Book and Other Essays on Disability* (Philadelphia: Temple University Press, 2003).

8. "Academy Awards and Images of Physical Disability," letter to the editor, *Los Angeles Times*, April 15, 1990, https://www.latimes.com/archives/la-xpm-1990 -04-15-ca-1601-story.html.

9. Art Blaser, "'Gump' Isn't the Answer for Real Understanding," *Los Angeles Times*, Feb. 20, 1995, https://www.latimes.com/archives/la-xpm-1995-02-20-ca -34026-story.html.

10. Mary Johnson, "'Million Dollar Baby' Cheap Shot at Disabled," *Seattle Post-Intelligencer*, Feb. 23, 2005, https://www.seattlepi.com/local/opinion/article /Million-Dollar-Baby-cheap-shot-at-disabled-1167105.php.

11. Lennard J. Davis, "Why 'Million Dollar Baby' Infuriates the Disabled," *Chicago Tribune*, Feb. 2, 2005, http://lists.cdu.edu.au/pipermail/csaa-forum/Week-of -Mon-20050207/000648.html.

12. Elsa Sjunneson-Henry, "I Belong Where the People Are: Disability and *The Shape of Water*," TOR.com (blog), Jan. 16, 2018, https://www.tor.com/2018/01/16 /i-belong-where-the-people-are-disability-and-the-shape-of-water.

13. Hanna Shaun Bar Nissim and R. J. Mitte, "Authentic Representation in Television: 2018," Ruderman Family Foundation, Feb. 2020, https://ruderman foundation.org/white_papers/the-ruderman-white-paper-on-authentic -representation-in-tv.

14. Kerry McLaughlin, "What Ignoring the Disability Community Costs Hollywood," Cutaway by SHIFT, Oct. 15, 2019, https://cutaway.shift.io/what-ignoring -the-disabled-community-costs-hollywood.

15. McLaughlin, "What Ignoring the Disability Community Costs Hollywood."

16. See Lisa de Moraes, "Final 2016–17 TV Rankings," *Deadline*, May 25, 2017, https://deadline.com/2017/05/2016-2017-tv-season-ratings-series-rankings-list -1202102340.

17. Amy Amatangelo, "Speechless Creator Scott Silveri Has a Lot to Say," *Paste Magazine*, Oct. 18, 2017, https://www.pastemagazine.com/tv/speechless/speechless-creator-scott-silveri-has-a-lot-to-say.

18. Ryan Lattanzio, "'Special': Ryan O'Connell on How His Show Made for '$2 and a Prayer' Struck Emmy Gold," *IndieWire*, Aug. 7, 2019, https://www.indiewire.com/2019/08/ryan-o-connell-special-netflix-emmys-interview-1202163023.

19. Keah Brown, "Ryan O'Connell Loves TV, and TV Loves Him Back," *Bonobos* (blog), April 12, 2019, https://blog.bonobos.com/netflix-special-show-ryan-oconnell.

20. See "CBS Is the First Entertainment Company to Sign Ruderman Family Foundation's Audition Pledge," Ruder Foundation press release, June 19, 2019, https://rudermanfoundation.org/press_releases/cbs-is-the-first-entertainment-company-to-sign-ruderman-family-foundations-audition-pledge.

21. Tyler Aquilina, "NBCUniversal Pledges to Include Actors with Disabilities in Auditions for All Film, TV projects," *Entertainment Weekly*, Jan. 30, 2021, https://ew.com/tv/nbcuniversal-pledges-auditions-for-actors-with-disabilities.

22. Interview with Keah Brown, Apr. 2019.

23. "Access to the Process," *Worklife* (Spring 1989): 16–17, https://www.google.com/books/edition/Worklife/FVCdZAHhZO4C.

24. Renee Fabian, "New Marvel Film 'The Eternals' Will Feature First Deaf Superhero," *Variety*, July 22, 2019, https://themighty.com/2019/07/marvel-eternals-deaf-superhero-lauren-ridloff.

25. Lauren Appelbaum, "Spotlight Q&A with Lauren Ridloff," RespectAbility.org, July 9, 2019, https://www.respectability.org/2019/07/spotlight-qa-with-lauren-ridloff.

26. Adam B. Vary, "'Eternals' Star Lauren Ridloff on Playing Marvel's First Deaf Superhero and the Need to 'Normalize Subtitles,'" *Variety*, Nov. 3, 2021, https://variety.com/2021/film/news/eternals-lauren-ridloff-deaf-superhero-marvel-studios-1235103428.

27. Vary, "'Eternals' Star Lauren Ridloff."

28. Abbey White, "Next Big Thing: 'Eternals' Star Lauren Ridloff on Becoming Marvel's First Deaf Superhero," *Hollywood Reporter*, Oct. 18, 2021, https://www.hollywoodreporter.com/movies/movie-features/lauren-ridloff-eternals-marvel-deaf-superhero-1235025797.

29. Vary, "'Eternals' Star Lauren Ridloff."

30. Mineli Gosami, "Marvel's First Deaf Superhero Lauren Ridloff Speaks Out," *Hearing Like Me* (blog), https://www.hearinglikeme.com/as-marvels-first-deaf-superhero-lauren-ridloff-speaks-out.

CHAPTER 10: WHAT'S SO FUNNY ABOUT DISABILITY?

1. Interview with Zach Anner, Jan. 2020.

2. Zach Anner, *If at Birth You Don't Succeed: My Adventures with Disaster and Destiny* (New York: Henry Holt, 2016), 71.

3. Interview with Anner.

4. Michael Rock, "Disability and Comedy: A History and Review," *AABR: Empowering People with Disabilities* (blog), Apr. 26, 2019, http://aabr.org/2019/04/26/disability-and-comedy-a-history-and-review.

5. Bruce Weber, "John Callahan, 59, Provocative Cartoonist," *New York Times*, July 30, 2010, https://www.nytimes.com/2010/07/28/arts/design/28callahan.html.

6. Lori A. Wood, "John Callahan: Back to the Drawing Board!" *Journal of the United Spinal Association*, Nov. 24, 2004, https://web.archive.org/web/20080110225355 /http://www.unitedspinal.org/publications/action/2004/11/24/john-callahan-back -to-the-drawing-board.

7. John Callahan, *Don't Worry, He Won't Get Far on Foot: The Autobiography of a Dangerous Man* (New York: William Morrow, 1989).

8. Matthew Singer, "Cartoonist John Callahan Was Offensive, Hilarious and One of Portland's Own. Now, He's Getting His Long-Delayed Close-Up," *Willamette Week*, July 18, 2018, https://www.wweek.com/culture/2018/07/18/cartoonist-john -callahan-was-offensive-hilarious-and-one-of-portlands-own-now-gus-van-sant -and-joaquin-phoenix-are-giving-him-his-long-delayed-close-up.

9. Timothy Egan, "Defiantly Incorrect," *New York Times Magazine*, June 7, 1992, https://www.nytimes.com/1992/06/07/magazine/defiantly-incorrect.html.

10. Egan, "Defiantly Incorrect."

11. Dennis McLellan, "John Callahan Dies at 59; Politically Incorrect Cartoonist Was a Quadriplegic," *Los Angeles Times*, July 29, 2010, https://www.latimes.com /local/obituaries/la-me-john-callahan-20100729-story.html.

12. "Josh Blue at Last Comic Standing!," June 8, 2006, https://youtu.be/qMSrpZi _6WM.

13. Interview with Josh Blue, Jan. 2020.

14. Shanna Lewis, "40 Years Ago, Denver Became the Birthplace of the Disability Rights Movement," Colorado Public Radio, Dec. 11, 2018, https://www.cpr.org /show-segment/40-years-ago-denver-became-the-birthplace-of-the-disability-rights -movement.

15. Sharon Lockyer, "From Comedy Targets to Comedy-Makers: Disability and Comedy in Live Performance," *Disability & Society* (Nov. 27, 2015), https://www .tandfonline.com/doi/full/10.1080/09687599.2015.1106402.

16. Ted Shiress, "Disability and Comedy: A Personal Perspective," *Guardian*, Sept. 12, 2013, https://www.theguardian.com/science/brain-flapping/2013/sep/12 /disability-comedy-personal-perspective.

17. Charles Walden Comedian, Sept. 15, 2007, https://www.youtube.com/watch ?v=V4cRgCEiocc.

18. Michael Stahl, "This Standup Comic Turned His Disability into Comedy Gold," *Narratively*, June 29, 2017, https://narratively.com/this-standup-comic -turned-his-disability-into-comedy-gold.

19. Natalie Angley, "She Lost Her Feet in an Accident. Now, Her Standup Comedy Helps Her Heal," CNN.com, Mar. 23, 2018, https://www.cnn.com/2018/03/23 /health/turning-points-danielle-perez-comedian/index.html.

20. Regina F. Graham, "I'm a Black, Disabled Actor. This Is How I'm Making My Place in Hollywood," *Refinery 29*, Sept. 16, 2020, https://www.refinery29.com /en-us/2020/09/9903981/lauren-ridloff-danielle-perez-disabled-actress-women -of-color.

21. *Disability Visibility Project* (podcast), episode 21, Mar. 25, 2018, https:// disabilityvisibilityproject.com/2018/03/25/ep-21-disabled-comedians.

22. *Disability Visibility Project* (podcast), episode 21.

23. Katie Dupere, "New Comic Series Hilariously Depicts What It's Like to Live with a Disability," Mashable.com, Oct. 19, 2016, https://mashable.com/2016/10/19/disability-comic-the-disabled-life.

24. Dupere, "New Comic Series."

25. Jessica Oddi and Lianna Oddi, *The Disabled Life* (blog), accessed Feb. 4, 2022, https://thedisabledlife.tumblr.com.

26. Connie Guglielmo, "'Comedy Is a Wall Breaker' for Letting People with Disabilities Be Themselves," CNET, Mar. 8, 2021, https://www.cnet.com/news/comedy-is-a-wall-breaker-for-letting-people-with-disabilities-be-themselves.

27. Guglielmo, "Comedy Is a Wall Breaker."

28. Maysoon Zayid, "Don't Bring Cotton Candy to a Nuclear War," in *Resistance and Hope: Essays by Disabled People*, ed. Alice Wong (San Francisco: Disability Visibility Project, 2018).

29. Maysoon Zayid, "I Got 99 Problems . . . Palsy Is Just One," TED Talks, Dec. 2013, https://www.ted.com/talks/maysoon_zayid_i_got_99_problems_palsy_is_just_one.

30. "Maysoon Zayid: 'Disability Is Not a Monolith,'" episode 2, *Able: A Series*, Amazon Originals, Sept. 12, 2019.

31. "Maysoon Zayid: 'Disability Is Not a Monolith.'"

32. Interview with Maysoon Zayid, Apr. 2020.

CHAPTER 11: HEALTH-CARE DISPARITIES

1. See "State of Alabama Emergency Operations Plan," https://int.nyt.com/data/documenthelper/6846-alabama-triage-guidelines/02cb4c58460e57ea9f05/optimized/full.pdf#page=1, accessed Nov. 22, 2021.

2. "Toolkit for COVID-19," Kansas Department of Health and Environment, Appendix B, p. 19, table 1, https://int.nyt.com/data/documenthelper/6847-kansas-triage-guidelines/02cb4c58460e57ea9f05/optimized/full.pdf#page=1, accessed Nov. 22, 2021; "Tennessee Hospital and ICU Triage Guidelines for Adults During Crisis: Standards of Care," Version 1.4, July 2016, p. 5, in *Guidance for the Ethical Allocation of Scarce Resources During a Community-Wide Public Health Emergency as Declared by the Governor of Tennessee*, Version 1.6, July 2016, https://int.nyt.com/data/documenthelper/6851-tennessee-triage-guidelines/02cb4c58460e57ea9f05/optimized/full.pdf#page=1.

3. "Scarce Resource Management and Crisis Standards of Care," Washington State Department of Health, https://int.nyt.com/data/documenthelper/6853-washington-state-triage-guidel/02cb4c58460e57ea9f05/optimized/full.pdf, accessed Nov. 22, 2021.

4. "Material Resource Allocation, Principles and Guidelines: COVID-19 Outbreak," University of Washington Medical Center, https://covid-19.uwmedicine.org/Screening%20and%20Testing%20Algorithms/Other%20Inpatient%20Clinical%20Guidance/Clinical%20Care%20in%20ICU/Material%20Resource%20Allocation.COVID19.docx, accessed Nov. 22, 2021.

5. "Letters: Disability Community Will Fight Any Attempt to Discriminate over Scarce Medical Resources," *Boston Globe*, Mar. 17, 2020, https://www.bostonglobe.com/2020/03/18/opinion/disabililty-community-will-fight-any-attempt-discriminate-over-scare-medical-resources.

6. Nicole Jennings, "Advocacy Group Says People with Disabilities Could Get Denied COVID-19 Treatment," *My Northwest*, Mar. 25, 2020, https://mynorthwest .com/1784739/virus-disabilities-discrimination.

7. "Preventing Discrimination in the Treatment of COVID-19 Patients: The Illegality of Medical Rationing on the Basis of Disability," Disability Rights Education and Defense Fund, Mar. 25, 2020, https://dredf.org/the-illegality-of-medical -rationing-on-the-basis-of-disability.

8. Ari Ne'eman, "I Will Not Apologize for My Needs," *New York Times*, Mar. 23, 2020, https://www.nytimes.com/2020/03/23/opinion/coronavirus-ventilators -triage-disability.html; Elaine Godfrey, "Americans with Disabilities Are Terrified," *Atlantic*, Apr. 3, 2020, https://www.theatlantic.com/politics/archive/2020/04/people -disabilities-worry-they-wont-get-treatment/609355; Jessica Slice, "My Disability Doesn't Shorten My Life Expectancy. Medical Rationing Might," *Washington Post*, Apr. 9, 2020, https://www.washingtonpost.com/outlook/2020/04/09/disability -medical-rationing; Abigail Abrams, "'This Is Really Life or Death.' For People with Disabilities, Coronavirus Is Making It Harder Than Ever to Receive Care," *Time*, Apr. 24, 2020, https://time.com/5826098/coronavirus-people-with-disabilities.

9. Joseph Shapiro, "People with Disabilities Say Rationing Care Policies Violate Civil Rights," National Public Radio, Mar. 23, 2020, https://www.npr.org/2020/03/23 /820398531/people-with-disabilities-say-rationing-care-policies-violate-civil-rights.

10. Sheri Fink, "U.S. Civil Rights Office Rejects Rationing Medical Care Based on Disability, Age," *New York Times*, Mar. 28, 2020, https://www.nytimes.com/2020 /03/28/us/coronavirus-disabilities-rationing-ventilators-triage.html.

11. Godfrey, "Americans with Disabilities Are Terrified."

12. "Declaration Under the Public Readiness and Emergency Preparedness Act for Medical Countermeasures Against COVID-19," US Dept. of Health and Human Services, Mar. 17, 2020, https://www.federalregister.gov/documents/2020/03/17/2020 -05484/declaration-under-the-public-readiness-and-emergency-preparedness-act -for-medical-countermeasures.

13. "Ventilator Allocation Guidelines," New York State Task Force on Life and the Law, New York State Department of Health, Nov. 2015, https://www.health.ny .gov/regulations/task_force/reports_publications/docs/ventilator_guidelines.pdf.

14. "Ventilator Allocation Guidelines."

15. Ari Ne'eman, "When It Comes to Rationing, Disability Rights Law Prohibits More than Prejudice," Hastings Center, Apr. 10, 2020, https://www.thehastingscenter .org/when-it-comes-to-rationing-disability-rights-law-prohibits-more-than-prejudice.

16. Ne'eman, "When It Comes to Rationing."

17. Shapiro "People with Disabilities Say Rationing Care Policies Violate Civil Rights."

18. "Republicans, Who Do You Think Is Bailing Out Your State?" editorial, *New York Times*, Apr. 27, 2020, https://www.nytimes.com/2020/04/27/opinion /coronavirus-state-budgets.html.

19. Shannon Young and Anna Gronewold, "Cuomo Threatens to Reject $6.7B in Federal Aid in Favor of Medicaid Redesign," *Politico*, Mar. 27, 2020, https://www .politico.com/states/new-york/albany/story/2020/03/27/cuomo-threatens-to -reject-67b-in-federal-aid-in-favor-of-medicaid-redesign-1269446.

20. Interview with Bryan O'Malley, May 2020.

21. Joe Eaton, "Nursing Home Workers Face Coronavirus with Low Pay, Inadequate Protection," *AARP* magazine, Apr. 29, 2020, https://www.aarp.org/caregiving /health/info-2020/nursing-home-workers-during-coronavirus.html.

22. "COVID-19 in Racial and Ethnic Minority Groups," US Centers for Disease Control and Prevention, https://www.cdc.gov/coronavirus/2019-ncov/need-extra -precautions/racial-ethnic-minorities.html, accessed Nov. 22, 2021.

23. Anita Cameron, "Racial Disparities in the Age of COVID-19," *Not Dead Yet* (blog), Apr. 23, 2020, https://notdeadyet.org/2020/04/anita-cameron-racial -disparities-in-the-age-of-covid-19.html.

24. Abrams, "This Is Really Life or Death."

25. See US Census data, "Disability Characteristics," 2017, https://data.census .gov/cedsci/table?tid=ACSST1Y2017.S1810&q=S1810, accessed Nov. 22, 2021.

26. Jessica Campisi, "Deaf Americans Are Urging the White House to Use Sign Language Interpreters at Coronavirus Briefings," CNN.com, Apr. 23, 2020, https:// www.cnn.com/2020/04/23/politics/white-house-interpreter-coronavirus-briefings -trnd/index.html.

27. Sarah Katz, "The Deaf Community Is Facing New Barriers as We Navigate Inaccessible Face Masks and Struggle to Follow News Broadcasts and Teleconferences—But the Tools for Accessibility Are Out There," *Business Insider*, Apr. 29, 2020, https://www.businessinsider.com/deaf-people-face-new-barriers-amidst -pandemic-accessible-tools-2020-4.

28. Abrams, "This Is Really Life or Death."

29. Amy Gaeta, "Disabled Communities in the COVID-19 Pandemic," *Disability Visibility Project* (blog), Mar. 26, 2020, https://disabilityvisibilityproject.com /2020/03/26/disabled-communities-in-the-covid-19-pandemic.

30. Leah Lakshmi Piepzna-Samarasinha, "How Disabled Mutual Aid Is Different Than Abled Mutual Aid," *Disability Visibility Project* (blog), Oct. 3, 2021, https:// disabilityvisibilityproject.com/2021/10/03/how-disabled-mutual-aid-is-different -than-abled-mutual-aid.

31. Piepzna-Samarasinha, "How Disabled Mutual Aid Is Different."

32. Teighlor McGee, "Minneapolis Uses Mutual Aid to Fight for Collective Liberation," *Bitch Media*, Nov. 1, 2021, https://www.bitchmedia.org/article/mutual -aid-collective-survival-minneapolis.

33. McGee, "Minneapolis Uses Mutual Aid."

34. See the Missing Billion website, https://www.themissingbillion.org, accessed Nov. 10, 2021.

35. Interview with Teresa Nguyen, Jan. 2020.

36. Neil Romano et al., "Organ Transplants and Discrimination Against People with Disabilities," National Council on Disability, Sept. 25, 2019, https://ncd.gov /sites/default/files/NCD_Organ_Transplant_508.pdf.

37. See "Employment First Advisory Partnership," Colorado Division of Vocational Rehabilitation, https://www.colorado.gov/pacific/dvr/employment-first -advisory-partnership, accessed Nov. 10, 2021.

38. Interview with Nguyen.

39. Rachel Bluth, "For the Disabled, a Doctor's Visit Can Be Literally an Obstacle Course—And the Laws Can't Help," *Washington Post*, Oct. 28, 2018, https:// www.washingtonpost.com/national/health-science/for-the-disabled-a-doctors

-visit-can-be-literally-an-obstacle-course-and-the-laws-cant-help/2018/10/26/1917
e04c-d628-11e8-aeb7-ddcad4a0a54e_story.html.

40. Silvia Yee, "Disability Discrimination in Health Care," Disability Rights Education and Defense Fund, Apr. 2012, https://dredf.org/public-policy/health -access-to-care-old/disability-discrimination-in-health-care.

41. Interview with June Isaacson Kailes, Sept. 29, 2007.

42. Interview with Isaacson Kailes.

43. Lisa I. Iezzoni et al., "Physicians' Perceptions of People with Disability and Their Health Care," *Health Affairs* 40, no. 2 (Feb. 2021), https://www.healthaffairs .org/doi/10.1377/hlthaff.2020.01452.

44. Iezzoni et al., "Physicians' Perceptions of People with Disability."

45. David Carlson et al., "Devaluing People with Disabilities: Medical Procedures That Violate Civil Rights," National Institute on Disability and Rehabilitation Research, May 2012, https://www.ndrn.org/wp-content/uploads/2012/05/Devaluing -People-with-Disabilities.pdf.

46. Laura VanPuymbrouck et al., "Explicit and Implicit Disability Attitudes of Healthcare Providers," *Rehabilitation Psychology*, Council on Quality and Leadership, 2020, https://www.c-q-l.org/wp-content/uploads/2020/03/CQL-2020-Van Puymbrouck-Friedman-Feldner-Health-Care-Providers-Disability-Attitudes.pdf.

47. Andrés J. Gallegos, "Misperceptions of People with Disabilities Lead to Low-Quality Care: How Policy Makers Can Counter the Harm and Injustice," *Health Affairs*, Apr. 1, 2021, https://www.healthaffairs.org/do/10.1377/hblog 20210325.480382/full.

48. National Council on Disability, Medical Futility and Disability Bias, Nov. 20, 2019, https://ncd.gov/sites/default/files/NCD_Medical_Futility_Report _508.pdf.

49. See "Quadriplegic COVID-19 Patient Starved by Texas Doctor Because of His Disability," June 26, 2020, https://www.youtube.com/watch?v=jq-_gtJnzZg.

50. Joseph Shapiro, "One Man's COVID-19 Death Raises the Worst Fears of Many People with Disabilities," NPR, July 31, 2020, https://www.npr.org/2020 /07/31/896882268/one-mans-covid-19-death-raises-the-worst-fears-of-many -people-with-disabilities.

CHAPTER 12: NOT DEAD YET VS. THE RIGHT TO DIE

1. Nicole Weisensee Egan, "Inside Terminally Ill Brittany Maynard's Decision to Die," *People*, Oct. 27, 2014, https://people.com/celebrity/brittany-maynard -death-with-dignity-terminally-ill-brain-cancer.

2. Josh Sanburn, "More States Considering Right-to-Die Laws After Brittany Maynard," *Time*, Jan. 22, 2015, http://time.com/3678199/brittany-maynard-death -with-dignity-legislation-california.

3. Megan Brenan, "Americans' Strong Support for Euthanasia Persists," Gallup, May 31, 2018, https://news.gallup.com/poll/235145/americans-strong-support -euthanasia-persists.aspx.

4. See testimony of Diane Coleman and Carol Gill before the Constitution Subcommittee of the US House Judiciary Committee, http://notdeadyet.org/testimony -of-diane-coleman-jd-and-carol-gill-ph-d-before-the-constitution-subcommittee -of-the-u-s-house-judiciary-committee, accessed Nov. 22, 2021.

5. "NDY's 24th Anniversary: Never Has the Fight for Our Lives Been More Urgent," Not Dead Yet (blog), Apr. 26, 2020, https://notdeadyet.org/2020/04/ndys -24th-anniversary-never-has-the-fight-for-our-lives-been-more-urgent.html.

6. H.R. 4149—Assisted Suicide Funding Restriction Act of 1996, 104th Congress (1995–1996), introduced Sept. 24, 1996, https://www.congress.gov/bill/104th -congress/house-bill/4149.

7. John Schwartz and James Estrin, "In Oregon, Choosing Death Over Suffering," *New York Times*, June 1, 2004, https://www.nytimes.com/2004/06/01/science /in-oregon-choosing-death-over-suffering.html, accessed Nov. 22, 2021.

8. Schwartz and Estrin, "In Oregon, Choosing Death Over Suffering."

9. Kevin McArdle, "Brittany Maynard's Husband Opens Up about 'Death with Dignity,'" *New Jersey 101.5*, Jan. 16, 2015, https://nj1015.com/brittany-maynards -husband-opens-up-about-death-with-dignity.

10. Marilyn Golden, "The Danger of Assisted Suicide Laws," CNN.com, Oct. 13, 2014, http://us.cnn.com/2014/10/13/opinion/golden-assisted-suicide/index.html.

11. See "NDY's Letter to Governor Jerry Brown Urging Veto of Assisted Suicide Bill," Sept. 21, 2015, http://notdeadyet.org/2015/09/ndys-letter-to-governor-jerry -brown-urging-veto-of-assisted-suicide-bill.html.

12. Paul K. Longmore, "The Strange Death of David Rivlin," *Western Journal of Medicine* 154, no. 5 (May 1991), https://www.ncbi.nlm.nih.gov/pmc/articles /PMC1002845.

13. Peter Applebome, "An Angry Man Fights to Die, Then Tests Life," *New York Times*, Feb. 7, 1990, https://www.nytimes.com/1990/02/07/us/an-angry-man-fights -to-die-then-tests-life.html.

14. "Larry McAfee, 39; Sought Right to Die," *New York Times*, Oct. 5, 1995, https://www.nytimes.com/1995/10/05/obituaries/larry-mcafee-39-sought-right -to-die.html.

15. Sheryl Gay Stolberg, "The Schiavo Case: Congress; Lawmakers Ready to Again Debate End-of-Life Issues," *New York Times*, Mar. 28, 2005, https://www.ny times.com/2005/03/28/politics/congress-ready-to-again-debate-endoflife-issues .html.

16. Jim Collar, "Following 'Last Dance' Prom, Wisconsin Teen Jerika Bolen Dies," *USA Today*, Sept. 22, 2016, https://www.usatoday.com/story/news/nation -now/2016/09/22/following-last-dance-prom-wisconsin-teen-jerika-bolen-dies /90855656.

17. See FDA, "FDA Approves First Drug for Spinal Muscular Atrophy," press release, Dec. 23, 2016, https://www.fda.gov/news-events/press-announcements /fda-approves-first-drug-spinal-muscular-atrophy.

18. Lori A. Roscoe et al., "A Comparison of Characteristics of Kevorkian Euthanasia Cases and Physician-Assisted Suicides in Oregon," *Gerontologist* 41, no. 4 (Aug. 2001), https://academic.oup.com/gerontologist/article/41/4/439/600708.

19. Lisa Belkin, "Doctor Tells of First Death Using His Suicide Device," *New York Times*, June 6, 1990, https://www.nytimes.com/1990/06/06/us/doctor-tells -of-first-death-using-his-suicide-device.html.

20. Ron Rosenbaum, "Angel of Death: The Trial of the Suicide Doctor," *Vanity Fair*, May 1991, https://www.vanityfair.com/magazine/1991/05/jack-kevorkian 199105.

21. Fred Charatan, "US Supreme Court Upholds Oregon's Death with Dignity Act," National Center for Biotechnology Information, Jan. 28, 2006, https://www .ncbi.nlm.nih.gov/pmc/articles/PMC1352080.

22. Jane E. Brody, "Personal Health" column, *New York Times*, June 18, 1997, http://www.nytimes.com/1997/06/18/us/personal-health-696889.html.

23. See "Oregon Death with Dignity Act 2020 Data Summary," Oregon Public Health Division, Center for Health Statistics, Feb. 26, 2021, https://www.oregon .gov/oha/PH/PROVIDERPARTNERRESOURCES/EVALUATIONRESEARCH /DEATHWITHDIGNITYACT/Documents/year23.pdf.

24. Karen Feldscher, "The Doctors Will See You Now," Harvard T.H. Chan School of Public Health, Mar. 4, 2019, https://www.hsph.harvard.edu/news/features /improving-doctors-diagnostic-accuracy.

25. Debbie Selby et al., "Clinician Accuracy When Estimating Survival Duration," *Journal of Pain and Symptom Management* 42, no. 4 (Oct. 2011): 578–88, https://www.sciencedirect.com/science/article/pii/S0885392411001369.

26. Paul Taylor, "Can Doctors Actually Predict How Long Patients Have Left?" *Globe and Mail*, June 17, 2016, https://www.theglobeandmail.com/life/health -and-fitness/health-advisor/can-doctors-actually-predict-how-long-patients-have -left/article30500639.

27. Bradford Richardson, "Diabetics Eligible for Physician-Assisted Suicide in Oregon, State Officials Say," *Washington Times*, Jan. 11, 2018, https://www .washingtontimes.com/news/2018/jan/11/diabetics-eligible-physician-assisted -suicide-oreg.

28. Erin Hoover Barnett, "A Family Struggles with the Question of Whether Mom Is Capable of Choosing to Die," *Oregonian*, Oct. 17, 1999, https://www .oregonlive.com/health/2015/02/physician-assisted_suicide_a_f.html.

29. Wesley J. Smith, "Suicide Unlimited in Oregon," *Weekly Standard*, Nov. 8, 1999, https://www.washingtonexaminer.com/weekly-standard/suicide-unlimited-in -oregon.

30. William Yardley, "First Death for Washington Assisted-Suicide Law," *New York Times*, May 22, 2009, https://www.nytimes.com/2009/05/23/us/23suicide.html.

31. See "Strategic Plan: Our Roadmap to Success," Compassion & Choices, https://compassionandchoices.org/about-us/strategic-plan/six, accessed Nov. 22, 2021.

CHAPTER 13: "EASY TO GET IN [BUT] IMPOSSIBLE TO GET OUT"

1. Perry Stein, "Disability Advocates Arrested During Health Care Protest at McConnell's Office," *Washington Post*, June 22, 2017, https://www.washingtonpost.com /local/public-safety/disability-advocates-arrested-during-health-care-protes-at -mcconnells-office/2017/06/22/f5dd9992-576f-11e7-ba90-f5875b7d1876_story.html.

2. Nellie Bly, *Ten Days in a Mad-House* (New York: Ian L. Munro Publishers, 1887).

3. "US: Concerns of Neglect in Nursing Homes," Human Rights Watch, Mar. 25, 2021, https://www.hrw.org/news/2021/03/25/us-concerns-neglect-nursing-homes#.

4. "Money Follows the Person," Centers for Medicaid and CHIP Services, https://www.medicaid.gov/medicaid/long-term-services-supports/money-follows -person/index.html, accessed Nov. 22, 2021.

5. "Anniversary of Americans with Disabilities Act: July 26, 2020," US Census Bureau, June 17, 2020, https://www.census.gov/newsroom/facts-for-features/2020

/disabilities-act.html; "Disability Impacts All of Us," US Centers for Disease Control and Prevention, last reviewed Sept. 16, 2020, https://www.cdc.gov/ncbddd/disability andhealth/infographic-disability-impacts-all.html.

6. "Anniversary of Americans with Disabilities Act: July 26, 2020."

7. Amie Lulinski et al., "The State of the States in Intellectual and Developmental Disabilities," Coleman Institute for Cognitive Disabilities, University of Colorado, 2018, https://www.colemaninstitute.org/wp-content/uploads/2018/04/SOS _SABE_brief_final.pdf.

8. Howard Gleckman, "Fiscal Cliff Deal Repeals CLASS Act, Creates Long-Term Care Commission," *Forbes*, Jan. 1, 2013, https://www.forbes.com/sites/howard gleckman/2013/01/01/fiscal-cliff-deal-repeals-class-act-creates-long-term-care -commission.

9. Mary Johnson, *Make Them Go Away: Clint Eastwood, Christopher Reeve & the Case Against Disability Rights* (Louisville, KY: Advocado Press, 2003), 188.

10. Florence DiGennaro Reed et al., "Barriers to Independent Living for Individuals with Disabilities and Seniors," *Behavior Analysis Practice* 7 (Oct. 2014), https://doi.org/10.1007/s40617-014-0011-6.

11. Christina T. Espinosa, "My Room or Yours? Home vs. Institutional Living and the Relationship to Quality of Life," University of Kentucky Human Development Institute, Fall 2015, https://www.hdi.uky.edu/wp-content/uploads/2015/10 /ResearchBrief_Fall2015.pdf.

12. Charlie Lakin, Sheryl Larson, and Shannon Kim, "The Effects of Community vs. Institutional Living on the Daily Living Skills of Persons with Developmental Disabilities?," *Evidence-Based Policy Brief*, Association of University Centers on Disabilities (Mar. 2011): 1, https://www.aucd.org/docs/councils/core/Evidence -Based%20Policy%20Brief_1.pdf.

13. See "Vital and Health Statistics," National Center for Health Statistics, series 3, no. 3, Feb. 2019, https://www.cdc.gov/nchs/fastats/nursing-home-care.htm.

14. Phil Galewitz, "Nursing Home Residents Get Aid to Move Out," *USA Today*, Apr. 21, 2010, https://usatoday30.usatoday.com/news/health/2010-04-21-nursing -homes_N.htm.

15. Stephanie Woodward, "I Was Pulled Out of My Wheelchair by Police. It Could Be Worse. Trumpcare Could Pass," *Vox Media*, June 28, 2017, https://www .vox.com/first-person/2017/6/27/15876442/healthcare-medicaid-cuts-disability -protests.

16. Rachael Scarborough King, "Opinion: For Families Like Mine, the Social Services in Biden's Budget Proposal Are a Choice Between Life and Death," CNN, Oct. 15, 2021, https://www.cnn.com/2021/10/15/opinions/home-care-funding -biden-build-back-better-budget-king/index.html.

17. "Our Union," Union of Domestic Workers, http://www.udwa.org/our-union, accessed Nov. 22, 2022.

18. Interview with Nancy Becker-Kennedy, Dec. 2019.

19. See "In-Home Supportive Services (IHSS): History of Major Program Changes," California Department of Social Services, May 2015, http://www.udwa .org/wp-content/uploads/2015/05/IHSS-History.pdf.

20. Daniel Sledge, "Linking Public Health and Individual Medicine: The Health Policy Approach of Surgeon General Thomas Parran," *American Journal of Public*

Health 107, no. 4 (Apr. 2017), https://www.ncbi.nlm.nih.gov/pmc/articles /PMC5343701.

21. Joan Headley, "Independent Living: The Role of Gini Laurie," *Rehabilitation Gazette* 38, no. 1 (Winter 1998), http://www.polioplace.org/sites/default/files/files /Rehabilitation_Gazette_Vol._38_No._1_Winter_1998_OCR.pdf.

22. Howard A. Rusk, "Companions of Medicare: Social Security Legislation of '65 Also Set Up Aids for the Poor and Disabled," *New York Times*, Aug. 7, 1966, https://timesmachine.nytimes.com/timesmachine/1966/08/07/82868829.html.

23. "Rusk, "Companions of Medicare."

24. "The Medicaid IMD Exclusion and Mental Illness Discrimination," a background paper from the Treatment Advocacy Center's Office of Research and Public Affairs, Aug. 2016, https://www.treatmentadvocacycenter.org/storage/documents /backgrounders/imd-exclusion-and-discrimination.pdf.

25. "Wyatt v. Stickney," *Disability Justice* (blog), https://disabilityjustice.org /wyatt-v-stickney, accessed Nov. 22, 2022.

26. "O'Connor v. Donaldson, 422 U.S. 563 (1975)," *Justia* (blog), https://supreme .justia.com/cases/federal/us/422/563, accessed Nov. 22, 2022.

27. Matt Reimann, "Willowbrook, the Institution That Shocked a Nation into Changing Its Laws," *Timeline*, June 14, 2017, https://timeline.com/willowbrook-the -institution-that-shocked-a-nation-into-changing-its-laws-c847acb44e0d.

28. "The Closing of Willowbrook," *Disability Justice* (blog), https://disability justice.org/the-closing-of-willowbrook, accessed Nov. 22, 2022.

29. See "Civil Rights of Institutionalized Persons," US Department of Justice, updated Nov. 18, 2021, https://www.justice.gov/crt/civil-rights-institutionalized -persons.

30. Christopher Jencks, *The Homeless* (Cambridge, MA: Harvard University Press, 1995).

31. See "HUD 2020 Continuum of Care Homeless Assistance Programs Homeless Populations and Subpopulations," US Department of Housing and Urban Development, Dec. 15, 2020, https://files.hudexchange.info/reports/published/CoC _PopSub_NatlTerrDC_2020.pdf.

32. Piepzna-Samarasinha, "How Disabled Mutual Aid Is Different Than Abled Mutual Aid."

CHAPTER 14: SPARKS OF ACTIVISM EVERYWHERE

1. "Report: 1 in 10 Politicians Has a Disability. That's a Gap in Representation," Rutgers University School of Management and Labor Relations' Program for Disability Research, Oct. 3, 2019, https://smlr.rutgers.edu/news-events/news/report -1-10-politicians-has-disability-thats-gap-representation .

2. Christy Hoppe, "Greg Abbott Pushes to Block Disabled Texans' Lawsuits Against State," *Dallas Morning News*, Feb. 15, 2014, https://www.dallasnews.com /news/politics/2014/02/16/greg-abbott-pushes-to-block-disabled-texans-lawsuits -against-state.

3. Naureen Khan, "Texas GOP Candidate Disappoints Disability Advocates," Al Jazeera America, Aug. 26, 2013, http://america.aljazeera.com/articles/2013/8/19 /gop-candidate-fortexgovernordisappointssomedisabilityadvocates.html.

4. Khan, "Texas GOP Candidate Disappoints Disability Advocates."

5. Ruth Igielnik, "A Political Profile of Disabled Americans," Pew Research Center, Sept. 22, 2016, https://www.pewresearch.org/fact-tank/2016/09/22/a-political-profile-of-disabled-americans.

6. Lisa Schur and Douglas Kruse, "Disability and Voting Accessibility in the 2020 Elections," Rutgers University, Feb. 16, 2021, https://www.eac.gov/sites/default/files/voters/Disability_and_voting_accessibility_in_the_2020_elections_final_report_on_survey_results.pdf.

7. Joseph Shapiro, "For Tammy Duckworth, War Injury Leads to Politics," NPR, Mar. 29, 2006, https://www.npr.org/transcripts/5308074.

8. Sheryl Gay Stolberg, "'It's About Time': A Baby Comes to the Senate Floor," *New York Times*, Apr. 19, 2018, https://www.nytimes.com/2018/04/19/us/politics/baby-duckworth-senate-floor.html.

9. Email interview with Sen. Tammy Duckworth, May 2020.

10. *Air Travel Consumer Report*, Office of Aviation Consumer Protection, Oct. 2021, p. 39, https://www.transportation.gov/individuals/aviation-consumer-protection/air-travel-consumer-reports-2021.

11. Yomi S. Wrong, "Which Airlines Damage the Most Wheelchairs? New Rules Mean You Can Find Out," *Los Angeles Times*, May 6, 2019, https://www.latimes.com/travel/la-tr-travel-all-systems-go-new-wheelchair-damage-reports-20190504-story.html.

12. Email interview with Duckworth.

13. Interview with Diego Mariscal, Jan. 2020.

14. "Disability Startup Network," 2Gether-International, https://2gether-international.org/pages/disability-startup-network, accessed Mar. 5, 2022.

15. "Segregated & Exploited: A Call to Action!," National Disability Rights Network, Jan. 2011, https://www.ndrn.org/wp-content/uploads/2019/03/Segregated-and-Exploited.pdf.

16. Frances A. Koestler, "The Workshops," chap. 14 in *The Unseen Minority* (Louisville, KY: American Printing House for the Blind, 2004), https://www.afb.org/online-library/unseen-minority-0/chapter-14.

17. William G. Whittaker, "Treatment of Workers with Disabilities under Section 14(c) of the Fair Labor Standards Act," Congressional Research Service Report for Congress, Feb. 9, 2005, https://hdl.handle.net/1813/78685.

18. Whittaker, "Treatment of Workers with Disabilities under Section 14(c)."

19. "Disability Militancy—the 1930s," *Disability History* (blog), Dec. 29, 2021, https://disabilityhistory.org/2021/12/29/disability-militancy-the-1930s/.

20. Alberto Migliore, "Sheltered Workshops," *International Encyclopedia of Rehabilitation* (Buffalo, NY: Center for International Rehabilitation Research Information & Exchange, 2010), http://wintac-s3.s3-us-west-2.amazonaws.com/topic-areas/ta_511/Migliore-2010-sheltered_workshops_0.pdf, accessed Mar. 5, 2022.

21. Hillel Aron, "Lawsuit Takes Aim at Sheltered Workshops, Where Disabled Workers Make Far Less than Minimum Wage," Fair Warning, Sept. 18, 2019, https://www.fairwarning.org/2019/09/hundreds-of-thousands-of-disabled-workers-still-make-less-than-minimum-wage.

22. See National Council on Disability, "Latest NCD Report Evaluates Progress Eliminating Subminimum Wage Employment for People with Disabilities," press

release, Oct. 16, 2018, https://ncd.gov/newsroom/2018/latest-ncd-report-evaluates
-progress-eliminating-subminimum-wage-employment-people.

23. "Segregated & Exploited: A Call to Action!" National Disability Rights
Network.

24. See "Employment First," Office of Disability Employment Policy, US Department of Labor, https://www.dol.gov/agencies/odep/initiatives/employment
-first, accessed Nov. 22, 2021.

25. Michelle Diament, "Suit: Focus on Sheltered Workshops Violates ADA,"
Disability Scoop, Jan. 31, 2012, https://www.disabilityscoop.com/2012/01/31/suit
-sheltered-workshops-ada/14881.

26. "Justice Department Reaches Landmark Settlement Agreement with State of
Oregon Regarding Americans with Disabilities Act," Department of Justice, Office
of Public Affairs, Dec. 30, 2015, https://www.justice.gov/opa/pr/justice-department
-reaches-landmark-settlement-agreement-state-oregon-regarding-americans.

27. Mike Duffy, "A Whole Class of Californians Can Be Paid Less Than Minimum Wage: Those with Disabilities," ABC-10 News, Sacramento, Sept. 29, 2021,
https://bit.ly/3C9stcF.

28. Margaret M. Quinlan and Benjamin R. Bates, "Bionic Woman (2007): Gender, Disability and Cyborgs," *Journal of Research in Special Educational Needs* 9, no.
1 (Mar. 3, 2009), https://www.researchgate.net/publication/230445618_Bionic
_Woman_2007_Gender_disability_and_cyborgs.

29. Lingling Zhang and Beth Haller, "Consuming Image: How Mass Media
Impact the Identity of People with Disabilities," *Communication Quarterly* 61, no. 3
(July 2013), https://www.researchgate.net/publication/263347381_Consuming
_Image_How_Mass_Media_Impact_the_Identity_of_People_with_Disabilities.

30. "Disability and the Media," United Nations Department of Economic and
Social Affairs/Disability, https://www.un.org/development/desa/disabilities
/resources/disability-and-the-media.html, accessed Nov. 22, 2021.

31. Interview with Storm Smith, Mar. 2020.

32. Jasmine E. Harris, "The Truth About Harvey Weinstein's Walker," *New York
Times*, Jan. 30, 2020, https://www.nytimes.com/2020/01/30/opinion/harvey
-weinstein-walker.html.

33. Interview with Jasmine E. Harris, Apr. 2020.

EPILOGUE: TRENDING OR TRULY EMPOWERING?

1. Kathryn Fink, "The Americans with Disabilities Act at 30," NPR's 1A, July 2,
2020, https://the1a.org/segments/the-americans-with-disabilities-act-at-30; Vilissa
Thompson and David J. Johns, "The Story of the Americans with Disabilities Act Is All
About Bridges," CNN.com, updated July 25, 2020, https://www.cnn.com/2020/07/25
/opinions/americans-with-disabilities-act-30th-anniversary-thompson-johns/index
.html; Shane Burcaw, "'More Work to Be Done': Man Highlights Changes Necessary
for Next 30 Years of ADA," Today.com (blog), July 24, 2020, https://www.today.com
/health/what-ada-americans-disabilities-act-30-year-anniversary-t186399; Orrin G.
Hatch, "I Helped Pass the Americans with Disabilities Act. Its Future Is Uncertain,"
USA Today, July 26, 2020, https://www.usatoday.com/story/opinion/2020/07/26
/americans-disabilities-act-anniversary-protect-legacy-column/5501105002.

2. Katie Hafner, "Once Science Fiction, Gene Editing Is Now a Looming Reality," *New York Times*, July 22, 2020, https://www.nytimes.com/2020/07/22/style /crispr-gene-editing-ethics.html.

3. Shapiro, *No Pity*, p. 322.

4. Alice Wong, ed., *Disability Visibility: First-Person Stories from the Twenty-First Century* (New York: Vintage Books, 2020), pp. xvi–xxi.

5. Marti Hause and Ari Melber, "Half of People Killed by Police Have a Disability: Report," NBCNightlyNews.com, Mar. 14, 2016, https://www.nbcnews.com/news /us-news/half-people-killed-police-suffer-mental-disability-report-n538371.

6. Eric Lutz, "Trump Considering 'Neurobehavioral' Tech to Predict Mass Shooters," *Vanity Fair*, Aug. 23, 2019, https://www.vanityfair.com/news/2019/08 /trump-considering-neurobehavioral-tech-to-predict-mass-shooters-gun-control.

7. See the Community Heroes website, https://communityheroes.net, accessed Dec. 3, 2021.

8. Interview with Tyrone Starkie, Feb. 17, 2020.

9. See the Invisible Disabilities Association website, https://invisibledisabilities .org, accessed Dec. 3, 2021.

10. See the All Wheels Up website, https://www.allwheelsup.org, accessed Mar. 5, 2022.

INDEX